THE BUSINESS GUIDE TO
MALAYSIA

Edited by
Loh Siew Cheang

Butterworth-Heinemann Asia,
an imprint of Reed Academic Publishing Asia,
a division of Reed Elsevier (Singapore) Pte Ltd.
1 Temasek Avenue
#17–01 Millenia Tower
Singapore 039192

ISBN 9810067941

Cover design by Fred Rose
Typeset by DOCUPRO, Sydney
Printed in Singapore by Kin Keong Printing Co. Pte. Ltd.

CONTENTS

ABOUT THE GENERAL EDITOR

Loh Siew Cheang is a practising lawyer and is the managing partner of a law firm based in Kuala Lumpur. He is well known in corporate, securities and investment circles, and advises many foreign companies doing business in Malaysia. He is a founding member and chairperson of Advoc Asia, an association of independent commercial law firms throughout Asia with corresponding law offices in Europe and North America. He is the author of *Corporate Powers—Controls, Remedies and Decision-making*, a book published by Butterworths through the *Malayan Law Journal*.

ABOUT THE CONTRIBUTORS

Dr Sulaiman Mahbob worked in the Economic Planning Unit of the Prime Minister's Department between 1971 and 1992, and later in the Ministry of Finance (Economics Division) Malaysia between 1986 and 1994. He also served as the Executive Director of the Malaysia Institute of Economic Research (MIER—an independent think-tank on economic policies) from 1994 to 1997. He is now Deputy Vice-Chancellor (Development) for the Northern University of Malaysia. Dr Sulaiman has an undergraduate degree in economics from the University of Malaya, a Masters degree from the University of London, and a PhD in development planning from Syracuse University, USA. He has been extensively involved in policy formulation and economic research.

William Leong graduated from the National University of Singapore as Bachelor of Laws (Honours) and was admitted as an Advocate and Solicitor of the High Court of Malaya in 1982. He was senior partner in Messrs Cheang & Ariff until 1994, when he joined a group of publicly listed companies as Executive Director. Thereafter he was Chief Operating Officer of one of the largest corporations in the Philippines, and at present he is the Executive Director of a publicly listed company in Malaysia. While in practice Mr Leong has advised foreign corporations doing business in Malaysia, as well as Malaysian corporations, in areas involving company and securities law.

Tan Keok Yin has, since 1981, been the Chief Executive Officer of the Federation of Malaysian Manufacturers (FMM), which is the premier economic organisation representing the manufacturing industry in Malaysia. He obtained a Bachelor of Arts (Honours) degree in Economics from the University of Malaya in 1966, serving as economist and then head of the Economics and Industries Division of Bank Negara Malaysia from 1966 to 1977. He was seconded as head of ASEAN and Regional Economic Groupings Division of the then Ministry of Trade and Industry from 1971 to 1972. Mr Tan is currently a director of Hong Leong Bank Berhad and Malaysian Pacific Industries Berhad.

Charles W Kraal is an Advocate and Solicitor, Malaya.

P Jayasingam graduated LLB and LLM (London). He was called to the English Bar in 1984, and is an Advocate and Solicitor of the High Court of Malaya. His practice is mainly confined to labour and industrial relations law.

Dr Lim Meng Seng was among the pioneers of management consulting in Malaysia, specialising in international marketing and business development, strategic planning, feasibility studies and technology transfer. He has served with the Ministry of Trade and Industry and the Ministry of Finance of the Government of Malaysia. He has a PhD in Economics from the Catholic Institute of Paris and is a Fellow of the Economic Development Institute, World Bank, Washington DC. He has served as business adviser and consultant to Malaysian companies, as well as foreign companies.

Chooi Tat Chew is an Executive Director with the Tax and Business Advisory Service of Price Waterhouse Malaysia. Tat Chew has more than eight years' experience with the Inland Revenue Department, where he was involved in the examination of tax returns, investigations and staff training. He has more than 20 years' experience in public accounting, with exposure to all aspects of taxation work, and is an associate member of the Institute of Chartered Secretaries and Administrators. He also has extensive exposure as project director of tax advisory and consulting assignments involving restructuring and reconstruction, reorganisation for public listing, privatisation and tax investigation and transfer pricing matters.

Boon Oon Seang, a former Director of the Internal Taxes Division of the Royal Customs and Excise Department, has over 33 years' experience in indirect taxes, namely, sales tax, service tax and excise duty. He studied the value-added tax in Korea, Indonesia, New Zealand and the Philippines, and has participated in various seminars on indirect taxes both locally and internationally. He is currently an Executive Director with Price Waterhouse Tax Services Sdn Bhd, specialising in indirect taxes.

Dato V L Kandan, Advocate and Solicitor, is President of the Malaysian Intellectual Property Association (MIPA), President of the ASEAN Intellectual Property Association (ASEAN IPA) and Vice-President of the Asian Patent Attorneys Association (APAA).

Low Chee Keong is an Associate Professor in Commercial Law in the School of Accountancy at the Chinese University of Hong Kong which he joined following his admission as an Advocate and Solicitor of the High Court of Malaya in 1992. He holds degrees in both economics and law from Monash University in Australia, and obtained his LLM from the University of Hong Kong. His research interests reflect his educational background and are evidenced by numerous scholarly articles on the areas of company and securities law. He is the author of *Securities Regulation in Malaysia*, as well as co-author of *Understanding Company Law in Malaysia* and *Understanding Company Law in Hong Kong*, and he presently serves on the editorial board of the *Journal of Chinese and Corporative Law* and *Current Commercial Law*.

Vinayak Pradhan graduated LLB (Honours) from the University of Singapore. He read in Chambers in Skrine & Co and, after having been called to the Malaysia Bar in 1974, worked as a legal assistant in Skrine & Co until his admission to the partnership in 1981. Mr Pradhan is a Fellow of the Chartered Institute of Arbitrators, United Kingdom, as well as a Fellow of the Malaysia Institute of Arbitrators. He was called to the Singapore Bar in 1991.

CHAPTER 1

THE MALAYSIAN ECONOMY—
CURRENT POSITION AND TRENDS
by Sulaiman B Mahbob

INTRODUCTION

Since 1989 there has been a period of very rapid economic growth for Malaysia. In large measure this has been the result of structural adjustment undertaken to bring the economy out of the unprecedented recession in the mid 1980s. Such efforts were, however, aided by a responsive private sector, high national savings and a large inflow of direct foreign investments, especially from Japan, the United States, Taiwan and Singapore, in search of locations with lower business and production costs. In addition, socio-political stability brought about by economic growth and the impact of the distributional strategies of the New Economic Policy 1971–90 was instrumental in the rapid turnaround of the economy after the recession in 1985. The impressive performance has led to considerable transformation of the economy, with manufacturing now accounting for the bulk of output and merchandise exports.

These economic changes, however, do come with some challenges. Among these are increasing price pressures and labour shortages. So far the country has been able to overcome these challenges. Considerable price stability has been attained in spite of the rapid economic growth and low unemployment. The challenge for Malaysia is to continue with its record of maintaining strong growth, yet to maintain price stability.

ECONOMIC GROWTH AND TRANSFORMATION

The economy expanded between 8% and 9% per annum between 1988 and 1995, making that period the fastest growing since Independence in 1957. This achievement may be compared with the current Sixth Malaysia Plan annual target of only 7.5%. This expansion has enabled Malaysians to enjoy a higher standard of living with per capita income rising from US$2050 in 1985 to US$3389 in 1994. Unemployment has fallen significantly from 8.3% in 1986 to a low of 2.9% in 1994 making the labour market very tight and forcing wage levels up. In terms of quality of life, average Malaysians have experienced improvements in their welfare. Life expectancy, a good indicator of this, has improved from 67.7 years in 1985 to 70.2 years in 1994 for males and from 72.4 years to 74.5 for females.

The sectoral composition of the total output has changed. Manufacturing accounted for 32% of GDP in 1994 compared with 20% in 1985, while that of agriculture declined from 21% to 15% during the same period. About 45% of the GDP consists of services which during 1988–95 grew rapidly at the rate of 9.4% annually. The major contribution to growth came from manufacturing, construction and services which have expanded at double digit rates in the past years, especially between 1990 and 1993. As a result of this change in output, the pattern of exports also changed; manufactures now account for the bulk (over 70%) of merchandise exports, compared with only about 32% in 1982.

Sectoral Shares of GDP

Year	Manufacturing	Agriculture	Construction	Services	Others
1985	19.7	20.8	4.8	43.5	11.2
1990	26.9	18.7	3.6	42.6	8.2
1994	31.7	14.5	4.2	44.5	5.1

Year	GDP Growth	Inflation	Unemployment
1986	1.2	0.7	8.5
1988	8.9	2.5	7.2
1989	9.2	2.8	6.3
1990	9.7	3.1	5.1
1991	8.7	4.4	4.3
1992	7.8	4.7	3.7
1993	8.3	3.6	3.0
1994	8.5	3.7	2.9

Economic diversification has been facilitated by the rapid progress of industrialisation which was given impetus by the Industrial Master Plan (IMP) covering the period from 1985 to 1995. Although Malaysia continues to be an important producer of primary materials, in particular natural rubber, palm oil and petroleum, it is also increasingly becoming a major producer of electronics and electrical products such as air-conditioners and textiles, in addition to being a major supplier of latex-dipped products.

The targets of the first IMP were exceeded for almost all industries for the period 1985 to 1992. Electronics and electrical production expanded by 30.5% compared with the target of 11% under the IMP. Textiles output increased by 14.7% compared with the target of 10.2%, while automobile output increased by 15.8% as against the target of 7.4%. Wood-based industries echoed a similar trend, with growth per annum estimated at 17.4% as compared to the targeted 6.1%.

The principal source of these changes has been the rapid inflow of direct foreign investments (DFI) from the East Asian economies, as well as from North America, in view of the attractiveness of the investment climate, in particular the political stability and availability of a comprehensive set of investment incentives. The liberalisation and deregulation measures undertaken in the late 1980s attracted DFI, which is still continuing to flow into the economy in a significant amount. The present policy is to allow foreign investors to hold equity up to 100% if exports account for over 50% of total output, and investments with shareholders' funds not exceeding RM2.5 million do not need licensing. DFI accounted for about 49.4% of total private investments in 1994. It is the current policy to step up domestic investments in view of the issues relating to heavy reliance on DFI, namely the increasing outflow of investment income in the nation's external account and its association with heavy importation of intermediate and capital goods.

Trend of FDI/DI Flows in Approved Manufacturing Projects,
1986–July 1995

Year	No. of Approved Projects	Foreign Investment (FDI) (RM mil)	Domestic Investment (DI) (RM mil)	Total Investment (RM mil)	DFI/Total Investment (%)	DI/Total Investment (%)
1986	447	1,687.9	3,475.3	5,163.2	32.7	67.3
1987	333	2,060.0	1,873.9	3,933.9	52.4	47.6
1988	732	4,878.0	4,215.9	9,093.9	53.6	46.4
1989	792	8,652.7	3,562.7	12,215.4	70.8	29.2
1990	906	17,629.1	10,539.0	28,168.1	62.6	37.4
1991	973	17,055.3	13,763.1	30,818.4	55.3	44.7
1992	874	17,772.1	10,003.0	27,775.1	64.0	36.0
1993	686	6,287.2	7,465.5	13,752.7	45.7	54.3
1994	870	11,339.1	11,612.2	22,951.3	49.4	50.6
Jan-July 1995	490	4,852.7	7,038.8	11,891.5	40.8	59.2

Source: MIDA

Despite the changes in the composition of total output, Malaysia is still beset with problems associated with its economic structure. The total manufacturing output still consists predominantly of electrical and electronics products and textile and rubber products. These three made up 70.8% of total manufacturing exports in 1994. Further, the production of these goods contributed a low value-added portion to the economy. In many cases the value-added component only comprised about 12–15% of total sales. Import content is still high, accounting for about 65% of total output value. Increases in DFI often led to increases in imports in the forms of investment and intermediate goods such as machinery and equipment. The balance of trade in the first seven months of 1995 indicated a negative of RM6.8 billion compared to only RM474 million for the same period the previous year.

This position is reflected in the current account of the balance of payments. Although the basic balance is good in view of the continued inflow of long-term capital investments, the current account has been under pressure since 1990. The trade balance is now in deficit while the outflow in services has been rising to an estimated RM15.7 billion in 1994. The trade balance changes between positive and negative. There is a tendency for imports to pick up to accompany increases in DFI but later to be moderated as they are translated into exports. However, what is of concern to the government is the widening services deficit. This is due to Malaysia's reliance on foreign suppliers of services such as freight and education. Malaysia's shipping capacity is still inadequate. It also has to send thousands of its students abroad, given the inadequate higher education facilities at home.

NATIONAL ECONOMIC MANAGEMENT

Malaysia has successfully steered its economy out of recession and has now been enjoying a period of rapid growth at the rates of 8–9% per annum for more than seven consecutive years. In fact it is now faced with the problems of managing success. After the recession the posture of national economic management evolved from one with a high presence of the public sector in the economy up to the mid 1980s to one which emphasises the greater role of the private sector. The government has actively pursued the policy of privatisation of its enterprises on the basis of its long-term plan for privatisation. It has also been strengthening its finances so as to achieve a balanced budget, which was attained in 1993 and 1994. In order to promote the private sector role in the economy, the government has continually reduced corporate taxes and provided support to private enterprises in the form of training and R&D incentives, as well as other financial and fiscal assistance. Double deduction of training expenses for tax calculation and the creation of funds for shipping and food production, as well as for training (the Human Resource Development Fund) are among the various assistance programs made available to the private sector.

The focus is now to enhance the role of science and technology in order to further modernise the economy and deepen the industrialisation process. Thus far Malaysia has relied heavily on labour-intensive export-oriented industries such as the textile, electrical and electronic industries. Technology is absolutely crucial for industrial development and implementation of heavy industries to take place. There is now increasing interest in expanding industries such as automobile production, and going into new production such as wafer fabrication and aerospace. For this purpose the government is now actively implementing a new industrial master plan (the New IMP), covering the period 1996–2005. An active government and private sector consultative group on high technology (MIGHT) has been set up to advise the government on matters related to greater adoption of high technology.

As a consequence of rapid growth, the nation has experienced price pressures and a tight labour market. Controlling inflation has acquired a prominent place in national economic management, especially in the formulation of its fiscal and monetary policies. The consumer price index has hovered around 3.5–4% annually and is becoming a persistent issue of concern with public policy focused on attaining zero inflation. The attainment of governmental budgetary balance and the strong anti-inflationary stance of monetary policies has contributed to containment of price escalation since 1993. However, the overall aggregate demand was still high throughout 1994 and 1995 and is expected to continue into 1996 and 1997 given the growth of expenditure in both the private and public sectors. This is partly due to the implementation during the period of major projects such as the new airport at Sepang and the light rail transit system (LRT) in Kuala Lumpur as well as the construction of the Commonwealth Games complex. These expenditures are made amid high employment and income levels and a tight labour market.

The zero inflation policy contained efforts not only in the form of monetary and fiscal policies but also greater consumerism and some price control. The latter covers a few essential items such as rice, sugar and cement. The effectiveness of price control as a measure to combat inflation is often doubted. It is no substitute for market forces in bringing about supply and demand equilibrium. In the long run it is better to encourage greater competition and market liberalisation rather than resorting to price controls. The government has attempted, through liberal imports, to increase food supply, especially because of the increase in food price indexes.

Both short-term and long-term measures to address the issues of labour and skill shortages have begun to be implemented. In the interim, the government has allowed the importation of labour to meet requirements in plantations, in agriculture and also in selected manufacturing and services. Many of these foreign workers have been imported from Indonesia, the Philippines and Bangladesh. But in the long run the aim is to produce a greater number of Malaysians skilled in various trades so as to meet the requirements of industry and of general economic modernisation. Thousands of Malaysian students are sent abroad annually to pursue technical and professional training while the general education system is increasingly oriented to science and technology. In addition, the private sector has been encouraged to provide skill training to its workers, and fiscal incentives are made available for this purpose.

Earlier the nation embarked on the implementation of infrastructural projects to improve the attractiveness of the country as an investment centre. Projects such as the north-south highway, ports, the power supply, the LRT and the privatisation of airports and ports have been implemented or are in advanced stage of implementation, in order to reduce bottlenecks and congestion and improve efficiency in the delivery and movement of goods and services in the country. This will help reduce costs of business in the country.

Total Manpower Requirements According to Year and Category of Occupation, 1990–98

Category of Occupation	Total
Engineering discipline	9,274
Science graduates	737
Other graduates	6,634
Technician	13,312
Craft skills	21,077
Operator CAD-CAM	8,996
Semi-skilled workers	162,480
Unskilled workers	92,485
Total	314,995

Source: Prospective Employment Survey, Ministry of Human Resources (1993)

Given the need for modernisation and further development of the services sector, as well as the importance of having an efficient economy, Malaysia has made efforts to improve its capital market. Measures to support and regulate the development of the securities industry, the development of the private debt and bond market as well as the market of derivatives and futures have been put in place. These include the establishment of a rating agency. In addition the country has established a tax haven in the island of Labuan to encourage offshore financial activities. Hopefully these measures will help nurture greater sophistication of the services industry, especially of financial services.

CHALLENGES AND PROSPECTS

It is the aim of the country to achieve developed-country status by the year 2020. For this purpose the economy has to grow at the rate of about 7% annually for three decades. This target is not unattainable as Malaysia has already been able to exceed that target for seven years since 1988. But to be a developed country, Malaysia must address its structural limitations, particularly on the role and contributions of high-tech industries and modern services. Manufacturing has to make a greater value-added contribution than it does now, and critical components in the value chain, such as wafer fabrication in the case of electronics, and engine production in the case of automobile industries, have to be undertaken in the country.

The challenges faced by the country include the need to acquire technologies and to upgrade the overall technical capability and skill of its workforce. New skills, such as CAD/CAM and design-based engineering and skills related to tool and die and mouldings, are essential to allow the industrial development process to take place. These become more critical as Malaysia advances in automobile production, micro-electronics, aerospace and advanced materials. As a medium-term measure Malaysia must continue to source technologies from abroad, for example, its attempt in the joint venture with a French automobile industry which will allow the transfer of technology in engine production.

The need to address the labour market will also receive attention from policy-makers. Wages have been rising in view of the high levels of demand and the tight labour market. In the short term, importation of labour has been resorted to, to meet employment requirements of the plantation and construction sectors, as well as of selected services. But continued reliance on foreign labour may depress wages and this in turn would delay firm decisions to embark on more capital-intensive production methods which would increase Malaysia's production capacity in the future. The policy on the use of foreign labour as an interim measure needs to be accompanied by greater bias towards investments with higher capital content so as to discourage labour-intensive industries from coming to Malaysia. There is already an indication that the capital size per approved project has been rising.

Enhancing the competitiveness of the economy will be a major macro-economic concern in the next five-year development plan, given these current issues. The challenge will be to continue to attract new investments, especially in new industries, to enable Malaysians to acquire new experience as well as expertise and skill. Malaysia needs increasingly to attract industries which demand less land and less labour content but more technology. In addition, the number of countries becoming more liberal and less regulated has increased. The Indian and Chinese governments have liberalised and deregulated their economies and have received a significant inflow of DFI. These countries will become the focus of private investments, especially with their generally low labour costs, thus providing some competition to Malaysia, especially for capital.

Related to this is the issue of rising costs. Although, relative to Japan, Hong Kong and Singapore, Malaysia's costs of production are still low, they are rising and may impact on its competitiveness. In order to address this, industries will have to improve their productivity at a rate greater than wage increases. Greater automation and computerisation, and the use of information technology as well as continued skill upgrading in the work force, are measures which are essential to address this issue and the overall efficiency of firms. This matter has greater urgency now with the withdrawal of the Generalised System of Preferences (GSP) by the United States in 1997 and the fast tracking of the ASEAN Free Trade Area (AFTA).

The government is now actively implementing its new IMP covering the period 1996–2005. The Ministry of International Trade and Industry has opted to use a cluster-based economic development approach as a basis of future industrial planning. A cluster approach entails planning for both horizontal and vertical integration of industries as a basis of future industrial growth. As stated earlier, a major limitation of the previous approach is its emphasis on macro targets, namely output, export and employment. While these serve their purposes, they do not fully address the issues of depth and linkages and the importance of supporting foundations such as technology and human resource development.

Notwithstanding these challenges, the prospects for the economy to grow on a sustainable basis at about 8% in the medium term cannot be doubted. Both public and private investment expenditure will play an important role in helping the process of growth. While major projects will be ready to assist business and industry, policies towards R&D, technology and human resource development are in place to help business planning in the future. That Malaysia weathered its worst recession in 1985 and insulated itself from world economic quandary in 1991 and 1992 provides hope and confidence that Malaysia is now in a better position to steer its economy to more sustained growth.

CHAPTER 2

JOINT VENTURE AGREEMENTS
by William Leong

We are not fit to lead an army on the march unless we are familiar with the face of the country—its mountains and forests, its pitfalls and precipices, its marshes and swamps.
We cannot enter into alliances until we are acquainted with the designs of our neighbours.
We shall be unable to turn natural advantages to account unless we make use of local guides.[1]

In deciding to invest in a foreign country and in implementing an investment plan, the investor is very much like the General in Sun Tzu's army. It is necessary to know the designs of the people being dealt with, the local conditions and regulatory set up, so as not to fall into precipices. More importantly, it is necessary to make full use of the advantages the country has to offer by using local advisers. It is not the intention and it is not within the scope of this work to provide a detailed exposition of the entire laws and policies relating to foreign investment in Malaysia. This would be encroaching on the expertise of consultants. However, following are some of the signposts and byways which a foreign investor needs to look out for during the investment process in Malaysia.

THE FOREIGN INVESTOR AND BUMIPUTRA PARTNERS

One of the first policy requirements that a foreign investor hears of when contemplating doing business in Malaysia is the National Development Policy (NDP) and the requirement to have a Malaysian joint venture with Bumiputra partners. Is this a legal requirement? Is there a way around such things ?

One of the follow up questions usually posed is: 'Can the shares in the joint venture company be registered in the local partner's name but held in trust for the foreign partner?' This is a common reaction when one hears for the first time of the need to have 30% of the shares in a joint venture company reserved for Bumiputras.

There are various reasons a party is reluctant to permit outsiders to have equity in a company, one of which is the need to maintain control of confidential information or technology or other proprietary interest.

To answer the question, it is necessary to understand the legal system in Malaysia, in particular the laws regulating contractual relationships, the NDP and the structure by which the NDP is implemented.

Depending on the situation, there may be no necessity to reserve any share for Bumiputra or Malaysian interests; or, if there is such a requirement, it may be in the nature of a moral obligation and not a legal obligation, so that violation of the requirement is not an offence that would make the transaction illegal. However, if it is a legal obligation, then failure to comply would be an offence and the arrangement would be illegal, with all the unpleasant consequences attendant on it. The requirement to reserve 30% Bumiputra interest is found in the Guidelines for the Regulation of Acquisition of Assets, Mergers and Takeovers.

THE GUIDELINES REGULATING THE ACQUISITION OF ASSETS, MERGERS AND TAKEOVERS

The Foreign Investment Committee (FIC) was established by the Government of Malaysia in 1974 to formulate policy guidelines on local and foreign investments in all sectors of the economy and to monitor the progress of investments. The policies of the FIC are contained in the Guidelines for the Regulation of Acquisition of Assets, Mergers and Takeovers. The following transactions require the approval of the FIC:

(1) Acquisition by foreigners of substantial fixed assets in Malaysia including the purchase of residential properties.

(2) Acquisition, mergers and takeovers of companies resulting in transfer of control to foreigners.

(3) Acquisition resulting in the transfer of 15% or more of the voting power of a company to foreigners.

(4) Joint venture agreements and technical know-how agreements if the agreements transfer control of Malaysian businesses to foreigners.

(5) Any merger or takeover by a Malaysian or foreign interest.

(6) Any other acquisitions exceeding RM5 million in value whether by a Malaysian or foreign interest.

ICA AND SIMILAR LEGISLATION

The Industrial Co-ordination Act 1975 (ICA) applies to persons engaging in any manufacturing activity. The Licensing Officer is the Secretary-General of the Ministry of International Trade and Industry (MITI) as gazetted under Gazette Notification PU (B) 31/78. The object of the Act is to ensure orderly growth in the manufacturing sector. Only manufacturing companies with shareholders' funds of RM2.5 million or more or who engage 75 or more full-time employees need apply for a licence under the ICA in this context:

'Manufacturing activity' is defined to mean the making, altering, blending, ornamenting, finishing or otherwise treating, or adapting any article or substance with a view to its use, sale, transport, delivery or disposal and includes the assembly of parts and ship repairing but shall not include any activity normally associated with retail or wholesale trade.

'Shareholders' funds' means the aggregate amount of a company's paid-up capital (in respect of preference shares and ordinary shares and not including any amount in respect of bonus shares to the extent they were issued out of capital reserve created by revaluation of fixed assets), reserves (other than any capital reserve which was created by revaluation of fixed assets and provisions for depreciation, renewals or replacements and diminutions in value of assets), balance of share premium account (not including any amount credited therein at the instance of issuing bonus shares at premium out of capital reserve by revaluation of fixed assets) and balance of profit and loss appropriation account.

'Full-time paid employee' means all persons normally working in the establishment for at least six hours a day and at least 20 days a month for 12 months during the year and who receive a salary. Persons such as travelling sales, engineering, maintenance and repair personnel, or who are paid by and are under the control of the establishment are also included. Full-time paid employees also include directors of incorporated enterprises except when paid solely for the attendance at Board of Directors meetings. Family workers who receive regular salaries or allowances and who contribute to the Employees Provident Fund (EPF) or other superannuation funds are also included in the definition.

The Licensing Officer is the Secretary General of the Ministry of International Trade and Industry as gazetted under Gazette Notification PU(B) 31/78. And in deciding whether to grant a manufacturing licence, the Licensing Officer is authorised to do so

subject to conditions, which conditions would include the requirement that the business reserve a certain portion of the equity for
Bumiputra and Malaysian interest. MITI has laid down guidelines
for foreign equity participation in the manufacturing business. The
guidelines are:

(1) No equity condition will be imposed on projects exporting 80%
or more of their production.

(2) The level of equity participation for other export-oriented
projects is as follows:

(a) for projects exporting between 51% and 79% of their produc-
     tion, foreign equity ownership of up to 79% may be allowed,
     depending on factors such as the level of technology, spin-off
     effects, size of the investment, location, value-addition and
     the utilisation of raw materials and components;

(b) for projects exporting between 29% and 50% of their produc-
     tion, foreign equity ownership of between 30% and 51% will
     be allowed, depending upon similar factors to those men-
     tioned above;

(c) for projects exporting less than 20% of their production,
     foreign ownership is allowed up to a maximum of 30%.

Notwithstanding this, for projects producing goods involving high
technology or which are priority products for the domestic market
as determined by the Government from time to time, foreign equity
ownership of up to 100% may be allowed.

The above guidelines do not apply to certain products or activities
where there are limits on the maximum level of foreign equity
ownership.

Where foreign equity is less than 100%, the balance of the equity
to be taken up by Malaysians should be allocated according to the
following principles:

(1) For projects initiated by foreigners and where no local partners
have been identified:

(a) if 70% or more of the equity is held by foreigners, the balance
     of the equity will be reserved for Bumiputras;

(b) if less than 70% of the equity is held by foreigners, 30% will
     be reserved for Bumiputras and the balance for non-
     Bumiputras. For example, if foreigners hold 60% of the
     equity, 30% will be reserved for Bumiputras and the remain-
     ing 10% for non-Bumiputras. If the equity reserved for

Bumiputras is not taken up, MITI will allocate part of the balance to non-Bumiputras.

(2) For projects initiated by Bumiputras on a joint venture basis with foreigners:

(a) if 70% or more of the equity is held by foreigners, the balance of equity will be reserved for the Bumiputra concerned;

(b) if less than 70% of the equity is held by foreigners, the balance will be reserved for Bumiputras. However, if Bumiputras are unable to take up the entire balance, MITI will allocate part of the balance to non-Bumiputras.

(3) For projects initiated by non-Bumiputras on a joint venture basis with foreigners:

(a) if 70% or more of equity is taken up by foreigners, the balance of the equity will be allocated to the non-Bumiputras concerned;

(b) if less than 70% of the equity is taken up by foreigners, 30% will be allocated to the non-Bumiputras concerned and the balance will be reserved for Bumiputras. However, under special circumstances, the non-Bumiputras may be permitted to take up the entire balance of the equity as decided by MITI.

For projects which involve the extraction or mining and processing of mineral ores, majority foreign equity participation of up to 100% is permitted. In determining the percentage, the following criteria will be taken into consideration:

(a) the level of investments, technology and risk involved in the projects;

(b) the availability of Malaysian expertise in the areas of exploration, mining and processing of the minerals concerned; and

(c) the degree of integration and level of value-addition involved in the projects.

What are the implications and consequences if the condition to reserve a certain portion of the equity is not complied with? Is the condition imposed by the FIC or MITI law or policy? If it is law, would the joint venture agreement become void? How is the contract affected by the non-compliance with the condition? To answer these questions, some understanding of the Malaysian legal system is necessary.

THE MALAYSIAN LEGAL SYSTEM

The Malaysian legal system has been influenced by five historical events. These are the establishment of the Malacca Sultanate at the beginning of the 15th century, the spread of Islam to South-East Asia, the migration of Chinese and Indians to Malaysian soil, particularly during the 19th century, British colonial rule and independence which was achieved on 31 August 1957.

Prior to the establishment of British colonial rule, the laws which were enforced in the Malay States were a mixture of Muslim and customary laws, and the Chinese and Indian settlers then were generally left to enforce law and order themselves through their headman or leader. During the British colonial era, general principles of English law were introduced and applied subject to the overriding qualification that English law would be applied with such modifications as local circumstances demanded. This pattern was continued upon termination of British colonial rule by the passage of the Civil Law Act, 1956. This statute in substance provided for the adoption in West Malaysia of the common law of England and the rules of equity as administered in that country as at 7 April 1956. In East Malaysia, English statutes of general application, in force in England on certain dates, were also adopted. In all cases, the adoption of English law is subject to the absence of provisions as may have been made by any written law in force in Malaysia, and the common law, the rules of equity and the statutes of general application shall be so far as circumstances of the States of Malaysia and their respective inhabitants permit and subject to such qualifications as local circumstances render necessary.

Since independence, Malaysia has built upon the legacy of its legal infrastructure and has produced a legal system which is its own, founded broadly on universal concepts of justice. Very simply, there are two sources of Malaysian law: written and unwritten. Written law consists of:

(1) The Federal Constitution.

(2) The respective constitutions of the 13 States which make up the federation.

(3) Principal and subsidiary legislation enacted under the legislative authority of Parliament.

(4) Principal and subsidiary legislation enacted by State Assemblies under powers conferred upon them by their respective constitutions.

Unwritten law consists of:

(1) The common law and the rules of equity as developed by Malaysian courts.

(2) Judicial decisions of superior courts.

(3) Customs which have acquired the status of law as recognised by the courts.

Since written laws have to be enacted by Parliament, the FIC guidelines are not written law. But the condition imposed by MITI is law, because the condition is imposed under the powers conferred on the Licensing Officer under the ICA, which is a statute enacted by Parliament. Therefore, one has to look at the industry in which the foreign investor wishes to participate and the laws governing the industry. As mentioned before, manufacturing is regulated by the ICA, banking and financial services by the Banking and Financial Industry Act, insurance by the Insurance Act and shipping by the Merchant Shipping Act. This is not an exhaustive list, but each requires a licence to be issued before the business can be carried out. In granting the licence, the authority concerned is empowered by the legislation or by the relevant subordinate legislation to issue the licence subject to conditions. The conditions may include the requirement to reserve a certain portion for Bumiputras.

If the industry is governed by some form of legislation and the requirement is a condition of the licence, the requirement has the force of law. Failure to comply may lead to the licence being withdrawn. The other consequence is that any arrangement to defeat the law, such as the use of a device to register the shares in a Bumiputra dummy holding in trust for a foreigner, would be illegal. In other words, should the dummy become smart and run away with the shares, the foreigner cannot seek the assistance of the courts to enforce the dummy's obligations.

If the industry is not regulated by any legislation but the transaction falls within the guidelines, the approval of the FIC is required. The FIC, in granting its approval, may do so subject to conditions which may include the need to reserve a certain portion of the equity for Bumiputras. If there is non-compliance with this condition, the FIC does not have any powers to punish the non-compliance. But there may be other means by which the foreigner can be persuaded to comply, such as the need to obtain work permits. In dealing with government agencies with regard to the joint venture agreement, the consequences of the failure to comply with the conditions of an FIC approval would have to be examined under the laws of contract.

THE LAW OF CONTRACT

A joint venture agreement, being a contract, is governed by the laws of contract in Malaysia. The applicable legislation is at present the Contracts Act 1950 (Act 136) (Revised 1974). There are, however, certain issues that have to be considered. One of these is whether certain principles of the English common law of contracts are applicable or whether the Contracts Act 1950 is exhaustive. There is a principle of the English common law that a contract is void if the contract is against public policy. If the FIC guidelines are taken to be public policy, non-compliance with them would, in accordance with the principle, be void.

It is therefore necessary to consider the origins of the Contracts Act 1950 and the applicability of English law. The Contracts Act 1950 has its forbears in the Indian Contracts Act 1872. When Malaysia was under the rule of the British, the British extended (with minor modifications) the Indian Contracts Act to the then Federated Malay States as the Contract Enactment 1899. The Indian Contracts Act was the product of the work of a number of India Law Commissions. In drafting the Act, the Law Commission to a large extent based its proposal on English common law at that time. The question is whether the Indian Contracts Act and, by extension, the Malaysian Contracts Act 1950 are a codification of English contract law. Besides the Contracts Act 1950, there is another piece of legislation that one has to consider: the Civil Law Act 1956 (Revised 1972). The relevant sections are ss 3 and 5, which provide for the application of English law in Malaysia. Section 3 is of general application and s 5 is limited to the application of English law in issues relating to 'commercial' matters.

The extent to which English contract law is applicable to Malaysia after the Contracts Act is dependent on the interpretation of ss 3 and 5 of the Civil Law Act 1956. The relevant part of s 3(1) provides:

Save in so far as other provision has been made or may hereafter be made by any written law in force in the Federation or any part thereof, the Court shall apply the common law and rules of equity as administered in England at the date of the coming into force of this Act: Provided always that the said Common law and rules of equity shall be applied so far as the circumstances of the States and the Settlements comprised in the Federation and their respective inhabitants permit and subject to such qualifications as the local circumstances render necessary.

Section 5 of the Civil Law Act 1956 provides as follows:

(1) In all questions or issues which arise or which have to be decided in the States of Johor, Kedah, Kelantan, Negeri Sembilan, Pahang, Perlis, Selangor and Tregganu with respect to the law of partnerships, corporations, banks and banking, principal and agents, carriers by air, land and sea, marine insurance, average, life and fire insurance and with respect to mercantile law generally, the law to be administered shall be the same as would be administered in England in the like case at the date of coming into force of this Ordinance, if such question or issue had arisen or had to be decided in England, unless in any case other provision is or shall be made by any written law.

(2) In all questions and issues which arise or which have to be decided in the States of Malacca and Penang with respect to the law concerning any of the matters referred to in the last preceding sub-section, the law to be administered shall be the same as would be administered in England in the like case at the corresponding period, if such question had arisen or had to be decided in England, unless in any case other provision is or shall be made by any written law.

It is clear from a reading of the two sections that s 5 introduces where applicable the whole of the law administered in England and the different language of s 3(1) suggests that State law is not included. It is more important to note that, under s 3, English law is only applicable subject to such qualifications as the local circumstances render necessary and in s 5(1) and (2) English law is to be administered unless in any case other provision is or shall be made by any written law.

With the passing of the Malaysian Contracts Act 1950, it would be appreciated that there is some force to the argument that 'other provision' has been made and therefore English law is not applicable.

There is a Federal Court decision, *Tan Mooi Liang v Lim Soon Seng* [1974] 2 *MLJ* 60 wherein the Federal Court held that, as the law of partnership in Malaysia was contained in the Contracts Act, English principles were inapplicable. There is a view that the interpretation of the Federal Court may be too wide and that a narrower interpretation should be followed. This narrower interpretation, according to Professor Sinnadurai (as he then was), is that if the issue before the court is covered by a particular provision of the law, be it different from English law, the issue should be determined by reference to that particular provision. If, however, there is no provision dealing with the issue in question, though there may be a general Act covering certain aspects of the law, the issue is to be settled by reference to English law on the matter not covered by the Act. Thus, unless the local legislation is intended to be a codification of the law, English principle should be applicable in areas not covered by the legislation.

From the above discussion, it will be seen that English principles of contract law would be applicable if the Malaysian Contracts Act is not a codification of the law of contract in Malaysia. There is equally strong judicial authority for both sides of the argument as to whether the Malaysian Contracts Act is or is not a code. The general consensus, however, is that when there are no provisions in the Contracts Act on a particular subject in the law of contract or if a particular subject is covered by the Act, but provisions relating to this subject are not exhaustive, English law would, by virtue of the Civil Law Act, be applicable. Where the Act makes certain provisions, even if this is different from English law or Indian law then the clear provisions of the section in the Act must be followed.

Contracts Act 1950 Section 24(e)

Section 24(e) of the Contracts Act 1950 provides that the court may declare any agreement to be void if the court regards the agreement to be immoral or opposed to public policy. What constitutes public policy? Is this the same concept as is understood by the common law in England? Are courts in Malaysia bound to apply the principles and the established heads of public policy that courts in England have to abide by? In the only reported decision, *Theresa Chong v Kin Khoon & Co* [1976] 2 *MLJ* 253, the Federal Court held that Malaysian courts are bound by the traditional heads of common law and that they should not invent a new head of public policy.

If the courts hold that the FIC guidelines are public policy, any agreement that contravenes the guidelines should, on the basis discussed above, be struck down by the courts as being against public policy under s 24(e).

Cases Involving the Guidelines

Courts in Malaysia have had the opportunity to consider the legal nature of the FIC guidelines. However, the several pronouncements have not been consistent. In one line of cases the courts have held that the FIC guidelines are not public policy. In *Ho Kok Cheong Sdn Bhd v Lim Tay Tiong* [1979] 2 *MLJ* 224 it was submitted on behalf of the defendants that the guidelines apply to the agreement and the requirements of the guidelines have not been complied with, and therefore the agreement is void and unenforceable as being in contravention of public policy, or alternatively the contravention renders the agreement illegal and unenforceable or the non-compliance renders the agreement voidable at the option of the first defendant in that case. Judge Wan Hamzah said:

> The guidelines were issued not pursuant to any power given by law, and in my opinion they have no force of law but are of advisory character merely. I do not think that non-compliance with the guidelines can be taken as an act opposed to public policy. The guidelines reflect the government's political policy, but government's policy is not public policy.

In *National Land Finance Co-operative Society Ltd v Sharidal Sdn Bhd* [1983] 2 *MLJ* 211 the respondents had agreed to buy certain immovable property. It was a condition of the agreement that the sale should be subject to the approval of the FIC. In the event, the FIC refused its approval but suggested that the property be transferred to a joint venture company with at least 30% of its equity held by Bumiputras. The respondents contended that the agreement became void when the FIC refused to approve the sale, while the appellants maintained that the agreement did not become void but subsisted because there was a conditional approval. The FIC, in reply to the application for its approval, stated:

> I am directed to inform you that the Foreign Investment Committee is not agreeable to the transaction to proceed as proposed. However, the FIC has no objection to the purchase of Sharidal Complex by National Land Finance Co-operative from Sharidal Sdn Bhd being undertaken on condition National Land Finance Co-operative Society Ltd incorporates a joint-venture company with Bumiputra holding at least 30% of the company's equity.

The Federal Court held that it would be a strain on the language if it was to agree with the appellants' view that the FIC approved the proposed sale. The court took the view that the FIC's letter was a rejection of the application for approval of the sale and went on to say that, in order for the appellants to argue that the FIC's letter was a conditional approval, it was necessary for them to show that the requirement to transfer the land to a joint venture company with at least 30% Bumiputra equity was within the contemplation of the parties when they signed the agreement.

There is as yet no decision by the courts directly on the legal status of the guidelines. It is unlikely that there will ever be such a pronouncement as each case will invariably turn on its own set of peculiar facts. What a foreign investor may need to look for is not an answer to this question but, knowing the precipices and pitfalls, ask what he needs to equip himself with to avoid them.

Remedies and protection

What can the foreign investor do to protect its interest in having to reserve 30% of its equity to a Bumiputra or Malaysian shareholder?

It is assumed that the joint venture vehicle used here will be a company limited by shares and incorporated under the Malaysian Companies Act 1965. This is the most practical and common form of joint venture vehicle used in the country.

Bearing in mind that the percentage of capital which is to be reserved is 30% or so, the majority of the shares are still held by the foreign investor. Unless otherwise provided, the common shares of a company are one vote per share. Therefore the foreign investor will have majority control of the company.

Notwithstanding the majority control, the foreign investor may ensure that its rights and interests are fully protected by having a shareholders' agreement; by having pre-emption rights; by reserving important decisions to require the express consent of the foreign investor; and by providing for the joint venture to be terminated on the occurrence of specific events and on termination for the transfer of the shares.

Shareholders' Agreement

The Articles of Association form the contract which deals with the rights and liabilities of shareholders as between the shareholders and the company. However, the Articles of Association of a company have to be registered with the Registrar of Companies and are available for inspection by the public, being a public document.

In many cases, the relationship between shareholders will be governed by certain terms and conditions which usually relate to confidential or technical information, or matters which the parties would not wish to be known to their commercial competitors. This can be contained in a shareholders' agreement which is a private document.

The foreign investor may set out in the shareholders' agreement provisions governing the rights of the parties in relation to matters which the foreign investor wishes to protect. Examples of these would be clauses relating to confidentiality and non-disclosure of know-how, technical information and matters of this nature. It is also usual to provide in the shareholders' agreement provisions relating to pre-emptive rights, termination, and restriction of the transfer of shares in the company.

Pre-emptive rights

Provisions for pre-emptive rights may be incorporated either in the Articles of Association or in the shareholders' agreement. Pre-emptive rights are the requirement in a proposed transfer first to offer the shares to the other shareholders in the company before they can be offered to third parties. The pre-emptive clause usually sets out in detail the procedure, time and also the price, or a mechanism for the determination of the price, to be offered. The language used has to be clear and precise because such clauses by their nature restrain the freedom to transfer a property or right of a person and courts are bound to view such restrictions strictly. It would also be appropriate to mention that it is a restriction, in the sense that the shares have first to be offered to the other shareholders, but that it cannot be an absolute prohibition against selling the shares. An absolute prohibition would be struck down by the courts and would be void.

Reservation of important decisions

It is also usual to provide in a shareholders' agreement that certain important decisions cannot be made without the express consent of one or both parties. It may also be provided that one or both shareholders may have a right of veto in respect of certain matters.

Although it is recognised that a shareholder may vote in the manner it deems fit, the conduct or act or resolution of the majority must not be oppressive or unfairly prejudicial to the minority shareholders under s 181 of the Companies Act 1965. Section 181 is similar to s 459 of the English Companies Act 1985. However, it was recognised by the Privy Council in the case of *Re Kong Thai Saw Mill* that the language of s 181 of the Companies Act 1965 is wider than the corresponding English provision.

There have been many cases in Malaysian courts where unhappy shareholders have sought the aid of the courts under s 181 of the Companies Act 1965 for relief against alleged oppressive acts of the majority. In view of this, obviously such clauses in the shareholders' agreement have to be drafted with great care to avoid having one party bound by the terms of the shareholders' agreement complain to the courts under the guise of s 181.

Termination and compulsory sale of the shares

The shareholders' agreement will set out the obligations and duties which each party will have to perform. It will also provide that, where there is a failure by one party to perform or comply with a term which is agreed to be important to the joint venture, such a failure will be a breach of contract which entitles the innocent party to terminate the joint venture.

It is also usual to provide that in such a situation the innocent party may, instead of having the company wound up, require the defaulting party to sell its shares, or in some cases require the defaulting party to buy out the innocent party.

This provision for the compulsory sale of the shares may also include instances where there is no breach or default but, as is common in business, where the parties are deadlocked. There are several methods by which this compulsory sale can work.

Put and call option

In many cases the joint venture business is dependent on the continued support of one of the parties and the other cannot continue the business effectively without this support. In such instances the appropriate mechanism for the termination of the joint venture is to allow the party that cannot effectively continue the business to have an option to put its shares to the other party. Similarly, the party that can effectively continue the business may have a call on the shares of the other party. To be valid, it is necessary that all the material terms of the option are spelt out in the agreement. Courts can only enforce the terms that the parties have agreed upon and cannot write the contract for the parties. Thus, terms such as the number of shares, the price and the manner in which the payment of the price and the delivery of the shares are to be made must be set out in full. Bearing in mind that the party continuing the business will in all probability be the foreign investor, the question will be how to enforce such a put and call option when the foreigner will not be legally entitled to buy the shares. This can be done by requiring the other party to sell the shares to a party nominated by the foreigner who qualifies to buy the shares. Such a solution is allowed under the provisions of the Contracts Act and the English principles of contract.

The most difficult part of such a provision is the setting out of the price. This is usually done by using a formula agreed to by the parties for determining a fair price for the shares. It is also common to provide that the auditors or a reputable firm of accountants determine the fair value of the shares. This, however, tends to be less favoured as the auditors have the unenviable task of determining what the fair value of a company's shares may be. It would be useful to set out in the agreement how the auditors are to determine fair value, otherwise one party may be able to challenge the valuation in court.

Russian roulette

Another method of disposing of the shares is to allow one party to offer to purchase the shares from the other at the price named by the offeror. The offeree may then be allowed, instead of selling the shares, to buy the offeror's shares at the price named. This ensures that the offeror will name a fair price to sell its own shares. Such a provision will be enforceable in the courts of Malaysia. However, for obvious reasons such a clause is not popular and there are no known decisions of the courts regarding such a clause.

Winding up

If the parties cannot continue to work together, a petition may be filed to have the company wound up under the Companies Act. The court may order a company to be wound up if it finds that it is just and equitable to do so. This can include a situation where the parties are deadlocked and cannot carry on operations any longer.

It is undesirable to allow an on-going profitable organisation to be wound up and, in some cases, the court may instead order one of the shareholders to buy out the other at a price to be determined by the court. It is definitely not in the interest of the parties for the court to intervene at this stage to order the shares to be bought or sold at a price which would depend to some extent on a finding by the court of fault of one of the parties. Therefore the price would not be determined by purely commercial reasons and valuation as such. In these circumstances, it is important that the joint venture agreement should have a mechanism for the buying out by one of the parties of the other, and the formulation of the price should be specifically expressed.

CONCLUSION

It is hoped that, in this short chapter, the foreign investor has been appraised of the several issues which need to be attended to so that he will be better prepared to enjoy his journey in investing in Malaysia, as many have done.

---

1 Sun Tzu in *The Art of War*.

CHAPTER 3

FOREIGN TRADE AND INVESTMENT
by Tan Keok Yin

IMPORTANCE OF FOREIGN TRADE TO MALAYSIA'S ECONOMY

Malaysia has an open economy, where the policy aims at further liberalisation and deregulation. Foreign trade plays an important role in the country's development, with exports accounting for 93.1% of the Gross National Product (GNP) in 1996. Imports are also significant, as they contributed 94.5% of GNP. In 1995, Malaysia was the 19th largest exporter in the world and the 17th largest importer. Foreign investment is particularly significant in the manufacturing sector, as Malaysia is committed to becoming an industrialised nation by the year 2020. Hence, the internationalisation of the Malaysian economy will be intensified between now and the 21st century in pursuit of its Vision 2020 objective.

Malaysia's Trade Performance

Malaysia's competitive strength in internationalisation lies specifically in its ability to maintain a commendable balance of trade, sustaining growth in the value of merchandise exports and growth in the export of commercial services. The Global Competitiveness Report, conducted by the World Economic Forum in 1997, ranked Malaysia ninth among 53 countries, indicating that the country's trade policies support the long-term international activities of the individual company. Malaysia has sustained double digit growth rates in trade for the past eight years, except for 1992 and 1996 when growth was 9% and 3.1% respectively.

Total merchandise trade increased by 22.6% in 1995 from RM309.6 [US$123.44] billion to RM379.8 [US$151.43] billion (exchange rate: US$1.00 = RM2.5081, 1995 average exchange rate). Export growth was 20.4%, increasing from RM153.9 [US$61.4] billion to RM185.3 billion. In US currency, Malaysia's export value was US$73.9 billion. Imports, which increased from RM155.9 [US$62.2] billion to RM194.5 billion, grew at 24.7%. Malaysia's value of imports in US currency was US$77.6 billion.

Consequently, Malaysia's share of world merchandise trade increased to 1.5% in 1995 as compared to 1.4% in 1994. Malaysia is ranked as the 19th largest exporter, ahead of developed nations such as Australia, Austria and Denmark; and 17th largest for imports, ahead of Austria, Australia, Sweden and Denmark.

In terms of per capita of export, at US$3894.7 Malaysia's was higher than countries such as the United States of America (which was the world's largest exporter), Australia and developing economies such as the Republic of Korea and Thailand. In terms of per capita import, Malaysia's achievement of US$4089.5 exceeded that of developed economies such as the United States of America, Japan, Australia and developing economies of the People's Republic of China and Thailand.

In comparison with selected ASEAN countries, namely Singapore, Thailand and Indonesia, Malaysia is the second largest trading nation in ASEAN after Singapore, whether in terms of value of trade or export and import per capita. Singapore led with an export value of US$188.3 billion and imports valued at US$200.7 billion. Singapore's export and import per capita were US$62,766.7 and US$66,900 respectively.

Thailand, at third placing, reported export and import values of US$55.8 billion and US$69.1 billion respectively. Its export and import per capita were respectively US$930 and US$1151.7. Indonesia's export and import values were US$45 billion and US$42.2 billion respectively. Its export and import per capita were respectively US$234.4 and US$219.8.

Major export and import products

Products exported by Malaysia were manufactured goods (77.4% of total exports in 1995) and primary commodities (21%). Manufactured exports comprised mainly electrical and electronic products and machinery, textiles, clothing and footwear, and wood products. Major primary commodity exports were palm oil and palm kernel oil, timber and crude oil.

The main products exported under the Generalised System of Preferences (GSP) by Malaysia were electrical and electronic products, machinery and transport equipment, palm oil and related products, rubber goods, furniture and parts, and wood manufactures.

Products imported by Malaysia were primarily machinery and transport equipment (60% of total imports or RM116,744.1

27

[US$46,546.83] million in 1995), manufactured goods (13.9% or RM26,978.9 [US$10,756.71] million) and chemicals (7.1% or RM13,785.1 [US$5496.23] million). Machinery and transport equipment imports included electrical machinery, apparatus, appliances, electrical and electronic products, aircraft and ships. Manufactured goods included non-ferrous metal, rubber, iron and steel products.

Direction of trade

Malaysia's largest trading partner is ASEAN, with Singapore accounting for the largest market share. Of Malaysia's total trade in 1995, 22.2% was with ASEAN countries. Japan was the second largest trading partner, holding a 20.2% share of total Malaysian trade. The United States of America came in third with 18.4%, and the European Union had 14.7% of total trade.

Major individual markets for exports were led by the United States of America (20.7% of total exports or RM38,318.8 [US$15,278.02] million), followed by Singapore (20.3% or RM37,599.4 [US$14,991.19] million) and Japan (12.7% or RM23,580.4 [US$9401.7] million). Major individual sources of imports were led by Japan (27.3% of total imports or RM53,120.3 [US$21,179.5] million), followed by the United States of America (16.3% or RM31,752.6 [US$12,660.02] million) and Singapore (12.4% or RM24,088.9 [US$9,604.44] million).

Malaysia also enjoys GSP privileges from the European Union, the United States of America, Japan, Canada, Sweden, Switzerland, Austria, Australia, Norway, Russia, Finland, New Zealand, Hungary, Republic of Czech and Slovak, Poland and the Cumulative Rules of Origin (CRO) to ASEAN countries. Of total Malaysian exports, 12.5% or RM23.14 [US$9.23] billion were exports under GSP schemes.

The highest share or 54.3% of total GSP exports was to the European Union, valued at RM12.6 [US$5.02] billion. On an individual country basis, GSP exports to the European Union were led by exports to the United Kingdom (16% of total GSP exports) at RM3700.9 [US$1475.58] million. This was followed by Germany, at 11.5% of total GSP exports and amounting to RM2669.2 [US$1064.23] million.

Malaysia's GSP exports to the United States of America in 1995 amounted to RM3350.4 [US$1335.83] million or 17.2% of total GSP exports. This was followed by GSP exports to Japan, which were 14.5% of total GSP exports or RM3.4 [US$1.36] billion.

Malaysia's trade with ASEAN

In terms of intra-ASEAN trade, Malaysia's exports to ASEAN countries in 1995 increased by 20.6% from RM41.8 [US$16.7] billion in 1994 to RM50.4 [US$20.1] billion. As noted above, Singapore was the main destination for Malaysian exports, accounting for 74.69% of total exports to ASEAN. Products exported to Singapore were mainly machinery and transport equipment (RM24.5 [US$9.8] billion), manufactured goods (RM2.9 [US$1.2] billion) and miscellaneous manufactured articles (RM2.6 [US$1.0] billion).

Thailand, with exports valued at RM7264.9 [US$2896.58] million or 14.4% of total exports to ASEAN, was Malaysia's second largest trading partner in ASEAN. Exports to Thailand comprised mainly machinery and transport equipment, mineral fuels, crude materials, manufactured goods and chemicals. Exports to Indonesia, amounting to RM2443.3 [US$974.16] million (or 4.8% of total exports to ASEAN), were the same products as Thailand with the exclusion of crude materials. Instead, Malaysia exported animal and vegetable oils to Indonesia.

Exports to the Philippines were worth RM1693.3 [US$675.13] million (or 3.4%), comprising mainly machinery and transport equipment, manufactured goods and crude minerals. For Brunei Darussalam, Malaysia's export to that country was RM742.3 [US$295.96] million (1.5%), trading in manufactured goods and food items. Malaysia's exports to Vietnam, the new ASEAN member, registered RM672.6 [US$268.17] million or 1.3% of exports to ASEAN. Exports to Vietnam were mainly manufactured goods and machinery and transport equipment.

Intra-ASEAN import trade grew by 15.5% in 1995, amounting to RM33.8 [US$13.5] billion. Import trade with Singapore, valued at RM24,088.9 [US$9604.4] million, constituted 71.4% of total imports from ASEAN. Thailand was the second most important source of imports for Malaysia, accounting for 15.2% of total ASEAN imports or RM5133.3 [US$2046.7] million. This was followed by Indonesia, 9.1% (or RM3057.5 [US$1219.1] million), the Philippines, 3.4% (or RM1153.5 [US$459.9] million), Brunei Darussalam, 0.03% (RM10.5 [US$4.2] million) and Vietnam, 0.9% (RM315.6 [US$125.8] million). The main imports from ASEAN were machinery and transport equipment, manufactured goods, chemicals, food items and miscellaneous manufactured articles.

Policy and Incentives for Export Promotion

In order to promote the expansion of Malaysia's trade, specifically export access in international markets, the government provides for several incentives to promote growth in exports. The foremost incentive for export-oriented firms to locate in Malaysia is through foreign equity guidelines.

No equity condition is imposed on projects that export 80% or more of their production. Projects exporting between 51% to 79% of their production are allowed foreign equity ownership of up to 79%. For those exporting between 20% to 50% of their production, the allowed level of foreign equity ownership is between 30% to 51%; and for those exporting less than 20%, foreign equity ownership is allowed up to a maximum of 30%.

In determining the percentage of approved foreign equity, the following factors are also considered: level of technology, size of investment, location of project, spin-off effect, value-added and utilisation of raw materials and components. Projects producing high technology or priority products for the domestic market may be allowed 100% foreign equity.

Export Credit Refinancing (ECR) Scheme

This incentive provides short-term credit to exporters at preferential rates of interest. The current maximum rate of interest is 5% per annum. The scheme, obtainable from commercial banks, comprises two facilities: the post-shipment facility and pre-shipment facility. Exporters may invoice exports in any currency, but financing is only available in Malaysian ringgit. Access to ECR is subject to the exporter obtaining this credit facility with any commercial bank.

Post-shipment facility is offered to exporters to obtain immediate funds upon shipment of eligible goods sold on credit terms of a minimum 30 days. The period of financing is according to the period of credit extended by the exporter to the foreign buyer, subject to a minimum of seven days and maximum of six months. Financing can be 100% of the value of export, subject to a maximum of RM30 [US$12] million and minimum of RM10,000 [US$4000]. Documents to be submitted to the commercial bank are the invoice, customs export declaration form and bill of lading.

Pre-shipment facility is offered to exporters of eligible products as well as domestic suppliers of component materials (indirect exporters) to obtain financing of working capital for production of goods for export. The period financed is between the receipt of an export order and the time of export, subject to a maximum of four months. The maximum amount of financing is 80% of the value of the export order under the order-based method or 70% of the value of eligible exports under the Certificate of Performance-based (CP-based) method.

The CP-based method uses the preceding 12 months' eligible exports to determine the amount of financing to be provided. Direct exporters must have exported a minimum of RM3 million of eligible products in the last financial year and the preceding 12 months. For exporters of agricultural products, the minimum export value is RM1 million for the last financial year. Application to obtain a CP should be made to the Central Bank of Malaysia through a commercial bank. The CP is valid for 12 months. Documents to be presented to the commercial bank include an export order or the CP.

Eligibility criteria for goods to qualify under ECR are:

(1) The product should not be listed in the 'Negative List' (list of products not eligible for ECR; please refer to Appendix I).

(2) The product should have a minimum value-added of 20%.

(3) The product should have a minimum 30% domestic resource content.

These criteria are implemented flexibly. Companies whose products do not meet these criteria may apply to the Central Bank of Malaysia for special consideration on a case-by-case basis. The local content and value-added criteria are currently exempted for crude rubber, vegetable oil products, cocoa products, agricultural food products, wooden articles, base metals and textile products.

Double deduction of expenses for the promotion of exports

Double deduction of expenses for the promotion of export of manufactured goods as well as agricultural produce is provided to companies to expand their markets overseas. Expenses which qualify for double deduction are:

- overseas advertising
- supply of free samples abroad
- export market research
- preparation of tenders for supply of goods overseas
- supply of technical information abroad
- exhibits and/or participation in trade or industrial exhibitions approved by the Ministry of International Trade and Industry
- services rendered for public relations work connected with export

- fares in respect of travel overseas for business by employees of companies
- accommodation and sustenance expenses incurred by the company's representative going overseas, subject to RM200 per day
- cost of maintaining sales offices overseas for the promotion of exports

This incentive is available to all resident companies. Companies enjoying pioneer status are allowed to accumulate these deductions to set off against their post-pioneer income.

Double deduction of export credit insurance premium

This is provided for premiums paid to any insurance company incorporated in Malaysia for the insurance of cargo exported.

Industrial Building Allowance (IBA)

This is provided for capital expenditure on the construction or purchase of buildings used as warehouses for storing goods for export or storage of imported goods for processing and re-export. The initial allowance is 10%. Thereafter, an allowance of 2% is given annually.

The cost of land is excluded from the qualifying expenditure. Other than construction costs, expenditure which could qualify for IBA is: architects' fees; costs of digging and laying foundations for drains, water pipes and electric cables; costs of preparing plans etc in connection with acquiring approval from local authorities for constructing the building; demolition costs incurred where an existing building has to be torn down to make way for new construction; construction costs which include labour, materials, haulage, management, supervision and other overhead charges or 'on cost'; incidental expenses on work carried out separately such as drainage, installation of water and electricity; and costs of installing fittings that form part of a building.

IBAs are also provided for buildings for use in the following areas:
- approved research projects
- approved research companies
- as a school or educational institution (allowance of 10% of expenditure annually for 10 years)
- accommodation for employees (IBA given as in the case of schools)
- child care facilities for employees (IBA given as in the case of schools).

Exemption on duty drawback

Exemption on duty drawback of customs duties on raw materials, components, machinery and/or equipment is provided in the following form:

(1) Full exemption from import duty on raw materials used in the manufacture of finished product for export; exemption is granted on provision that the raw material/component is not manufactured locally or the local manufactured raw material/component is of unacceptable quality and price.

(2) Full import duty exemption for companies located in Sabah, Sarawak and designated areas in Peninsular Malaysia's Eastern Corridor, regardless of whether the final product is for export or domestic consumption.

(3) Drawback of excise duty on parts, ingredients or packaging materials used in the manufacture of final products for export.

(4) Drawback on sales tax for duty-paid goods used in the manufacture of final products for export.

(5) Exemption from import duty and sales tax on machinery and equipment.

(6) Drawback of import duty on all duty-paid goods used as parts or ingredients or packaging materials in the manufacture of goods for export.

Institutions and Facilities for Export Promotion

Infrastructure set up to support the promotion of trade includes the following:

Malaysia External Trade Development Corporation (MATRADE)
Malaysia Export Credit Insurance Berhad (MECIB)
Malaysian Trade Missions Overseas
Foreign Currency Exchange Accounts
Free Zones and Licensed Manufacturing Warehouses
Trade and Bilateral Payment Agreements/Arrangements

Malaysia External Trade Development Corporation (MATRADE)

A statutory body set up under the Ministry of International Trade and Industry, MATRADE began operations in March 1993 as the successor to the Malaysian Export Centre (MEXPO). MATRADE offers the following services to manufacturers and exporters: commercial intelligence on export markets; foreign trade inquiries;

training programs and services to upgrade marketing skills, particularly SMIs; advisory services on market access, pricing, packaging and shipping; participation in international trade fairs, local exhibitions, selling missions, in-coming trade/buying missions; trade publications such as *Malaysia Trade Quarterly, Trade Digest, Malaysia Business Update* and *World Trade Fairs Calendar.*

MATRADE has 25 trade offices overseas to carry out its trade promotion activities. They are located in:

Sydney, Australia	Rotterdam, Netherlands
Sao Paulo, Brazil	Moscow, Russia
Toronto, Canada	Jeddah, Saudi Arabia
Santiago, Chile	Johannesburg, South Africa
Beijing, China	Seoul, Republic of Korea
Paris, France	Singapore, Republic of
Koln, Germany	Taipei, Taiwan
Hong Kong	Dubai, United Arab Emirates
Milan, Italy	Los Angeles, United States of America
Osaka, Japan	New York, United States of America
Tokyo, Japan	London, United Kingdom
Nairobi, Kenya	Ho Chi Minh City, Vietnam
Safat, Kuwait	

MATRADE also administers the Industrial Technical Assistance Fund (ITAF) scheme for market development, or ITAF 4. Assistance is given to majority Malaysian-owned (70% Malaysian equity) small and medium-size industries to produce promotional materials for overseas publicity as well as subsidising the cost of participation in overseas trade missions and trade fairs. In 1995, a total of RM1.1 [US$0.44] million was disbursed to 154 projects.

MATRADE can be contacted at the following address:

> The Chief Executive
> Malaysia External Trade Development Corporation (MATRADE)
> 7th Floor Wisma Sime Darby
> Jalan Raja Laut
> 50350 Kuala Lumpur
>
> Tel: 603–2928122   Fax: 603–2921130

Malaysia Export Credit Insurance Berhad (MECIB)

A government-owned export credit insurance company, MECIB offers various insurance policies, bankers' guarantees and buyer credit. Insurance policies offered by MECIB include the following:

(1) Comprehensive short-term policy covering non-payment, whether arising from commercial or non-commercial risks, of goods and commodities exported on credit terms of not more than 180 days or if required, up to 720 days; coverage for these policies commences from the date of shipment.

(2) Comprehensive short-term policy covering goods produced specifically under contract for sale to foreign buyers, particularly for the nature of goods which could result in substantial losses in the event of contracts being frustrated in the pre-shipment period; coverage commences from the date of contract.

(3) Specific policies to cover export of capital or semi-capital goods/services with long manufacturing or payment periods and high contract values; these policies are tailored to the needs and features of each project and credit terms must be for a minimum of two years and a maximum of eight years.

(4) Policies which insure Malaysian confirming banks against insolvency or default of the overseas issuing bank or economic and political risk resulting in non-payment.

(5) Letter of authority arrangements to allow exporters to assign their claim payment rights over transactions insured under a comprehensive or specific policy in order to obtain post-shipment export loans.

(6) Bankers' guarantees for export financing services provided by MECIB insures commercial banks against losses arising from an exporter/supplier's failure to repay his export loans/advances. These guarantees cover 75% of losses for pre-shipment loans/advances, and 85% loss for post-shipment loans/advances. Only the principal sum is covered; the maximum repayment term is up to 180 days from the date that the loan/advance was made.

Foreign currency exchange accounts

Effective 1 December 1994, exporters in Malaysia are permitted to retain a portion of their export proceeds in foreign currency with a designated bank. The exporter could maintain either a one-foreign-currency account or a multi-currency account. Overnight limits for these accounts are as follows:

Average monthly export receipts	Overnight limits
More than RM20 million	Up to equivalent of US$10 million
Between RM10 to RM20 million	Up to equivalent of US$5 million
Between RM5 to RM10 million	Up to equivalent of US$3 million
Not more than RM5 million	Up to equivalent of US$1 million

Average monthly export receipts are determined from export proceeds in the preceding 12 months. The limit for new exporters without any track record is US$1 million.

The designated banks in Malaysia are:

Bank Bumiputra Malaysia Berhad
Bank of Commerce (M) Berhad
DCB Bank Berhad
Hongkong Bank Malaysia Berhad
Malayan Banking Berhad
OCBC Bank (Malaysia) Berhad
Public Bank Berhad

Free Zones and Licensed Manufacturing Warehouses

Free Zones and Licensed Manufacturing Warehouses are facilities offered to export-oriented manufacturing establishments to enjoy minimum customs control and formalities in their import of raw materials, parts, machinery and equipment, as well as in the export of finished products. While Free Zones are actual geographical zones/areas of operations, Licensed Manufacturing Warehouses are simply buildings established where Free Zones could not be set up. Licensed Manufacturing Warehouses are also used as a 'mechanism' to disperse industries.

To date there are 14 Free Zones, namely at Bayan Lepas, Prai, Prai Wharf, Batu Berendam, Tanjung Kling, Sungei Way, Ampang Hulu Kelang, Telok Panglima Garang, Johor Port, Jelapang, Kinta, Tanjung Gelang and Sama Jaya.

The criteria for setting up in Free Zones and Licensed Manufacturing Warehouses are: (a) the entire production is exported, although companies exporting not less than 80% of their production could be considered for approval; (b) raw materials/components used in the finished product are mainly imported, although companies are encouraged to use local raw materials/components where possible.

Trade and bilateral payment agreements/arrangements

As at June 1996, Malaysia concluded trade agreements with a range of 42 countries as diverse as OECD economies to developing economies and newly emerging countries. These 42 countries are:

Albania	Korea, Republic of
Argentina	Kyrgyz Republic
Australia	Lebanon
Bangladesh	Libya
Bosnia	Mali
Brazil	Namibia
Bulgaria	New Zealand
Chile	Pakistan
China (PRC)	Peru
Croatia	Poland
Egypt	Romania
Germany	Russia
Ghana	Tunisia
Hungary	Turkey
Indonesia	Turkmenistan
Iran	United Arab Emirates
Iraq	Uruguay
Japan	Venezuela
Jordan	Vietnam
Kazakhstan	Zimbabwe
Korea, Democratic Republic of	

Bilateral payment agreements/arrangements covering reciprocal payments and credit arrangements, bilateral payments, palm oil credit and arrangement, and memorandum of understanding have been signed with 25 countries, namely:

Albania	Nigeria
Algeria (2 arrangements)	Pakistan
Argentina	Peru
Botswana	Romania
Chile	Seychelles
Fiji	Sudan (2 arrangements)
Iran (2 arrangements)	Tunisia
Iraq	Turkmenistan
Laos PDR	Uzbekistan

Mexico	Venezuela
Mozambique	Vietnam
Myanmar	Zimbabwe

International Procurement Centres

In order to encourage trading activities in Malaysia, the 1997 national budget introduced a package of incentives for the establishment of International Procurement Centres (IPCs). The promotion of IPCs is aimed at developing Malaysia as a marketing and distribution centre for multinationals. Concurrently, IPCs would widen the market for local products, especially those of small and medium scale companies. The country's services industry would also be developed, particularly the use of domestic port and airport facilities and services.

The package of incentives offered to approved IPCs is:

- approval of a number of expatriate posts based on the requirements of IPCs;
- approval to operate one or more foreign currency accounts with any licensed commercial bank to retain export proceeds without any limit imposed;
- approval to enter into foreign exchange forward contracts to sell forward export proceeds based on projected sales;
- exemption from the Ministry of Domestic Trade and Consumer Affairs foreign equity ownership requirements for wholesale and retail trade; and
- approval to bring in raw materials, components or finished products without payment of custom duties into Free Zones or Licensed Manufacturing Warehouses for repacking, cargo consolidation and integration before distribution to final consumers.

In order to qualify for IPC status, companies should fulfil the following criteria:

- locally incorporated under Malaysia's Companies Act 1965 with minimum paid-up capital of RM0.5 [US$0.20] million;
- a minimum total business spending of RM1.5 [US$0.60] million per year;
- a minimum annual business turnover of RM100 [US$39.87] million; and
- goods to be handled directly through Malaysian ports and airports.

The agency responsible for processing and improving all applications for IPC status is the Ministry of International Trade and Industry.

Future Foreign Trade and Promotion Strategies

New markets in which Malaysia is actively expanding, as well as new sources of imports, include the following:

(1) Dynamic North-East Asian economies of the People's Republic of China, Hong Kong, Taiwan and Republic of Korea.

(2) Southern countries (excluding ASEAN and People's Republic of China): (a) South Asian countries of India, Pakistan, Bangladesh and Afghanistan; (b) South American countries of Argentina, Brazil, Chile, Colombia, Mexico, Panama, Uruguay and Venezuela; (c) West Asian countries of Saudi Arabia, United Arab Emirates, Iran and Yemen; (d) African countries of South Africa, Tanzania, Uganda, Ghana, Egypt, Cote D'Ivore, Kenya, Mauritius, Nigeria, Cameroon, Mozambique and Angola; (e) Indo-Chinese countries of Cambodia, Laos and Vietnam; (f) Oceania, Papua New Guinea and Myanmar.

Total trade with dynamic North-East Asian economies, valued at RM52.2 [US$20.81] billion, grew by 28.3% in 1995. The value of exports to these countries increased from RM21.1 [US$8.4] billion to RM25.8 [US$10.3] billion in 1995, registering growth of 22.7%. The proportion of exports to these countries to total exports similarly increased from 13.7% to 13.9%. Taiwan and Hong Kong were the more important export destinations in the region, particularly in manufactured goods, where Hong Kong was the largest market, and machinery and transport equipment, where Hong Kong remained the largest market.

Growth in imports was equally strong at 34.4%, increasing from RM19.6 [US$7.81] billion to RM26.4 [US$10.53] billion in the same period. The share of imports to these countries compared to total imports improved from 12.6% to 13.6%. Taiwan and the Republic of Korea were the more important suppliers of goods to Malaysia. Both countries were the principal suppliers of machinery and transport equipment. Taiwan was the principal supplier for Malaysia's imports of electrical machinery and chemicals.

Trade with southern countries (excluding ASEAN and the People's Republic of China) in 1995 was RM20,973.10 [US$8362.11] million, recording a growth of 19.9% over 1994's trade of RM17,486.90 [US$6972.17] million. Exports to southern countries were RM14,453.70 [US$5762.81] million in 1995, ie an increase of 23.2% over 1994's RM11,734.50 [US$5721.36] million. Consequently, the share of exports to southern countries against total exports increased from 7.6% in 1994 to 7.8% in 1995. Major export markets for Malaysia were countries from the South Asian region with

RM4547.3 [US$1813.05] million worth of exports, followed by West Asian countries with RM4022.7 [US$1603.88] million exports and South American countries with RM2928.5 [US$1167.62] million exports.

On an individual country basis, exports to India recorded the highest value at RM2084 [US$830.91] million, followed by Pakistan at RM1790.2 [US$713.77] million and the United Arab Emirates at RM1720.6 [US$686.02] million. Exports to the south (excluding ASEAN) comprised mainly animal and vegetable oils (valued at RM7.2 [US$2.87] billion or 36.5% of total exports to these countries), followed by machinery and transport equipment (at RM5.5 [US$2.19] billion) and manufactured goods (at RM2.3 [US$0.92] billion).

Imports from southern countries (excluding ASEAN and the People's Republic of China) increased from RM5043.60 [US$2010.92] million to RM6519.4 [US$2599.34] million, registering a growth of 29.3%. The share of imports from southern countries to total imports improved from 3.2% in 1994 to 3.4% in 1995. Principal suppliers of imports to Malaysia were the South American countries (at RM2344.3 [US$934.7] million), South Asian countries (at RM1634.5 [US$651.7] million) and West Asian countries (at RM1168.7 [US$466] million).

On an individual country basis, principal suppliers of goods to Malaysia according to the value of imports recorded were India (at RM1378.9 [US$549.8] million), Brazil (at RM770.9 [US$307.4] million) and Argentina (at RM649.9 [US$259.12] million). Machinery and transport equipment, manufactured goods and food were the largest import items in 1995.

New products into which Malaysia is diversifying in terms of export could be observed in the change in constitution of manufactured exports. It was noted that, despite the continued dominance of electrical and electronic products, textiles, apparel and footwear, and wood products, there was also a growing contribution from higher value-added products as well as increased exports of intermediate and capital goods in 1995.

Export of chemicals and chemical products increased its share of total exports from 3.5% in 1994 to 4% in 1995. Office machinery and automatic data processing equipment also registered strong growth (at 37.2%, the strongest among the major categories in the electrical and electronic products group). Telecommunications and sound recording apparatus and equipment (growth of 17.7%), general industrial machinery, equipment and parts (28.4%), electrical, apparatus resistors (32.5%) were among the top performers. Other manufactured exports included transport equipment, manufactures of metal, optical and scientific equipment and non-metallic mineral products.

General Trading Companies (GTCs) have been initiated by the government to enhance exports of indigenous Malaysian products and services, particularly to countries in the south. Administered by MATRADE, GTCs undertake feasibility studies, establish distribution centres, advertise and promote the exports of Malaysian-made products and services to the countries concerned. Currently, GTCs identified by the government include Sime Darby Corporation Sdn Bhd, Guthrie Malaysia Trading Corp Sdn Bhd, Edaran Otomobil Nasional (EON) and Malaysia South-South Corporation Bhd (MASSCORP).

The government has already instituted a financial aid program to GTCs by providing seed money to draw up action programs in the following areas: EON in Central and Eastern Europe, Russia and the Central Asian Republic; Sime Darby in Africa; Guthrie in South America and MASSCORP in Indo-China and Myanmar.

Regional Economic Cooperation which includes the ASEAN Free Trade Area (AFTA) and the various growth triangles, namely the Indonesia-Malaysia-Singapore Growth Triangle (more popularly known as SIJORI), the Indonesia-Malaysia-Thailand Growth Triangle (IMT-GT), the Brunei Darussalam-Indonesia-Malaysia-Philippines East ASEAN Growth Area (BIMP-EAGA), are important strategies to strengthen trade between ASEAN countries as well as to accelerate development of the respective ASEAN nations.

Internationally, these regional cooperation frameworks enlarge the market size of ASEAN countries through conglomeration of individual national markets into a common regional free trade area. In addition, the formation of a common free trade area or growth triangle would contribute to the mobility of goods, services, capital and resources, including human resources, through the gradual reduction of tariffs under the Common Effective Preferential Tariff Scheme, and removal of non-tariff barriers.

The Common Effective Preferential Tariff (CEPT) Scheme sets a time-frame of 10 years in which tariffs among ASEAN countries would be reduced to 0%. Between 1994 and 1995, Malaysia offered more than 80% of its products or a total of 8840 items for tariff reduction. Of this, 3545 items are offered on the Fast Track, ie reduction from the existing tariff rate (from less than 5% to above

20%) to 0% within five to seven years; and 5295 items on the Normal Track which is to reach 0% within seven to ten years.

Working on such a schedule, AFTA is expected to be realised in the year 2003, making ASEAN as a whole a much more attractive centre for investment and trade in the East Asian region.

Other regional and international developments affecting Malaysia's trade expansion strategies are the enlargement of the European Union, the North American Free Trade Agreement, the East Asia Economic Caucus, Asia-Pacific Economic Cooperation, South-South Cooperation, Group of 15, Southern African Development Community, Economic Cooperation Organisation and Organisation of Islamic Countries.

Taking cognisance of the fact that Malaysia will be totally graduated out of the European Union's GSP scheme and of increasing pressures from industrialised nations to comply with environmental and social requirements in international trade, Malaysian exports will have to ensure greater cost competitiveness as well as meet with the requirements laid down.

Concurrently, Malaysia is expanding its trade network through close cooperation in the form of trade missions, agreements, financial aid to establish GTCs, networking and participating in joint trade and economic development committees with member countries of the South-South Cooperation, G–15, Organisation of Islamic Countries, Economic Cooperation Organisation and Southern African Development Community.

FOREIGN INVESTMENTS

Foreign Investment Trends in Malaysia

Foreign capital inflow into Malaysia began slowly in the 1960s with net inflow ranging from RM90 million to RM300 million, rising to between RM300 million and RM1.4 billion in the 1970–79 period. In the early 1980s, foreign direct investment (FDI) increased in significance, registering between RM1.9 billion and RM3.3 billion, especially in the oil sector. When Malaysia was beset with economic recession in the years 1985–86, FDI flows into the country decreased to RM1.1 billion in 1987. The government then provided generous fiscal incentives as well as a relaxed foreign investment policy, particularly with respect to equity ownership, under the Promotion of Investment Act 1986.

From 1987 until 1993, FDI flows into Malaysia increased substantially, especially in the manufacturing sector and to a lesser extent in the agricultural and property sectors. It was in this period, ie beginning in 1987, that the manufacturing sector overtook the agricultural sector as the main engine of growth of the economy. Foreign investment influenced Malaysia's industrial growth from import-substitution in the early 1960s into export-orientation in the 1970s and, encouraged by government investment incentives and strategies, entered into the era of heavy industrialisation. The World Investment Report 1995 reported that Malaysia received the second highest volume of FDI inflow among ASEAN countries in 1993. Malaysia received FDI inflow of US$5.2 billion, behind Singapore's US$6.8 billion. Malaysia's total FDI stock as at 1993 was US$26.9 billion.

Foreign investment performance in 1995

In 1994, FDIs slowed down owing to the after-effects of lower approved investments in the manufacturing sector in the period 1991–93 because of the global decline in FDI funds, as well as increasing competition for investments from emerging low-cost economies such as Vietnam, Cambodia, China and Eastern Europe. Consequently, the government launched its Domestic Investment Initiative program to encourage greater domestic investment and reinvestment activity. This resulted in a strong performance in domestic investment, which exceeded foreign investments in the 1993–95 period.

In addition, Malaysia has begun the shift into more capital-intensive industries, particularly to overcome constraints in labour supply and loss of comparative advantage labour-intensive operations. Projects, unless exempted, should have capital investment per employee of at least RM55,000 (US$21,928.95). Consequently, capital investment per employee in Malaysia rose from RM69,159 (US$27,574.26) in 1989 to RM168,157 (US$67,045.57) in 1994 and RM177,448 (US$70,749.97) in 1995.

The above developments saw investments, in particular foreign investments, concentrated in higher-tech projects such as the manufacture of motherboards and communication cards, computers, disk media substrates, advanced technical ceramic packages for semiconductors, polished and unpolished glass panels, finished and unfinished glass funnels for cathode ray tubes, colour monitors/PCBs, petroleum products and chemicals, eg specialty polyester copolymers.

In 1995, capital investment per employee in the electrical and electronic products industry rose from RM42,115 [US$16,791.60] in 1991 to RM79,149 [US$31,557.35]. During the same period, capital investment per employee in the textiles and textile products industry increased over one and a half times from RM53,629 [US$21,382.32] to RM136,831 [US$54,555.64]. Similarly in the transport equipment industry, capital investment per employee increased by 85% from RM140,539 [US$56,034.095] to RM259,959 [US$103,647.78].

Foreign investments in the manufacturing sector

As noted above, foreign investment approved in the manufacturing sector in 1995 amounted to RM9143.6 [US$3645.63] million, dropping by 19.4% over 1994's value of foreign investments (RM11,339.1 [US$4520.99] million). Of this amount, RM6312.5 [US$2516.85] million was invested in new projects (compared to RM6388.3 [US$2547.07] million in 1994) and RM2831.1 [US$1128.78] million in expansion/diversification of existing operations (RM4950.8 [US$1973.92] million in 1994).

By industry sub-sectors, foreign investment was highest in the electrical and electronics industry (RM2373.70 [US$946.41] million) followed by chemicals and chemical products (RM1825.81 [US$727.97] million) and non-metalic mineral products (RM1254.91 [US$500.34] million) in 1995.

Industries which have had a higher value of foreign investments than domestic investments over the years are electrical and electronics, textiles and textile products, chemicals and chemical products, plastic products, machinery manufacturing, scientific and measuring equipment.

The source of FDI in the manufacturing sector in 1995 was mainly Japan (RM2096.32 [US$835.82] million), the United States of America (RM1801.64 [US$718.33] million), Taiwan (RM1442.21 [US$575.02] million), Singapore (RM1008.65 [US$402.16] million), Republic of Korea (RM604.35 [US$240.96] million) and India (RM472.68 [US$188.46] million. Investment from these six countries accounted for 81.2% of total foreign investment approved in the sector.

Japan's investments were mainly in non-metallic mineral products, and electrical and electronic products. Japanese investments were substantially in the production of polished and unpolished glass panels, finished and unfinished glass funnels for cathode ray tubes, and advanced technical ceramic packages for semiconductors.

The United States of America's investments were mainly in the electrical and electronic products industry (50% of total US investments) to produce computers, motherboards, communication cards, disk media substrates and in the chemicals and chemical products industry, specialty polyester copolymers.

Singapore's investments were more diversified but still generally concentrated in the electrical and electronic products, wood and wood products, fabricated metal products and chemicals and chemical products industries.

Of Taiwan's investments, 49% was in the electrical and electronics products industry, particularly in the production of computer monitors and in petroleum refineries products.

Of the Republic of Korea's investments, 96% was concentrated in one wholly-owned project to produce computer monitors/PCB assemblies.

Investment Policy and Incentives

Industrial Coordination Act (ICA) 1975

The Industrial Coordination Act (ICA) 1975 requires person(s) engaging in any manufacturing activity to obtain a licence from the Licensing Officer. Pertinent details of this Act are as follows:

Objective: (a) To ensure orderly development and growth of the manufacturing sector; and (b) to facilitate the collection of industrial information vital to the formulation of plans and policies for the manufacturing sector.

Coverage: (a) Manufacturing companies with shareholders' funds of RM2.5 [US$1.0] million and above, or (b) employing 75 or more full-time employees.

Definitions: (1) Manufacturing activity—making, altering, blending, ornamenting, finishing or otherwise treating or adapting any article or substance with a view to its use, sale, transport, delivery or disposal, and includes assembly of parts and ship repairing; but does not include wholesale or retail trade.

(2) Shareholders' funds are the aggregate amount of a company's:

(a) paid-up capital (preference and ordinary shares but not including bonus shares issued out of capital reserve created by the revaluation of fixed assets);

(b) reserves (other than capital reserve created by the revaluation of fixed assets, provisions for depreciation, renewals or replacements and diminution in value of assets);

(c)   balance of share premium account but not including the amount credited at the instance of issue of bonus shares at premium out of capital reserve by the revaluation of fixed assets;

(d)   balance of profit and loss appropriation account.

(3) Full-time paid employees include:

(a)   all persons normally working for at least six hours a day and at least 20 days a month for 12 months during the year and receiving a salary;

(b)   travelling sales, engineering, maintenance and repair personnel are included;

(c)   directors of incorporated enterprises except when paid solely for attendance at Board of Directors' meetings are included;

(d)   family members receiving regular salaries or allowances and contributing to the Employees Provident Fund or other superannuation funds are included.

Exempted activities: (a) Companies engaged in manufacturing activity with less than RM2.5 [US$1.0] million shareholders' fund, ie small and medium-size industries (SMIs); (b) milling of oil palm fresh fruits into palm oil; (c) production and processing of natural rubber of all types, including latex, skim sheets, crepe, scrap, technically-specified rubber, non-standard and modified rubber or any other unvulcanised form of natural rubber prepared by any patented or technically specified procedure; (d) milling of padi into rice.

Licensing officer: (a) The Secretary-General of the Ministry of International Trade and Industry (MITI) is the Licensing Officer; (b) The Licensing Officer may prescribe conditions deemed expedient and necessary, such as equity and employment structure, distributorship and quality standards on application for a manufacturing licence.

Application for a manufacturing licence should be submitted to:

Director-General
Malaysian Industrial Development Authority (MIDA)
6th Floor Wisma Damansara
Jalan Semantan
PO Box 10618
50720 Kuala Lumpur

Tel:603–2553633   Fax:603–2557970

Investors intending to set up manufacturing projects in Sabah or Sarawak are also required to submit copies of their applications to the respective State governments.

Other than the ICA, investment, including equity ownership, policies and taxation measures have been liberalised and deregulated since 1987. These policies and measures, which have continued in line with Malaysia's open economy, include guidelines on protection of foreign investments, acquisition and control by foreign interests, and corporate taxation.

Guidelines on protection of foreign investments

These cover equity policy, distribution of Malaysian equity, investment guarantee agreements and settlement of investment disputes under the Convention of Settlement of Investment Disputes.

In encouraging foreign investment in Malaysia, it is the policy of the government to encourage joint ventures with Malaysian investors. Nonetheless, as mentioned previously, foreign equity may be allowed up to:

- 100% for projects exporting 80% or more of production
- 79% for projects exporting between 51% to 79% of production
- 30% to 51% for projects exporting between 20% to 50% of production
- a maximum of 30% for projects exporting 20% of production
- 100% for products of high technology or priority products for domestic use.

In projects involving extraction or mining and processing of mineral ores, majority foreign equity participation of up to 100% is permitted. Criteria taken into consideration are the level of investments, technology and risk involved in the project; the availability of Malaysian expertise in the project concerned; and the degree of integration and level of value-added in the project.

Investment guarantee agreements

These have been signed with 48 countries and associations as at June 1996. These countries are:

Albania	Kyrgyz Republic
Argentina	Laos, People's Demorcratic Republic
Austria	Mongolia
ASEAN	Namibia
Bangladesh	Netherlands
Belgo-Luxembourg	Norway
Bosnia Herzegovina	Organisation of Islamic Conference
Cambodia	Pakistan, Islamic Republic of

Canada	Papua New Guinea
Chile	Peru
China	Poland
Croatia	Romania
Denmark	Spain
Finland	Sri Lanka
France	Sweden
Germany	Switzerland
Hungary	Turkmenistan
India, Republic of	Taiwan
Indonesia	United Arab Emirates
Italy	United Kingdom
Jordan	United States of America
Kazakhstan	Uruguay
Korea	Vietnam
Kuwait	Zimbabwe

These agreements provide foreign investors with the following: protection against nationalisation and expropriation; prompt and adequate compensation in the event of nationalisation or expropriation; free transfer of profits, capital and other fees; and settlement of investment disputes under the Convention on Settlement of Investment Disputes of which Malaysia has been a member since 1966.

The Ministry of International Trade and Industry issues letters of coverage under the respective investment guarantee agreements to approved projects in Malaysia.

Acquisition and control by foreign interests

This is subject to approval by the Foreign Investment Committee (FIC) under the following circumstances:

(a) acquisition of substantial fixed assets;

(b) acquisition of assets, mergers and takeovers of any local business or company resulting in transfer of ownership or control to foreign interests;

(c) acquisition of shares in a local company resulting in 15% or more voting rights being held by ONE foreign interest or associated group of foreign interests;

(d) acquisition of shares in a local company resulting in 30% or more voting rights being held by foreign interests;

(e) control of a local company or business through joint-venture, management, technical assistance or by any means;

(f) acquisition of shares in a local company that is deemed to be a merger or takeover where more than 15% of voting rights are owned by foreign interests (merger or takeover is any form of transaction involving transfer of more than 50% of voting rights in a local company or group of local companies from one party to another);

(g) a restructuring scheme involving the transfer of more than 50% of voting rights in a local company or group of local companies from one party to another, where more than 15% of voting rights are owned by foreign interests;

(h) acquisition of a local company which increases voting rights of foreign interests to above 15%;

(i) subscription of shares in any local company where foreign interests hold more than 15% of voting rights.

The Secretariat of the Foreign Investment Committee is located at the Economic Planning Unit of the Prime Minister's Department.

Corporate taxation

Corporate taxation in Malaysia is 30% with effect from year of assessment 1995. Notwithstanding the above, a non-resident person, whether an individual or a company, is liable to income tax at rates shown below on the gross amount of the following types of income:

Interest derived from Malaysia	15%
Royalty derived from Malaysia	10%
Section 4A income	10%

Section 4A income is:

(1) Income from services rendered in connection with the use of property or rights belonging to/or the installation or operation of any plant, machinery or other apparatus purchased from the person being taxed.

(2) Income recovered from providing technical advice, assistance or services rendered in connection with the technical arrangement or administration of any scientific, industrial or commercial undertaking, ventures, project or scheme.

(3) Rents or other payments (not film rentals) under any agreement or arrangement for use of any movable property.

Malaysia has signed Avoidance of Double Taxation Agreements with 47 countries (as at 8 June 1996) in Europe, Asia, Australasia and the Pacific, America and Africa. These countries are:

Albania
Austria
Australia
Bangladesh
Belgium
Canada
China
Fiji
France
Germany
Hungary
India
Indonesia
Iran
Italy
Japan
Jordan
Malta
Mauritius
Mongolia
Netherlands
New Zealand
Norway

Pakistan
Papua New Guinea
Philippines
Poland
Romania
Russia
Saudi Arabia
Singapore
South Korea
Sri Lanka
Sudan
Sweden
Switzerland
Thailand
Turkey
United Arab Emirates
United Kingdom
United States of America (limited
 to shipping and air transport)
Vietnam
Yugoslavia
Zimbabwe

Incentives

Promotion of Investments Act 1986

This Act provides incentives for investment in the manufacturing, agricultural and tourism sectors. Tax incentives provided are pioneer status or investment tax allowance and reinvestment allowance.

Pioneer status grants partial exemption from payment of income tax. Tax need only be paid on 30% of a company's statutory income. Exemption is for a five year period, commencing from the date of production, as determined by the Minister of International Trade and Industry. The level of technology, industrial linkage, value-added and local content are other factors that are taken into consideration in determining a company's eligibility to receive pioneer status.

As an additional incentive to locate in Sabah, Sarawak and designated areas in the Eastern Corridor of Peninsular Malaysia, companies need only pay tax on 15% of their statutory income. The

Eastern Corridor covers Kelantan, Terengganu, Pahang excluding Lipis, Raub, Jerantut and Cameron Highlands (unless otherwise indicated for approved industrial estates) and Mersing in Johor. Dividends paid out of tax-exempt income to shareholders are also exempt from tax.

Investment tax allowance is granted to qualifying capital expenditure incurred within five years from the date of approval of the incentive. The allowance given is 60% and this could be used to set off against a maximum of 70% of statutory income in the year of assessment. Any unused allowance can be carried forward to subsequent years until the whole amount is used up. Of the statutory income, 30% will be taxed at the prevailing company tax rate.

Companies located in Sabah, Sarawak and designated areas of the Eastern Corridor of Peninsular Malaysia are granted an allowance of 80% in respect of qualifying capital expenditure. The allowance can be used to set off against a maximum of 85% of statutory income in the year of assessment. Dividends paid out of tax-exempt income to shareholders are also exempted from tax.

Products or activities must be promoted activities or products to be eligible to receive pioneer status or investment tax allowance. The list of promoted activities or promoted products is determined by the Minister of International Trade and Industry. The list is available to the public upon request from the Ministry or the Malaysian Industrial Development Authority (MIDA).

Reinvestment allowance is granted to manufacturing companies which incur qualifying capital expenditure for the expansion, modernisation, upgrading and diversification (into related products) of their operations. The allowance, which is 60% of capital expenditure incurred, is not granted to companies enjoying pioneer status or investment tax allowance or industrial adjustment allowance.

Reinvestment allowance, used to offset adjusted profits against 70% of statutory income, is transferred to an exempt income account. Dividends distributed from this exempt income account are also tax exempt in the hands of shareholders. Redistributions of these exempt dividends are also tax exempt. In the 1997 national budget, this reinvestment allowance was further expanded to provide an allowance of 60% of capital expenditure to be offset against 100% of statutory income (as in the scheme granted to encourage industries to locate in the Eastern Corridor of Peninsular Malaysia, Sabah and Sarawak) for firms to reinvest in equipment which could significantly improve their productivity level. This allowance is effective from year of assessment 1998.

Other incentives

Other incentives for investments include incentives for: high-technology industries; strategic industries; research and development; training; small-scale companies; storage, treatment and disposal of toxic and hazardous wastes; operational headquarters (OHQs); and infrastructure allowance.

Incentives for high-technology industries

These are granted to companies producing promoted products in new and emerging technologies. These incentives are: full tax exemption at statutory income level for five years, or investment tax allowance of 60% on qualifying capital expenditure incurred within a period of five years, to be set off against the statutory income for each assessment year without any restriction.

Criteria to be fulfilled by the high-technology company are: local research and development expenditure to gross sales should be at least 1% on an annual basis (companies are allowed a three-year grace period from the date of operation/commencement of business to comply with this requirement); the percentage of science and technical graduates in the total workforce should be at least 7%.

Promoted activities and products for high-technology companies include the following:

(1) Advanced electronics covering: design, development and manufacture of computers or peripherals, and micro-processor applications; development and production of communication equipment; and design and production of integrated circuits.

(2) Equipment/instrumentation which encompasses: design, development and manufacture of medical equipment, medical implants or devices, scientific equipment; and development and production of high pressure water cutting equipment.

(3) Biotechnology which includes: development, testing and production of pharmaceuticals, fine chemicals, food or feed supplements, and biodiagnostics; development and production of cell cultures and biopolymers; and development and production of biotechnology processes for waste treatment.

(4) Automation and flexible manufacturing systems which cover the development and production of computer process control systems/equipment, process instrumentation, robotic equipment and computer numerical control machine tools.

(5) Electro-optics and non-linear optics which cover the development and production of optical lenses, laser application equipment, fibre-optic communication equipment.

(6) Advanced materials involving the application or production of polymers or biopolymers, superconductors, fine ceramics or advanced ceramics and high strength composites.

(7) Optoelectronics which cover the development and production of optoelectronics system components, optical system components, photo-couplers and semiconductor lasers.

(8) Software engineering involving the development and production of neural networks, pattern recognition systems, machine vision and fuzzy logic systems.

(9) Alternative energy sources covering the development and production of fuel cells, polymer batteries, solar cells and renewable energy.

(10) Aerospace which covers the following: manufacture and assembly of aircraft; manufacture of aircraft equipment, components, accessories or parts thereof; modification and conversion of aircraft; and refurbishment or re-manufacture of aircraft equipment, components, accessories or parts thereof.

Incentives for strategic industries

These may be granted to projects of national importance where there is heavy capital investment and high technology generating extensive linkages. The project must also have a significant impact on the Malaysian economy. Incentives provided are: full tax exemption at the statutory income level for a period of 10 years; and investment tax allowance of 100% in qualifying capital expenditure incurred within five years to be offset against statutory income for each assessment year without any restriction.

Incentives for research and development (R&D)

Incentives for R&D activities are:

(1) Revenue expenditure incurred on research related to business that is directly undertaken, or on its behalf, is eligible for double deduction.

(2) Investment tax allowance of 50% on qualifying expenditure on R&D activity for 10 years, limited to 70% of statutory income for each assessment year.

(3) Industrial building allowance for building used for approved research.

(4) Capital allowances for plant and machinery used on an approved research project.

(5) Double deduction for cash consideration made to approved research institutions and payments used for services of an R&D company or contract R&D company.

Companies established to undertake R&D receive the following incentives:

(1) Tax exemption for five years; dividends received by shareholders are also tax exempt and accumulated losses can be carried forward to the post-tax relief period.

(2) Investment tax allowance of 100% on qualifying capital expenditure for 10 years to carry out R&D activities for holding/affiliate or associate companies, to be set off against statutory income, limited to 70%; either the R&D company receives this allowance and its holding/affiliate company does not qualify for double deduction, or the R&D company forgoes this benefit to allow the holding/affiliate company to claim double deduction.

(3) Industrial building allowance for buildings used for carrying out R&D.

Income tax exemption for five years will also be given to new-technology-based firms.

Incentives for training

(1) Investment tax allowance of 100% for 10 years to companies intending to undertake technical or vocational training, abated from statutory income limited to 70% of such income for each assessment year.

(2) Single deduction for contribution in cash to a technical or vocational training institution established and maintained by a statutory body.

(3) Exemption from import duty, sales tax, excise duty for machinery, equipment and materials used for training.

(4) Double deduction for expenses incurred by companies (employing less than 50 to a minimum of 10 Malaysian workers and paid-up capital of less than RM2.5 [US$1.0] million) for approved training in approved training institutions. (Companies with more than 50 Malaysian workers or a minimum of 10 but less than 50 Malaysian workers with paid-up capital of RM2.5 [US$1.0] million and above are required to contribute 1% of the wages of their employees to the Human Resources Development Fund; in return, they can claim for reimbursement up to a maximum of 80% of training expenditure incurred. Effective 1 January 1995, companies employing less than

50 but with a minimum of 10 Malaysian employees and with paid-up capital of RM2.5 million and above would also have to contribute to the HRDF.)

(5) Industrial building allowance for expenditure incurred on buildings used for training.

(6) Existing companies providing technical or vocational training which incur new investment to upgrade training equipment or expand training capacity are eligible to receive industrial building allowance.

Incentives for small-scale companies

(1) Incentives provided under the Promotion of Investments Act 1986, namely pioneer status, investment tax allowance or reinvestment allowance. Small-scale companies are companies whose shareholders' funds do not exceed RM500,000 [US$200,000], incorporated in Malaysia under the Companies Act 1965 and which have at least 70% Malaysian equity. An additional incentive provided is full exemption from customs duty on raw materials, components, machinery and equipment not available locally.

(2) The industrial technical assistance fund (ITAF) provides matching grants for consultancy services, product development and design, quality and productivity improvement, and market development schemes undertaken by small-scale industries.

Incentives for storage, treatment and disposal of toxic and hazardous wastes

(1) Pioneer status for five years to companies directly involved in such activities in an integrated manner.

(2) Companies which are waste generators themselves and wish to establish similar facilities, whether on-site or off-site, are eligible for a special allowance of an initial rate of 40% and an annual allowance of 20% for all capital expenditure.

(3) Import duty and sales tax exemption are also extended to both types of companies for machinery, equipment, raw materials and components used in such activities.

Incentives for Operational Headquarters (OHQs)

(1) Tax incentives of a concessionary rate of tax at 10% on business income arising from certain services rendered; profit after the 10% concessionary tax can be credited to an exempt account from which tax-exempt dividend could be declared; the rate applies

for five years from the date of approval with the possibility of extension of another five years.

(2) Services qualifying for tax at the concessionary 10% rate include provision of services by OHQs to offices outside Malaysia in the following: general management and administration; business planning; procurement of raw materials and components; technical support; marketing control and sales promotion; training and personnel management; research and development work; assistance in obtaining credit facilities; the service sector, and commercial and investment banking services.

(3) The 1997 national budget provided an additional incentive in the form of Pioneer Status with 100% tax exemption or investment tax allowance of 60% to be offset against 100% of statutory income to small-scale companies which produce intermediate goods for the international market and capable of achieving world class standards, whether in terms of price, quality or capacity. Pioneer Status would be provided for a period of 10 years and is effective after budget day, ie 25 October 1996.

(4) An indirect incentive to assist in the growth and development of small-scale companies, specifically to promote and strengthen links with larger-size firms, the 1997 national budget also provided incentive for large-size firms. The incentive allows large-size firms to deduct off their income tax expenditures incurred towards training the employees of their vendors (small-scale companies). Other deductible expenses include expenditure for product development and testing and factory auditing to ensure quality in the products of their vendor (small-scale companies). This income deduction is effective from year of assessment 1997.

(5) With effect from year of assessment 1995, incentives for OHQs are extended to:

1. locally-owned companies setting up OHQs in Malaysia;
2. all economic sectors including manufacturing, services, agriculture, construction and mining;
3. foreign exchange control regulations are relaxed to allow OHQs to: borrow freely in foreign currency without Central Bank approval for treasury and management operations for related companies outside Malaysia; borrow freely in ringgit up to RM10 million for any use in Malaysia; freely invest in foreign securities and lend to related companies outside Malaysia; open foreign currency accounts with designated financial institutions, including offshore banks in Labuan; and use foreign professional services if such services are not available in Malaysia.

4. OHQs are given priority in access to services such as telex, telephone and telefax;

5. OHQs are provided expatriate posts based on organisational structure, the extent of regional coverage, experience and qualification of expatriates; work permits are for a duration of three to five years and multiple entry visas, equivalent to length of service in the country;

6. OHQs are allowed to acquire fixed assets as long as these assets are used for the purpose of carrying out their operations;

7. OHQs are freely permitted to repatriate profits and fees, subject to completion of an exchange control form where applicable.

Infrastructure allowance

• Infrastructure allowance of 100% on qualifying expenditure is provided for projects located in Sabah, Sarawak and designated areas of the Eastern Corridor of Peninsular Malaysia which require construction by investors of infrastructure such as bridges, jetties, connecting roads, substations etc.

Infrastructure to Support Foreign Investment

Key agencies involved in providing advisory services to promote investments as well as on major issues on foreign investments are the Malaysian Industrial Development Authority (MIDA), MIDA's Advisory Services Centre on Investment and the Centre on Investment at State level.

Malaysian Industrial Development Authority (MIDA)

MIDA is a statutory body under the Ministry of International Trade and Industry, charged with the functions of:

(a) promoting investment activity in Malaysia, whether domestic or foreign;

(b) undertaking planning and research on industrial strategy, licensing and incentives;

(c) formulating strategies for international cooperation especially with reference to ASEAN;

(d) providing statistics on the manufacturing sector;

(e) maintaining a Registry of Investors and Contract Manufacturers;

(f) handling inquiries on policies, procedures and investment opportunities in the manufacturing sector;

(g) providing secretariat services to the following Committees: the Action Committee on Industries, the Committee on Exemption of Duties on Machinery and Equipment, the Committee on Double Deduction for Approved Training in the manufacturing sector, the Committee for Approved Research and Development;

(h) operating the Advisory Services Centre on Investment.

Headed by its Director-General, MIDA has 10 divisions, namely:

Administration, Finance and Central Services Division
Planning and Research Division
Industrial Promotion Division
Transport & Machinery Industries Division
Metal and Engineering Supporting Division
Electrical and Electronic Industries Division
Textile and Miscellaneous Industries Division
Mineral and Paper Industries Division
Agro-Industries Division
Chemical Industries Division.

MIDA has branch offices in all 13 States of Malaysia. Its overseas network covers the Asia-Pacific region, Europe and the United States of America, specifically in the following countries:

Sydney, Australia
Paris, France
Koln, Germany
Hong Kong
Milan, Italy
Osaka, Japan
Tokyo, Japan
Seoul, Korea

Singapore
Stockholm, Sweden
Taipei, Taiwan
London, United Kingdom
Chicago, United States of America
Los Angeles, United States of America
New York, United States of America

MIDA's Advisory Services Centre on Investment is the Coordinating Centre on Investment in Malaysia. Acting as a one-stop centre, it provides investors with the necessary approvals at the federal level in respect of investments in manufacturing. MIDA should also be approached for the granting of tax incentives for manufacturing, integrated agriculture, hotels and tourism projects. Acting through its Advisory Services Centre, MIDA receives, processes and conveys the decisions of the relevant authorities to investors who have submitted applications to set up operations or for tax incentives.

Applications handled by MIDA are:

(1) Application for manufacturing licences under the Industrial Coordination Act 1975.

(2) Application for tax incentives under the Promotions of Investment Act 1986.

(3) Application for expatriate posts for new projects.

(4) Application for double deduction of expenditure on approved training.

(5) Application for tariff protection.

(6) Application for exemption from import duty on raw materials and component parts, and customs and sales duties on machinery or equipment.

(7) Application for extension of business visit pass (not exceeding three months) relating to manufacturing projects.

(8) Application for approval to employ women workers for night shift and overtime work exceeding 64 hours per month.

(9) Requests for verification or amendment of tariff codes.

(10) Approvals of technology transfer agreements.

To perform such a variety of functions, senior officers from the following ministries and departments are stationed at MIDA's Advisory Services Centre:

Ministry of Finance
Ministry of Human Resources
Immigration Department
Royal Customs and Excise Department
Factories and Machineries Department
Department of Environment
Tenaga Nasional Berhad
Telekom Malaysia Berhad

Centres of investment at State level operate along the same lines as MIDA's Advisory Services Centre, ie to act as a one-stop centre for investors to obtain the relevant approvals from State governments. Among the key approvals which investors are required to obtain from State governments are:

(1) Obtaining land in industrial estates, including an application to convert the use of land to industrial.

(2) Approval for factory building plans, including extensions.

(3) Certificate of Fitness for buildings.

(4) Application for water supply.

(5) Signboard and advertisement permit.

(6) Canteen licences.

Presently, nine States have set up such centres, which are in Johor, Kelantan, Melaka, Negeri Sembilan, Pahang, Perak, Sabah, Selangor and Terengganu.

In the States of Kedah, Perlis and Penang, applications are submitted directly to the relevant local authorities. In the event of complications, the State Economic Development Corporations would act as coordinator between the various agencies to convene a meeting to resolve and expedite the approval of such applications.

These State Centres of Investment are located either at the State Economic Development Corporations in Johor, Kelantan, Melaka, Pahang and Perak; or at State Economic Planning Units in Negeri Sembilan, Selangor and Terengganu; or at the Department of Industrial Research and Development (DIRD) in Sabah and at the Ministry of Industrial Development (MID) in Sarawak.

Future Investment and Promotion Strategies

Malaysia's future investment and promotion strategies are guided by the following objectives:

- To strengthen the competitiveness of the industrial sector, specifically with respect to:

    (a) developing a dynamic, integrated and diversified manufacturing sector with strong intra and inter-links with the other sectors;

    (b) promoting and developing higher value-added content, knowledge and high-technology industries;

    (c) developing a technically proficient and productive industrial work-force;

    (d) enhancing indigenous technological capabilities;

    (e) enhancing the export capabilities of small and medium-size industries;

    (f) strengthening development of support and ancillary industries to develop stronger links between multinational companies and large local corporations as anchor companies to spearhead Malaysia's globalisation drive;

    (g) developing and expanding market opportunities under the ASEAN Free Trade Area and World Trade Organisation (WTO), particularly opportunities in new and emerging economies at regional and global level;

(h) enhancing domestic investment activity;

(i) encouraging the inflow of appropriate foreign capital and technology.

- To develop and strengthen the services sector in line with liberalisation under the WTO and also to improve Malaysia's balance of payment.

As observed from the incentives provided, steps are already being taken to encourage the growth of higher value-added and technological production in Malaysia. It is expected that further developments with respect to investment would be:

(1) Liberalisation of the services sector in line with WTO requirements to ensure more competitive rates for services, including transportation and telecommunications facilities, to support industrial development.

(2) Requirements for new areas of support services for manufacturing particularly in construction of prototypes and testing.

(3) Increased investments in automation equipment, computer numerically-controlled machine tools and laser technology for application in manufacturing.

References

Bank Negara Malaysia Annual Report 1996

MIDA, *Malaysia Investment in the Manufacturing Sector, Policies, Incentives and Facilities*

Ministry of Finance, *Economic Report 1996/97*

Ministry of International Trade and Industry, *Malaysia's International Trade and Industry Report 1995/96*

NEGATIVE LIST OF GOODS

(Harmonized Commodity Description & Coding System)

Section I	**Live animals; Animal products**
(01–05)	Nil
Section II	**Vegetable products**
(06–14)	Nil
Section III	**Animal or vegetable fats and oils and their cleavage products; Prepared edible fats animal and vegetable waxes**
(15)	
	Nil
Section IV	**Prepared foodstuffs; Beverages, spirits and vinegar; Tobacco and manufactured tobacco substitutes**
(16–24)	
1802.00 000	Cocoa shells, husks, skins and other cocoa waste
24.01	Unmanufactured tobacco; tobacco refuse
Section V	**Mineral products**
(25–27)	
2501.00	Salt (including table salt and denatured salt) and pure sodium chloride, whether or not in aqueous solution; sea water
	Except: 2501.00 100—Pure sodium chloride; table salt
2502.00 000	Unroasted iron pyrites
25.03	Sulphur of all kinds; other than sublimed sulphur, precipitated sulphur and colloidal sulphur
25.04	Natural graphite
25.05	Natural sands of all kinds, whether or not coloured, other than metal-bearing sands falling within Heading 26
25.06	Quartz (other than natural sands); quartzite, whether or not roughly trimmed or merely cut, by sawing or otherwise into blocks or slabs of a rectangular (including square) shape

25.08	Other clays (not including expanded clays of Heading No 68.06), and alusite, kyanite and sillimanite whether or not calcined; mullite; chamotte or dinas earths
2509.00 000	Chalk
25.10–25.22	Raw building materials (eg natural salts of calcium, barium, silicon, magnesium, pumice stone, slate, marble, granite, sandstone, pebbles, gravel, macadam, dolomite, gypsum & anhydrite, etc) Except: 2511.10 000—Natural barium sulphate (barytes) 2522.20 000—Slake lime
25.25	Mica, including splittings; mica waste
25.26	Natural steatite, whether or not roughly trimmed or merely cut, by sawing or otherwise, into blocks or slabs of a rectangular (including square) shape; talc
2527.00 000	Natural cryolite; natural chiolite
25.28	Natural borates and concentrates thereof (whether or not calcined), but not including borates separated from natural brine; natural boric acid containing not more than 85% or H_3BO_3 calculated on the dry weight
25.29	Feldspar; leucite; nepheline and nepheline syenite; fluorspar
25.30	Mineral substances not elsewhere specified or included
26	Ores, slag and ash
27	Mineral fuels, mineral oils and products of their distillation; bituminous substances; mineral waxes
Section VI	**Products of the chemical and allied industries**
(28–38)	Nil
Section VII	**Plastics and articles thereof; Rubber and articles thereof**
(39–40)	Nil
Section VIII (41–43)	**Raw hides and skins, leather, furskins and articles thereof; Saddlery and harness; Travel goods, handbags and similar containers, Articles of animal gut (other than silk-worm gut)**
41	Raw hides and skins (other than furskins) and leather Except: 4104.10 200—dressed leather 4104.29 000—other dressed leather 4107.10 200—dressed leather

4107.90 200—dressed leather

4108.00 000—chamois (including combination chamois) leather

4109.00 000—Patent leather and patent laminated leather; metallised leather

4111.00 000—Composition leather with a basis of leather or leather fibre, in slabs, sheets or strips, whether or not in rolls

43   Furskins and artificial fur; manufactures thereof.

Except: 4304.00—Artificial fur and articles thereof

Section IX (44–46)	**Wood and articles of wood; Wood charcoal; Cork and articles of cork; Manufactures of straw, of esparto or of other plaiting materials, basketware and wickerwork**
44.01	Fuel wood in logs, in billets, in twigs, in faggots or in similar forms; wood in chips or particles; sawdust and wood waste and scrap whether or not agglomerated in logs, briquettes, pellets or similar forms
4402.00 000	Wood charcoal (including shell and nut charcoal), whether or not agglomerated
44.03	Wood in the rough, whether or not stripped of its bark of sapwood, or roughly squared
44.04	Hoopwood; split poles; piles, pickets and stakes of wood, pointed but not sawn lengthwise; wooden sticks, roughly trimmed but not turned, bent or otherwise worked, suitable for the manufacture of walking-sticks, umbrellas, tool handles or the like, chipwood and the like
Section X (47–49)	**Pulp of wood or of other fibrous cellulosic material; Waste and scrap of paper or paperboard; Paper and paperboard and articles thereof**
47.07	Waste and scrap of paper or paperboard
Section XI (50–63)	**Textiles and textile articles**
5001.00 000	Silkworm cocoons suitable for reeling
5002.00 000	Raw silk (not thrown)
50.03	Silk waste (including cocoons unsuitable for reeling, yarn waste and garnetted stock)
51.01	Wool, not carded or combed

51.02	Fine or coarse animal hair not carded or combed
51.03	Waste of wool or of fine or coarse animal hair, including yarn waste but excluding garnetted stock
5104.00 000	Garnetted stock of wool or of fine or coarse animal hair
5201.00 000	Cotton, not carded or combed
52.02	Cotton waste (including yarn waste and garnetted stock)
5203.00 000	Cotton, carded or combed
53.01	Flax, raw or processed but not spun; flax tow and waste (including yarn waste and garnetted stock)
53.02	True hemp (cannabis sativa L), raw or processed but not spun; tow and waste of true hemp (including yarn waste and garnetted stock)
53.03	Jute and other textile bast fibres (excluding flax, true hemp and ramie), raw or processed but not spun; tow and waste of these fibres (including yarn waste and garnetted stock)
53.04	Sisal and other textile fibres of the genus Agave, raw or processed but not spun; tow and waste of these fibres (including yarn waste and garnetted stock)
53.05	Coconut, abaca (Manila hemp or Musa textile Nee), ramie and other vegetable textile fibres, not elsewhere specified or included, raw or processed but not spun; tow noils and waste of these fibres (including yarn waste and garnetted stock)
	Except: 5305.11 000—Raw coconut (coir)
	5305.19 000—Other
53.06	Flax yarn
5308.90 110	Ramie yarn not put up for retail sale
5308.90 120	Ramie yarn put up for retail sale
60	'Military Clothing' under this Section
61	'Military Clothing' under this Section
62	'Military Clothing' under this Section
6309.00 000	Worn clothing and other worn articles
63.10	Used or new rags, scrap twine, cordage, rope and cables and worn cut articles of twine, cordage, rope or cables, of textile materials

Section XII (64–67)	**Footwear, headgear, umbrellas, sun umbrellas, walking-sticks, seat-sticks, whips, riding-crops and parts thereof; Prepared feathers and articles made therewith; Artificial flowers; articles of human hair**
	Nil
Section XIII (68–70)	**Articles of stone, plaster, cement, asbestos, mica or similar materials; Ceramic products; glass and glassware**
	Nil
Section XIV (71)	**Natural or cultured pearls; Precious or semi-precious stones, precious metals, metals clad with precious metal, and articles thereof; Imitation jewellery; coin**
	All Items
	Except: 71.13.—Articles of jewellery and parts thereof, of precious metal or of metal clad with precious metal
	71.14.—Articles of goldsmiths' or silversmiths' wares and parts thereof, of precious metal or of metal clad with precious metal
	71.15.—Other articles of precious metal or of metal clad with precious metal
	71.16.—Articles of natural or cultured pearls, precious or semi-precious stones (natural, synthetic or reconstructed)
	71.71. —Imitation jewellery
Section XV (72–83)	**Base metals and articles of base metal**
72.02	Ferro-alloys
72.04	Ferrous waste and scrap; remelting scrap ingots of iron or steel
	Except: 7204.21 000—Alloy steel (of stainless steel)
	7204.29 000—Alloy steel (other)
72.06	Iron and non-alloy steel in ingots or other primary forms, (excluding iron of Heading No 72.03)
74.01	Copper mattes; cement copper (precipitated copper)
7402.00 000	Copper waste and scrap
75.01	Nickel mattes, nickel oxide and other intermediate products of nickel metallurgy

75.02	Unwrought nickel
7503.00 000	Nickel waste and scrap
78.01	Unwrought lead
	Except: 7801.10 000—Refined lead
	7801.91 000—Lead alloy
7802.00 000	Lead waste and scrap
79.01	Unwrought zinc
7902.00 000	Zinc waste and scrap
8002.00 000	Tin waste and scrap
81	Other base metals; cermets; articles thereof
Section XVI (84–85)	**Machinery and mechanical appliances; electrical equipment; Parts thereof; Sound recorders and reproducers, television image and sound recorders and reproducers, and parts, and accessories thereof**
	Nil
Section XVII (86–89)	**Vehicles, aircraft, vessels and associated transport equipment**
8804.00 900	Parachutes (including dirigible parachutes) and rotochutes; parts thereof and accessories thereto
Section XVIII (90–92)	**Optical, photographic, cinematographic, measuring, checking, precision, medical and surgical instruments and apparatus; Clocks and watches; Musical instrument parts and accessories thereof**
	Nil
Section XIX	**Arms and ammunition; Parts and accessories thereof**
(93)	All Items
Section XX	**Miscellaneous manufactured articles**
(94–96)	Nil
Section XXI	**Works of art, collectors' pieces, and antiques**
(97–98)	All Items

Appendix II

DIRECTION OF TRADE FOR EXPORTS
RM million (figures in brackets are in US$ million)

COUNTRY	1991	1992	1993	1994	1995
ASEAN	27,659.12	30,529.63	33,734.67	41,792.27	49,719.08
	[10,244.12]	[11,742.16]	[12,494.32]	[16,662.92]	[19,823.40]
Singapore	22,029.81	23,859.69	26,259.32	31,842.70	37,584.81
	[8,159.19]	[9,176.80]	[9,725.67]	[12,695.95]	[14,985.37]
Thailand	3,012.78	3,784.84	4,360.12	5,802.20	7,258.04
	[1,115.84]	[1,455.71]	[1,614.86]	[2,313.38]	[2,893.84]
Indonesia	1,385.65	1,288.58	1,397.78	1,868.24	2,441.22
	[513.20]	[495.61]	[517.70]	[744.88]	[973.33]
Philippines	908.20	1,215.37	1,233.98	1,590.47	1,692.23
	[336.37]	[467.45]	[457.03]	[634.13]	[674.71]
Brunei	322.68	381.16	483.47	688.66	742.78
	[119.51]	[146.60]	[179.06]	[274.57]	[296.15]
United States of America	15,984.06	19,279.30	24,641.24	32,523.51	38,278.48
	[5,920.02]	[7,415.12]	[9,126.38]	[12,967.39]	[15,261.94]
European Union	13,979.66	15,406.55	17,573.70	21,990.84	26,273.52
	[5,177.65]	[5,925.60]	[6,508.78]	[8,767.93]	[10,475.47]
United Kingdom	4,139.28	4,176.12	5,120.88	5,841.06	7,483.53
	[1,533.07]	[1,606.20]	[1,896.62]	[2,328.88]	[2,983.74]

Germany	3,421.03 [1,267.05]	4,155.77 [1,598.37]	4,432.23 [1,641.57]	5,087.20 [2,028.31]	5,926.61 [2,362.99]
Netherlands	2,279.97 [844.43]	2,523.56 [970.60]	2,952.34 [1,093.46]	3,544.74 [1,413.32]	4,505.27 [1,796.29]
France	1,308.65 [484.68]	1,437.78 [970.60]	1,713.07 [634.47]	2,094.03 [834.91]	1,852.46 [738.59]
Belgium	1,046.76 [387.69]	1,217.95 [468.44]	1,450.11 [537.08]	1,962.80 [782.58]	1,967.61 [784.50]
Japan	14,839.61 [5,496.15]	13,921.11 [5,354.27]	15,741.13 [5,830.05]	18,550.68 [7,396.31]	23,449.00 [9,349.31]
Korea, Republic of	4,168.46 [1,543.87]	3,549.07 [1,365.03]	4,189.28 [1,551.58]	4,311.14 [1,718.89]	5,162.05 [2,058.15]
Hong Kong	3,172.00 [1,174.81]	3,925.00 [1,509.62]	5,001.74 [1,852.50]	7,100.90 [2,831.19]	9,899.31 [3,946.94]
Taiwan	2,565.70 [950.26]	3,228.72 [1,241.82]	3,888.14 [1,440.05]	4,590.29 [1,830.19]	5,813.27 [2,317.80]
China, People's Republic of	1,760.75 [652.13]	1,960.93 [754.20]	3,094.70 [1,146.18]	5,062.83 [2,018.59]	4,904.43 [1,955.44]
Australia	1,613.66 [597.65]	1,732.04 [666.17]	1,616.95 [598.87]	2,410.13 [960.94]	2,824.63 [1,126.20]

Source: External Trade Summary, Department of Statistics

69

MAJOR SOURCES OF IMPORTS
RM million (figures in brackets are in US$ million)

COUNTRY	1991	1992	1993	1994	1995
ASEAN	20,053.87	20,721.76	23,203.57	29,232.56	33,432.61
	[7,427.36]	[7,969.91]	[8,593.91]	[11,655.26]	[13,329.86]
Singapore	15,713.67	15,969.57	17,872.70	21,991.28	24,079.93
	[5,819.88]	[6,142.14]	[6,619.52]	[8,768.10]	[9,600.87]
Thailand	2,452.07	2,515.61	2,916.04	3,856.61	5,131.53
	[908.17]	[967.54]	[1,080.01]	[1,537.66]	[2,045.98]
Indonesia	1,390.04	1,621.26	1,843.93	2,461.38	3,057.31
	[514.83]	[623.56]	[682.94]	[981.37]	[1,218.97]
Philippines	493.81	611.17	563.59	841.01	1,153.52
	[182.89]	[235.06]	[208.74]	[335.32]	[459.92]
Brunei	4.29	4.14	7.31	82.29	10.33
	[1.59]	[1.59]	[2.71]	[32.81]	[4.12]
United States of America	15,457.91	16,023.54	19,856.58	26,020.91	31,412.97
	[5,725.15]	[6,162.90]	[7,354.29]	[10,374.75]	[12,524.61]
European Union	13,786.31	12,643.71	13,636.75	23,043.94	29,960.32
	[5,106.04]	[4,862.96]	[5,050.65]	[9,187.81]	[11,945.42]
United Kingdom	4,669.27	3,465.60	3,673.02	4,998.31	5,479.62
	[1,729.36]	[1,332.92]	[1,360.38]	[1,992.87]	[2,184.77]

Germany				
4,397.02	4,270.67	4,504.58	6,542.68	8,612.63
[1,628.52]	[1,642.56]	[1,668.36]	[2,608.62]	[3,433.93]
France				
1,384.43	1,322.11	1,675.11	4,068.96	5,917.46
[512.75]	[508.50]	[620.41]	[1,622.33]	[2,359.34]
Italy				
1,222.70	1,337.89	1,505.96	2,113.54	2,462.58
[452.85]	[514.57]	[557.76]	[842.69]	[981.85]
Netherlands				
909.40	859.46	921.04	1,056.95	1,313.30
[336.81]	[330.56]	[341.12]	[421.41]	[523.62]
Japan				
26,289.25	26,366.09	32,255.38	41,627.52	53,088.81
[9,736.76]	[10,140.80]	[11,946.44]	[16,559.36]	[21,166.94]
Taiwan				
5,505.70	5,760.50	6,296.96	7,960.27	9,913.68
[2,039.15]	[2,215.58]	[2,332.21]	[3,173.82]	[3,665.60]
China, People's Republic of				
2,212.90	2,481.66	2,821.11	3,577.36	4,298.25
[819.59]	[954.48]	[1,044.86]	[1,426.32]	[1,713.75]
Hong Kong				
2,061.00	2,301.76	2,371.24	3,105.94	4,193.70
[763.33]	[885.29]	[878.24]	[1,238.36]	[1,672.06]
Korea, Republic of				
2,743.31	3,102.93	3,601.94	4,978.42	7,965.30
[1,016.04]	[1,193.43]	[1,334.05]	[1,984.94]	[3,175.83]
Australia				
3,232.72	2,699.02	3,323.69	4,618.86	5,259.39
[1,197.30]	[1,038.08]	[1,231.00]	[1,841.58]	[2,096.96]

Source: External Trade Summary, Department of Statistics

CHAPTER 4

FINANCING
by Charles Kraal

INTRODUCTION

The banking and financial industry in Malaysia has experienced rapid growth in the last decade. A wide variety of credit facilities is now available to a local borrower. However, to the non-resident, the availability of domestic credit facilities is subject to certain restrictions especially: (a) exchange control restrictions provided under the Exchange Control Notices of Malaysia (ECM) No 6 which deals with provision of credit facilities to non-residents generally, and ECM 8 which deals with domestic credit facilities to non-resident controlled companies; and (b) the availability of domestic security for credit facilities.

The first restriction mentioned above is purely legal and is subject to certain qualifications, especially with regard to short-term trade financing where the tenure of credit is less than 12 months. The second restriction, however, is a practical one as the local banking ethos is more inclined towards domestic, as opposed to global, asset-backed financing.

The first restriction is an extension of the controls placed by the Central Bank of Malaysia (Bank Negara Malaysia) with respect to local and foreign currency exchange. The provisions are not overly prohibitive and do not appear to have affected the level of foreign investment in the country. However, the level of foreign investment is perhaps not an accurate yardstick to measure the effect of exchange control restrictions. This is discussed at greater length in this chapter.

The second restriction, ie security for credit facilities, is the one that causes most problems to non-resident investors who may not have sufficient external sources of funding. As mentioned earlier, the local banking ethos is more inclined towards locally available assets as security, and these normally take the form of real property, guarantees, stocks, shares and bonds. Global asset-backed financing is uncommon and, in limited circumstances, utilised only by the larger banking concerns or by foreign controlled local banks. Further, although in theory intellectual property rights may also be utilised as security, such concepts are generally far more uncommon in practice.

DOMESTIC FINANCING FOR NON-RESIDENTS

The use of the term 'non-resident' as opposed to 'foreign' investor is because the exchange control restrictions referred to earlier deal with provisions of credit facilities to non-residents.

According to ECM 1 the term 'non-resident' means 'any person other than a resident'.

The ECM goes on to define 'resident' as:

(i) a citizen of Malaysia excluding a person who has obtained permanent resident status of a territory outside Malaysia and is residing outside Malaysia;

(ii) a non-citizen of Malaysia who has obtained permanent resident status of Malaysia and is residing permanently in Malaysia; or

(iii) a person, whether body corporate or unincorporated, whether head office or branch, incorporated or registered with or approved by any authority in Malaysia.

(b) an overseas branch/regional office/sales office/representative office as resident company;

(c) Embassies, Consulates, High Commissions, Jupranational or international organisations; or

(d) a Malaysian citizen who has obtained permanent resident status of a territory outside Malaysia and is residing in Malaysia.

Further the exchange control restrictions also deal with the provision of domestic credit facilities to non-resident controlled companies (referred to as 'NRCCs'). An NRCC means a company in Malaysia where:

(a) more than 50% of the shareholding is held by non-residents and/or NRCCs; or

(b) it is a branch of a company incorporated outside Malaysia; or

(c) the majority shareholding is held by residents but the ultimate right of control is held by non-residents and/or NRCCs; or

73

(d)   although the ultimate right of control is held by residents, the majority shareholding is held by non-residents and/or NRCCs.

ECM 6 deals with the provision of credit facilities to non-residents generally. It distinguishes between financing for the purpose of acquisition of residential property in Malaysia (excluding purchase of land only) and financing for any other purpose. In the later case, a non-resident who maintains an external account is permitted to obtain such credit facilities provided the total credit facilities of the non-resident from all banking institutions does not exceed RM200,000 whereas the latter specifically permits credit facilities for the acquisition of residential property for private accommodation and is subject to the following restrictions:

(1) The non-resident has a valid work permit with at least one year before expiry at the date of the application for the facility.

(2) The facility must not exceed 60% of the purchase price or construction costs.

(3) The residential property is for the non-resident's own accommodation.

(4) The non-resident must not own any other residential property in Malaysia whether individually or jointly.

ECM 1 also permits stockbroking companies to extend financing to non-residents for the purchase of shares listed in the Kuala Lumpur Stock Exchange only. It is obvious that the permitted domestic financing for non-resident individuals is limited. However, this does not mean that credit facilities other than those enumerated above are prohibited. ECM 1 provides that, where a non-resident requires any other credit facilities, the prior permission of the Exchange Controller must be obtained.

The relevant exchange control restrictions with respect to the provision of domestic credit facilities to NRCCs is to be found in ECM 8.

ECM 8 general permission is granted for following purposes:

(1) The issue of guarantees by a resident on behalf of an NRCC excluding trade financing guarantee (ie facilities guaranteeing payment for the purchase of goods).

(2) The extension of credit facilities by residents to NRCCs for any amount in ringgit or foreign currency for short-term trade financing where the tenure of credit is less than 12 months.

(3) The extension of credit facilities by residents to NRCCs up to an aggregate limit of RM10 million in ringgit or foreign currency for any other credit facility.

However, in cases falling within (2) and (3) above it is further provided that credit facilities in foreign currency must be extended by licensed banks or licensed merchant banks and, in cases where credit facilities are extended by banking institutions, at least 60% of short-term trade financing and 60% of other types of credit facilities must be extended by Malaysian-owned banking institutions.

In any other case which does not fall within the ambit of those generally permitted, the NRCC must seek the approval of the Exchange Controller. The criteria for such approval include:

(1) Whether the credit facility is for productive purposes. 'Productive purposes' is not defined in the ECM and therefore affords a wide degree of latitude on the part of the Exchange Controller.

(2) The NRCC should have a domestic debt (including the facility for which approval is sought) to eligible capital funds ratio not exceeding 3:1. For this purpose 'domestic debt' excludes short-term trade financing and guarantees, and 'eligible capital funds' means the sum total of: (i) paid up capital; (ii) preference shares (excluding redeemable preference shares issued to residents who are not ordinary shareholders); (iii) share premium; (iv) accumulated profits (less losses); (v) concessional credit facilities from non-resident shareholders; and (vi) revaluation reserves for public listed companies.

SECURITY FOR CREDIT OBTAINED

Assuming that the non-resident or NRCC is either permitted to obtain or has obtained approval for the credit facility sought, this of course does not mean that the domestic banks and financial institutions are going to blaze a trail to the non-resident or NRCC offering credit without requiring anything more.

Generally all banks and financial institutions would require security in the form of locally available assets or local guarantees. It is only in exceptional circumstances that local banking and financial institutions would accept global asset-backed security of foreign guarantees. Such exceptional circumstances usually involve sterling corporate credibility and projected cash receipts which minimise any risk of default.

By far the most welcome form of security is real property. Apart from this, other common types of securities include guarantees; deposits or pledges of stocks, shares, bonds etc; a right of set-off over deposits of cash; assignments of assets or debts owed to the borrower; corporate debentures; and bills of exchange, trust receipts or letters of hypothecation.

This list is not exhaustive. However, for the non-resident or NRCC such security may not be available. The alternative then would be to seek local participation on a joint venture basis where the local partner would be responsible for the obtaining of credit and/or provision of security for credit facilities required for the venture.

CONCLUSION

Local financing is generally geared towards providing short-term credit facilities to non-residents and NRCCs. This is in line with the current policy of encouraging foreign equity participation in the local economy.

CHAPTER 5

EMPLOYMENT LAW—
RIGHTS AND LIABILITIES
by P Jayasingam

LEGISLATION

The main body of employment law in Malaysia is found in three principal pieces of legislation and subsidiary legislation made thereunder. These are the Employment Act 1955, the Industrial Relations Act 1967 and the Trade Unions Act 1959.

However, employers in Malaysia will also have to contend with other pieces of legislation which concern the rights and liabilities of both employers and employees. These are:
(1) Employees Provident Fund Act 1991.
(2) Employees Social Security Act 1969.
(3) Workmen's Compensation Act 1952.
(4) Worker's Minimum Standards of Housing and Amenities Act 1990.
(5) Wages Council Act 1947.
(6) Children and Young Persons (Employment) Act 1966.
(7) Occupational Safety and Health Act 1994.
(8) Human Resources Development Act 1992.

These pieces of legislation are geared towards regulating the terms and conditions of service of workers or employees, imposing obligations on employers towards their employees and vice versa, as well as regulating the relationship between trade unions of workers and employers.

Although this chapter will deal mainly with the three principal pieces of legislation above, brief comments will be made on the other legislation referred to.

GENERAL

Employers will be heartened to note that management rights have been enshrined in s 13(3) of the Industrial Relations Act 1967, which reads as follows:

Notwithstanding subsection (1), no trade union of workmen may include in its proposals for a collective agreement a proposal in relation to any of the following matters, that is to say

(a) the promotion by the employer of any workman from a lower grade or category to a higher grade or category;

(b) the transfer by an employer of a workman within the organisation of an employer's profession, business, trade or work, provided that such transfer does not entail a change to the detriment of a workman in regard to his terms of employment;

(c) the employment by an employer of any person that he may appoint in the event of a vacancy arising in his establishment;

(d) the termination by an employer of the services of a workman by reason of redundancy or by reason of the reorganisation of an employer's profession, business, trade or work or the criteria for such termination;

(e) the dismissal and reinstatement of a workman by an employer;

(f) the assignment or allocation by an employer of duties or specific tasks to a workman that are consistent or compatible with the terms of his employment.

These are non-negotiable rights of an employer subject only to s 5 of the Industrial Relations Act 1967. In brief, an employer must exercise these rights for proper cause, failing which it is answerable to the Industrial Court as to the propriety or otherwise of the exercise of these rights.

The significance of s 13(3) of the Industrial Relations Act 1967 is that it seeks to identify the rights of an employer over individual employees and a remedy for improper exercise of such rights as provided for under ss 20 and 26 of the Industrial Relations Act 1967. This effectively excludes trade union intervention in the exercise of these rights (whether properly exercised or not) by the use of collective coercive action in the form of strikes. Section 44(e) of the Industrial Relations Act 1967 prohibits strikes over any dispute involving the subject matter of s 13(3) of the Act.

Much controversy surrounds s 13(3) of the Industrial Relations Act 1967, as the International Labour Organisation has viewed it as a contravention of ILO Convention No 98 (which Malaysia ratified in 1961), in that it restricts the full right to free collective bargaining. In any case, the government has thus far argued in favour of retaining this section as a means of preserving industrial harmony while at the same time not sacrificing the right of the aggrieved individual by giving him a right to redress any unfairness by the employer.

The rest of the rights of the employer are only subject to the contract of employment. However, in relation to employees within the scope of the Employment Act 1955, ss 7 and 7A of this Act merely ensure that no contractual provision would be inferior to the provisions of the Act. As a general guideline, the Employment Act 1955 covers employees earning up to RM1500 per month. However, the First Schedule to the Employment Act 1955 provides for various exceptions to this rule, which covers the following categories of workers:

(1) Manual workers.

(2) Supervisors of manual workers.

(3) Persons engaged in the operation and maintenance of mechanically propelled vehicles operated for the transport of passengers or goods or for reward or for commercial purposes.

(4) Persons engaged on any vessel registered in Malaysia.

The rights and liabilities of employers differ for organised and unorganised industries. There is only one section of the Industrial Relations Act 1967 that protects unorganised workers, ie s 20. Whereas an employee in an organised industry can take any grievance through his union to the Industrial Court, an employee in an unorganised industry can only ventilate a grievance on his dismissal without just cause or excuse.

In any case, potential employers (investors) need to understand both individual employment rights and collective labour relations in order to operate within the legal framework created by the body of the employment law.

INDIVIDUAL EMPLOYMENT LAW

A contract of employment is formed by an agreement, whether express or implied, whether in writing or oral, whereby an employee agrees to work and an employer agrees to employ the person as an employee. This agreement to employ must come within the definition of a contract of service, as opposed to a contract for service, to involve the employer in the liabilities of the law.

There is no coverage through labour laws at all for those whose income is derived under contracts for services, as they are deemed to be self-employed or own-account business people. There are other government bodies and cooperatives to regulate the relationship between the self-employed and the principals. Examples of these are found in the fishing, land development, rubber smallholders and rice farming industries.

The Employment Act 1955 is the only statute which provides for floor level rights on working hours, overtime rates, annual leave, sick leave, public holidays, maternity leave, rest days etc. Those outside the scope of this Act are only protected in terms of what their contracts of employment specify.

Employees covered by the Employment Act 1955 have recourse under s 69 of the Act to make claims for moneys under the statute or under their contracts of service. Orders made by the presiding labour officer are enforceable through normal execution procedures in the civil courts. Appeal against these orders lie in the High Court of Malaya.

OBLIGATIONS OF THE EMPLOYER

Duty to Provide Work

The general rule is that the employer is not under an obligation to provide work for his employees so long as the wages due under the contract of employment are paid to an employee who is ready and willing to work. There may be instances where the employer is unable to provide work, for example, when there is a lack of orders or when there is a strike. This means the employer will not be in breach of contract by failing to provide work in such circumstances. However, there are certain circumstances where the failure to provide work will be considered a breach of contract. These circumstances can be summarised as follows:

(1) Where work is available but not given which results in the employee suffering a loss of reputation.

(2) Where the failure to provide work leads to a reduction in the employee's actual or potential earings.[1]

(3) Where an employee needs practice in order to maintain and develop his skills in employment.

(4) Contracts where not only payment is envisaged but also publicity from the performance.[2]

In the case of *Collier v Sunday Referee Publishing Co Ltd* [1940] 2 KB 647 Asquith J held as follows:

> It is true that a contract of employment does not necessarily, or perhaps normally, oblige the master to provide the servant with work. Provided I pay my cook her wages regularly, she cannot complain if I choose to take all of my meals out.

It must be noted, however, that the above view is subject to the exceptions enumerated in the earlier paragraph. Where there are collective agreements which stipulate total working hours or days per week, caution must be exercised. In the case of *Perangsang Pasifik Sdn Bhd v National Mining Workers Union* (1985) ILR 227 [Award No 51 of 1985] and in the case of *Mount Pleasure Holdings Bhd Prai v Kesatuan Pekerja-Pekerja Perusahaan Membuat Tekstil & Pakaian, P Pinang & S Prai* (1985) ILR 120 [Award No 290 of 1984], the Industrial Court held that the employer must provide work for the hours or days per week stated in the collective agreement and that the employee could not reduce the working hours or days per week even in order to avoid retrenchment.

Obligation to Pay Wages

The contract of employment will normally contain an express term which will determine the remuneration to be paid to the employee. The general rule at common law is that an employer must pay the wages of his employees if the employees are ready, willing and able to work even if no work is provided by the employer. This principle will apply to all categories of workers, whether they are monthly rated, daily rated, hourly rated or piece rated.[3]

However, an employer may, by statute, be required to make deductions from the employee's wages. Such deductions if made will be lawful.

Duty to Ensure the Employee's Safety

The employer is under a common law duty to:

(1) Provide the employee with proper equipment, tools and appliances, which are safe for work.[4]

(2) Provide a safe system of work for its employees. This would involve the provision of warnings, protective clothing, special instructions and training and supervision on all aspects of safety at work. If there are safety precautions laid down, these must be brought to the employee's attention. If safety equipment is provided, it must be available for use with all necessary instruction and information for its proper use.

(3) Engage reasonably competent fellow employees. This obligation would require an employer to employ a competent person so as to ensure that that person poses no risk to fellow employees.

In relation to these duties, the standard of care required of the employer is 'the care which an ordinary prudent employer would take in all the circumstances'.[5]

In furtherance of these duties, the Occupational Safety and Health Act 1994 was passed by Parliament to ensure employees' safety at work. This Act will be dealt with briefly in a later part of this chapter.

Implied Duty of Mutual Respect

This is a twofold duty. On the one hand employers are required to treat their employees with due respect and consideration and, on the other hand, the employer must refrain from taking any action which will seriously injure or destroy the employees' trust and confidence upon which the employment relationship is based.

In *Lewis v Motorworld Garages Ltd* (1986) ICR 157 the Court of Appeal held as follows:

> that whether an employee had been entitled to terminate his contract of employment without notice by reason of the employer's conduct depended not upon whether the employer had intended the conduct to be repudiatory or could reasonably have believed that it would be accepted as such, but upon whether the employer's conduct, viewed objectively, evinced an intention no longer to be bound by the contract; that where an employer had breached an express term of an employment contract but the employee had affirmed the contract, that breach could nevertheless subsequently amount to a repudiatory breach of the implied contractual obligation of trust and confidence.

OBLIGATIONS OF THE EMPLOYEE

The prime obligation of an employee is to be available and ready for work during the hours stipulated for such work (except in the case of sickness etc). In *Seaboard World Airlines Inc v Transport and General Workers Union* (1973) ICR 458, it was held that contracts normally provide for the performance of broadly specified types of work for a specified period of working hours. It would not be a breach of contract by the employer to ask the employee to do work as specified in the contract, within those times. The fact that the actual workload increased, because business improved or other employees resigned, would not be grounds for the employee to refuse to carry out the additional workload. The employee, in other words, is not entitled to idle time, other than stipulated break times.

Duty to Obey All Lawful and Reasonable Orders

It is an implied term of the contract of employment that an employee is required to obey all lawful and reasonable instructions or orders of the employer. Lawful order in this context means any order which is not inconsistent with written law. A reasonable order on the other hand refers to any order which is within the scope of the employment. An employee may without any breach of the express or implied provisions of his contract disobey an order which is either unlawful or unreasonable. Where, however, an employee is doubtful as to the legality of the order it would be prudent for the employee to obey the given order under protest.[6]

Duty to Provide Faithful and Honest Service

The employment relationship is one of a fiduciary character. In the circumstances, whenever the employer engages a worker he expects the worker to faithfully discharge his service and to protect and further his interest. If the employee acts in a manner which is inconsistent with this fiduciary relationship, the employee may be dismissed from service. This obligation to provide faithful and honest service is an implied term and need not be in writing. Examples of this duty include the following:

(1) The employee is required not to place himself in a position where his interest conflicts with his duties.[7]

(2) The employee is prohibited from making any secret profit without his employer's leave.[8]

(3) The employee is prevented from misusing his employer's confidential information.[9]

(4) The employee is prohibited from doing anything which may injure the interest of the employer.

(5) The employee is prohibited from being involved in or associated with business which is competitive with that of his employer.

Duty to Exercise Skill and Care

In carrying out his duties the employee, by implication, owes his employer a duty to exercise reasonable care and skill in the discharge of such duties. This involves ensuring that the employer's property and business are not subjected to any damage. Additionally, the employee must not subject his master, fellow workers, third parties or even himself to harm or the risk of harm. An employee who fails to exercise skill and care in the discharge of his duties is guilty of the misconduct of negligence and may be subjected to disciplinary action.[10]

Duty to Adapt to New Methods and Techniques

As a general rule, an employee is required to adapt to new methods and techniques that may be required of him from time to time by his employer. However, such new methods or techniques should not involve changes which fundamentally alter the character of the employee's existing contract. If such changes are necessary, it would be advisable for the employer to obtain the employee's consent before implementing them.

COLLECTIVE LABOUR RELATIONS

Trade unions of workers and of employers and individual employers are given the right in law to negotiate collective agreements which are binding not only on the parties who signed them but also on their successors, transferees and assignees. A collective agreement is also binding on all workers employed in the company to whom the agreement relates, irrespective of whether they are members of the trade union of workers or not: s 17 of the Industrial Relations Act 1967.

The provisions of the Trade Unions Act 1959 and the Industrial Relations Act 1967 interlink and create a legal framework within which employers and trade unions conduct their relationship and create the legal rights of each.

Registration of Trade Unions

The Trade Unions Act 1959 governs the registration of trade unions. A trade union is defined under s 2 of the Act as follows:

'trade union' or 'union' means any association or combination of workmen or employers, being workmen whose place of work is in West Malaysia, Sabah or Sarawak, as the case may be, or employers employing workmen in West Malaysia, Sabah or Sarawak, as the case may be:

(a) within any particular trade, occupation or industry or within any similar trades, occupations or industries; and

(b)   whether temporary or permanent; and

(c)   having among its objects one or more of the following objects:

    (i)   the regulation of relations between workmen and employers, for the purposes of promoting good industrial relations between workmen and employers, improving the working conditions of workmen or enhancing their economic and social status, or increasing productivity;

    (ia)   the regulation of relations between workmen and workmen, or between employers and employers;

    (ii)   the representation of either workmen or employers in trade disputes;

    (iia)   the conducting of, or dealing with, trade disputes and matters related thereto; or

    (iii)   the promotion or organisation or financing of strikes or lock-outs in any trade or industry or the provision of pay or other benefits for its members during a strike or lock-out;

It can be seen from the above definition that general or omnibus unions are prohibited. Membership of a trade union must consist of workers who are from a similar trade, industry, occupation or establishment. Statutory bodies, local authorities and public sector employees can only be represented by their own unions. Additionally, West Malaysian workers, Sabah workers and Sarawak workers must have their own separate unions.

It is also significant to note that the objects of a trade union are clearly spelled out in the definition and that no organisation, howsoever formed, may act as a trade union and carry out any of these objectives. Section 67 of the Trade Unions Act 1959 makes any society or company unlawful if it includes any of the objects of a trade union in its activities.

Rights of a Registered Trade Union

The right of a registered trade union can be briefly summarised as follows:

(1) The right to represent individual members of their union, in their individual grievances.

(2) The right to trade union leave. This right is provided for in s 6 of the Industrial Relations Act 1967 in very wide terms. Section 59(1)(f) of that Act is a penal provision against employers who seek to discipline trade union officers who have taken time off for trade union activities in accordance with s 6 of the Act.

(3) Sections 20, 21 and 22 of the Trade Unions Act 1959 make civil suits against trade unions in respect of damages for breach of contract and claims in tort unmaintainable in a civil court.

Recognition of Trade Unions

Where a trade union has established that its membership strength has attained a simple majority of workers, the employer will have to grant recognition to the union or face an order of the Minister of Human Resources to do so. The granting of recognition will entitle the union to represent all workers in the company within the scope of representation, including non-members, in collective bargaining. Once recognition is granted, even if the union loses its majority position in the company, recognition cannot be withdrawn.

There is a distinction in the rights of a trade union prior to and after the granting or order of recognition. The trade union has the right to represent *only* its members prior to recognition. It can at that stage only enforce the existing contractual or statutory rights of its members. It cannot seek to *improve* the terms and conditions of employment of its members, but only to preserve their existing rights.

After recognition, however, the situation is completely different. The trade union now represents 'all workmen' in the company. This refers to all the workers within the scope of the union's membership according to its own constitution and further subject only to s 5(2)(b) and (c) and s 9(1) of the Industrial Relations Act 1967. These sections exclude from the scope the recognition those employees engaged in managerial, executive, security and confidential capacities, unless that trade union specifically caters for employees in each of these capacities. Section 9(5) of the Industrial Relations Act 1967 confers on the Honourable Minister of Human Resources the power to decide whether or not a worker is employed in any of these capacities.

Although the whole of s 9 of the Industrial Relations Act 1967 is designed to provide a smooth procedure for the conclusion of a claim for recognition, challenges to the Honourable Minister's decision as to the majority of the membership, the capacity of the workers as well as to the competency of the trade union to represent the workers, to the Superior Courts have sometimes occasioned delays of up to five or more years.

In any case, in order to maintain the status quo between the parties during the pendency of a claim for recognition, s 10 of the Industrial Relations Act 1967 prohibits the union from picketing or striking, and the employer from locking out or terminating any workers (save for misconduct), during this period.

With a view to industrial harmony, s 11 of the Industrial Relations Act 1967 prevents another union from seeking to claim recognition in respect of the same workers until after a lapse of three years from the date recognition is granted to one union. Where a claim for recognition fails, for instance, due to lack of a simple majority of members, that union cannot make a second attempt to claim recognition until after six months from the date on which the first attempt failed.

The most significant effect of a grant or order of recognition is that, thereafter, all terms and conditions of employment are determined by consensus. Neither the employer nor the trade union can unilaterally decide the dispute. The only authority that can make a decision on any such dispute is the Industrial Court.

Thus, the corner-stone of the system for maintaining industrial harmony is the imposition of an obligation on both parties to resolve disputes through consultation and consensus.

Collective Bargaining

The objective of a trade union after securing recognition is to commence collective bargaining.

Save for the restrictions in ss 13(3) and 15 of the Industrial Relations Act 1967, a trade union is free to negotiate on all matters falling within the definition of a trade dispute in the Act.

A trade dispute is defined in s 2 of the Industrial Relations Act 1967 as follows:

'trade dispute' means any dispute between an employer and his workmen which is connected with the employment or non-employment or the terms of employment or the conditions of work of any such workmen;

Collective bargaining is defined in the same section as follows:

'collective bargaining' means negotiating with a view to the conclusion of a collective agreement;

The union, as a matter of practice, forwards wide ambit proposals for collective agreement so that there is room to reduce and/or give up certain claims during negotiations. The employer is required to respond within 14 days to the proposal (s 13(4) of the Industrial Relations Act 1967) and commence collective bargaining within 30 days of the acceptance. Failing this, the Director-General of Industrial Relations may intervene to assist the parties to commence collective bargaining. If the assistance of the Director-General of Industrial Relations fails, a trade dispute is then deemed to exist.

The Honourable Minister may at this stage intervene and have the dispute referred to the Industrial Court: s 26 of the Industrial Relations Act 1967. The union, failing such a reference, may resort to industrial action.

In practice, most industrial actions in Malaysia occur during breakdowns in collective bargaining. Section 44(6) of the Industrial Relations Act 1967 prohibits strikes once a dispute has been referred to the Industrial Court.

Industrial Action

Strikes

What constitutes a strike has been defined in s 2 of the Industrial Relations Act 1967. In brief, it means a total cessation of work by a body of workers under a common understanding. It also includes a partial cessation of work by a number of workers acting in combination. The incidence of strikes is not alarming in Malaysia, but other forms of industrial action, equally or more damaging, are carried out. A strike is either lawful or unlawful. Justification is not an issue at all. The right to strike within the law is not subject to being reasonable or justified.

Work to rule

A work to rule is a strict adherence to rules and regulations of the company with a complete refusal to cooperate. An instance of such work to rule is refusal to work overtime (non-essential services). It includes a boycott of non-employment activities such as the company's annual dinner, long service awards, company sports and family day.

Picket

The law on picketing is covered by s 40 of the Industrial Relations Act 1967. Picketing outside working hours, at or near the place of work, is lawful as long as it is in contemplation or furtherance of a trade dispute and the picket is carried out without leading to a breach of the peace.

The attendant adverse publicity of a picket is what the union generally depends on to succeed in its claims. Further, a picket is a testing point for the leadership to assess support of its membership for a strike, if necessary.

Go-slow

This action refers to a physical slow down of work and falls within the definition of a strike. Such action would be automatically unlawful as the preconditions for a lawful strike will be absent (eg a secret ballot). Additionally, a strike within the premises of the company would be unlawful per se.

Collective Agreements

A collective agreement is defined by s 2 of the Industrial Relations Act 1967 as follows:

> 'collective agreement' means an agreement in writing concluded between an employer or a trade union of employers on the one hand and a trade union of workmen on the other relating to the terms and conditions of employment and work of workmen or concerning relations between such parties.

The collective agreement entered into between the parties must have a valid period of at least three years and must incorporate procedures to resolve disputes on implementation and interpretation of the agreement. It is common for the parties to include a stipulation that the agreement will continue to remain in force until superseded by a new agreement.

By virtue of s 44(d) of the Industrial Relations Act 1967, strikes and lockouts are prohibited over any of the matters covered by the collective agreement during its validity. In practice, employers and trade unions provide for the collective agreement to continue even after the three-year period until a new agreement is concluded.

Effect of a Collective Agreement

Upon conclusion, a signed copy of the collective agreement must be deposited with the Registrar of the Industrial Court for cognisance. Once taken cognisance of by the Industrial Court, the collective agreement is deemed to be an Award of the Court. It binds all workers within the union's scope of representation irrespective of whether they are members of the union or not. It will also bind all successors, transferees or assignees of the employer or the trade union of employers.

Enforcement of Collective Agreements

Interpretation

Section 33 of the Industrial Relations Act 1967 allows the parties to a collective agreement or the Minister of Human Resources to refer any term of the collective agreement to the Industrial Court to render an interpretation thereto or to effect such modifications as may be necessary to resolve an ambiguity in the wording of the terms.

The Industrial Court adopts the principles of statutory interpretation in giving meaning to the words in a collective agreement, even though the drafting of the agreement was by 'lay-persons'. This underscores the importance of using the correct words in the agreement.

Non-compliance

Section 56 of the Industrial Relations Act 1967 allows the parties to the agreement, as well as individual workers, to lodge a complaint of non-compliance against one party to the agreement. If the allegation in non-compliance is substantiated, the court may order the offending party to comply with the relevant provision. The Award of the Industrial Court may be registered and subsequently enforced as a decision of the Sessions Court or High Court.

The Industrial Court may if 'special circumstances' exist vary the agreement under s 56(2)(c) of the Industrial Relations Act 1967 to accommodate the circumstances. Attempts by employers to use financial losses to vary agreements have thus far failed.

Dispute Settlement Machinery

The preamble to the Industrial Relations Act 1967 provides as follows:

> An Act to provide for the regulation of the relations between employers and workmen and their trade unions and the prevention and settlement of any differences or disputes arising from their relationship and generally to deal with trade disputes and matters arising therefrom.

Negotiations

This is the first stage of dispute settlement and it envisages both parties discussing their disputes directly with a view to reaching an amicable solution through consensus. Agreements reached and taken cognisance of by the Industrial Court are enforceable.

Conciliation

The machinery of the Industrial Relations Department is available when direct negotiations reach a deadlock. The conciliator acts as a neutral party to find common ground between the two parties and to find a mutually acceptable solution.

The conciliator also steps in when unions resort to industrial action to advance their claims.

Industrial adjudication

Where the dispute or matter cannot be resolved by conciliation, the Minister of Human Resources is vested with the discretion to refer the matter to the Industrial Court for an Award. Once a reference has been made, strikes in relation to the subject matter of the reference are prohibited.

INDUSTRIAL COURT

The Industrial Court is a statutory court constituted under the Industrial Relations Act 1967. Being a creature of statute, the Court's powers and duties are prescribed by its enabling legislation.

Section 29 of the Industrial Relations Act 1967 outlines the various powers that may be exercised by the court when deliberating upon the matter before it. In exercising its discretion, the court is also enjoined to take various factors into account, as set out by s 30 of the Industrial Relations Act 1967. The section reads as follows:

(1) The Court shall have power in relation to a trade dispute referred to it or in relation to a reference to it under section 20(3), to make an award (including an interim award) relating to all or any of the issues.

(2) Where the Court is not unanimous on any question or matter to be determined, a decision shall be taken by a majority of members and, if there is no majority decision, by the President or Chairman.

(3) The Court shall make its award without delay and where practicable within thirty days from the date of reference to it of the trade dispute or of a reference to it under section 20(3).

(4) In making its award in respect of a trade dispute, the Court shall have regard to the public interest, the financial implications and the effect of the award on the economy of the country, and on the industry concerned, and also to the probable effect in related or similar industries.

(5) The Court shall act according to equity, good conscience and the substantial merits of the case without regard to technicalities and legal form.

(5A) In making its award, the Court may take into consideration any agreement of code relating to employment practices between organisations representative of employers and workmen respectively where such agreement or code has been approved by the Minister.

(6) In making its award, the Court shall not be restricted to the specific relief claimed by the parties or to the demands made by the parties in the course of the trade dispute or in the matter of the reference to it under section 20(3) but may include in the award any matter or thing which it thinks necessary or expedient for the purpose of settling the trade dispute or the reference to it under section 20(3).

(7) An award may specify the period during which it shall continue, and may be retrospective to such date as is specified in the award:

Provided that the retrospective date of the award may not, except in the case of a decision of the Court under section 33 or an award of the Court for the reinstatement of a workman on a reference to it in respect of the dismissal of a workman, be earlier than six months from the date on which the dispute was referred to the Court.

(8) The award of the Court shall be signed by the President or the Chairman of any Division or in the event of the President or the Chairman for any reason being unable to sign the award by the remaining members.

(9) The Court may rectify in any award any clerical error or mistake arising from any accidental slip or omission.

The Industrial Relations Act 1967, by virtue of s 33A(1), provides for a limited right of appeal. This is fortified by s 33B(1) and (2) which precludes a party from pursuing an appeal through any forum other than that which is provided for in the Act.

Prerogative Writs and Industrial Court Awards

Notwithstanding the provisions of s 33B(1) and (2) of the Industrial Relations Act 1967, which basically preclude appeals against findings of fact and law, an aggrieved party may challenge the Award of the Industrial Court through prerogative writs in judicial review proceedings. However, judicial review relates to jurisdictional errors only, and may be based on the following grounds:

(1) That the Industrial Court acted without jurisdiction and/or erred in law.

(2) That the Industrial Court acted in excess of its jurisdiction.

(3) That the Industrial Court reached its decision without taking into account all relevant matters.

(4) That the Industrial Court took into account irrelevant matters.

(5) That the Industrial Court arrived at a decision which was so unreasonable that no reasonable person or body of persons could have come to the conclusion that it did.

DISMISSAL OR TERMINATION

Under s 20 of the Industrial Relations Act 1967, a worker who considers himself dismissed without just cause or excuse may file a representation for his reinstatement with the Director-General of Industrial Relations within 60 days of the dismissal. His right under s 20 of the Act will lapse if he fails to make his representation on time. The Director-General of Industrial Relations may take such steps as he deems necessary and expedient to arrive at an amicable settlement. If, however, no settlement can be reached, the Director-General must notify the Minister of Human Resources who may, if he sees fit, refer the matter to the Industrial Court for an Award.

Under the Industrial Relations Act 1967, a 'workman' is defined in s 2 as follows:

> 'workman' means any person, including an apprentice, employed by an employer under a contract of employment to work for hire or reward and for the purposes of any proceedings in relation to a trade dispute includes any such person who has been dismissed, discharged or retrenched in connection with or as consequence of that dispute or whose dismissal, discharge or retrenchment has led to that dispute.

The term 'workman' has been given a broad definition by courts and encompasses even general managers and high ranking employees. The only persons who may not be covered by the phrase 'workman' are persons who can properly be regarded as independent contractors[11] who can be taken to be in business on their own account.

Although a worker's contract of service may contain a termination clause, employers must realise that Malaysian law does not recognise any significant difference between a termination of the contract in accordance with a termination clause and an outright dismissal. Therefore, although the employer may regard the matter as one of contractual termination, the worker may regard the matter as a dismissal without just cause or excuse.[12]

This principle has been extended to cover employees on probation. Under the law an employee, albeit under probation, is nevertheless a worker in the context of the Industrial Relations Act. If the worker is not confirmed at the end of the period of probation he may regard this non-confirmation as a dismissal without just cause or excuse and may file a representation for reinstatement like any other worker.

The adjudication of a representation for reinstatement materially differs from an ordinary civil case, where the plaintiff would shoulder the burden of proof. Although an employer may be likened to a defendant while the worker may be likened to a plaintiff, in a case before the Industrial Court, the employer bears the legal and evidential burden of setting out the reasons for dismissing the worker, to establish the same on a balance of probabilities and to prove further that the dismissal was with just cause or excuse. This will require the employer to produce all relevant witnesses and documents to the court, an obligation which can prove to be difficult in view of the fact that a period of two years will have elapsed before the matter comes up for trial. The absence of such material witnesses or documents can be fatal to the employer's case before the Industrial Court.

Usually the employer's decision to dismiss a worker follows a domestic inquiry into his conduct. Following recent decisions of the Federal Court, the failure to hold a domestic inquiry, or the holding of a defective inquiry, prior to the dismissal of a worker is not fatal to the employer's case.[13] The function of the Industrial Court is to determine whether or not the dismissal of the worker is justified having regard to all the evidence presented before it. These Federal Court decisions also abolished the distinction drawn between employees covered by the Employment Act 1955 (s 14 of the Act imposed a mandatory requirement of 'due inquiry' prior to a dismissal) and persons not covered by that Act, for the purposes of proceedings filed under s 20 of the Industrial Relations Act 1967. Be that as it may, the recent Supreme Court case of *Said Dharmalingam bin Abdullah v Malaysian Breweries (Malaya) Sdn Bhd* (1997) 1 AMR 1063 reopened the controversy again by suggesting that a due inquiry must be held for employees covered by the Employment Act 1955. However, an employee who is covered by the Employment Act 1955 may institute a claim under s 69 of that Act for termination benefits in the labour department if the mandatory 'due inquiry' provision is not complied with.

In deliberating upon a case of dismissal, the Industrial Court is required to act according to equity and good conscience and to consider the substantial merits of the case without regard to technicalities and legal form: s 30(5) of the Industrial Relations Act 1967. In this connection the Industrial Court will take into account the seriousness of the misconduct, the employee's designation and past record as well as the general standard of discipline practised by the company.

CONSTRUCTIVE DISMISSAL AND FORCED RESIGNATION

Under the law a dismissal includes not only straightforward dismissals by the employer but also forced resignations and constructive dismissals. A resignation obtained by duress or coercion will be treated as a dismissal in law.[14]

A constructive dismissal arises where the employer commits a fundamental breach of the contract. If the worker accepts this repudiation of the contract on the part of the employer (conduct of the employer which evinces an intention no longer to be bound by the contract or conduct which is tantamount to forcing the worker out) soon after by treating himself as dismissed, he may file a representation under s 20 of the Industrial Relations Act 1967.[15]

If the court is satisfied that there has in fact been a fundamental breach of contract as alleged or a resignation procured by coercion, it will then be incumbent upon the employer to justify its actions.

FIXED TERM CONTRACTS

Malaysian law, and in particular the Industrial Relations Act 1967, espouses the principle of security of tenure in employment.

A contract for a specified period or for the performance of a specified task terminates at the end of the contract period in the absence of an express renewal. However, if the purpose of the worker's employment has all the hallmarks of regular employment, a non-renewal of the contract will in law be treated as a dismissal, and the employer would bear the burden of establishing that the non-renewal was with just cause or excuse.[16]

REDUNDANCY

It is well established in industrial law that the reorganisation of a business is a function which falls within the power and prerogative of management. As long as this power is exercised in a bona fide manner, no arbitrator ought to interfere with this exercise of the employer's right. There is, therefore, a clear judicial recognition of the company's right to determine the structure and workings of its business, even if its decisions have the effect of rendering part of its work-force surplus and therefore redundant. In this context, it is irrelevant that the company was making profits at the time of the retrenchment exercise.

A redundancy situation exists where the court is satisfied that the company is no longer in need of the services rendered by the worker in question because the worker concerned is surplus to the requirements of the company. In such circumstances, the affected worker may be retrenched.

The selection of workers for retrenchment is generally subject to the principle of 'last in, first out'. However, the employer may adopt other methods of selection provided there is justification to depart from the 'last in, first out' principle and the method of selection adopted by the employer is a clear and objective one. The 'last in, first out' principle, is, however, of no application where the redundancy relates to a single position.

Quite apart from establishing redundancy from a factual and evidential point of view, the company's bona fides are an important factor to bear in mind. It is well founded in law that, where a redundancy situation is created solely for the aim of removing a certain employee, courts will not hesitate to interfere even if redundancy has in fact been established to the hilt.

TRANSFER

As a general rule transfer is regarded as an implied right of the employer. This implied right permits the employer to transfer the employee to another branch of the company, notwithstanding the absence of an express clause, as long as the branch was in existence at the time of the employee's employment. However, the employer would require express contractual authority to transfer an employee to associated or subsidiary companies or to branches not in existence at the time of appointment.

Notwithstanding the presence of either an express or implied right of transfer, a worker may either refuse to comply with a transfer order or claim constructive dismissal if the employer acts capriciously, or is motivated by mala fides. Furthermore, courts tend to interfere with the transfer order if it causes a financial burden to the worker.

RETIREMENT

A worker may not be retired from service in the absence of a contractually agreed retirement age whether express or implied. In the absence of such a right the employee may consider himself dismissed if he is forced to retire against his will.[17]

PROBATIONERS

The general law is that a probationer has no substantive right to his post. He holds no lien on the post. He is on trial to prove his fitness for the post for which he offers his services. His character, suitability and capacity as an employee are to be tested during the probationary period and his employment comes to an end if, during or at the end of the probationary period, he is found to be unsuitable and his employer terminates his probation according to the contract.

However, a probationer so terminated can question the decision through s 20 of the Industrial Relations Act 1967. Should the matter be referred to the Industrial Court for a decision, the court will want to be satisfied that the termination was a bona fide exercise of the power conferred by the contract. If the court is convinced that there was an unfair labour practice it will interfere with the termination and accord proper relief to the worker. In the recent case of *Khabah bte Abbas v Pesaka Capital Corp Sdn Bhd* (1997) 1 *MLJ* 376, the Court of Appeal held that an employee on probation would enjoy the same rights as a permanent employee or confirmed employee and, therefore, his or her services could not be terminated without just cause or excuse.

EMPLOYEES PROVIDENT FUND ACT 1991 (EPF ACT)

The purpose of the EPF Act is to provide a compulsory savings scheme to act as a retirement fund for workers in the private sector who in general do not enjoy a pension. The Act aims to set up a contributory fund. Employers are required to make a contribution totalling 12% of employees' wages while employees are required to contribute a sum totalling 11% of their wages. Although the Act places an obligation to contribute on both the employer and employee, the responsibility for the contributions of both parties rests with the employer. To this end, the Act permits the employer to deduct the employees' contribution directly from his wages.

Under the Employees Provident Fund (Amendment) Act 1995, an employee who contributes to the fund is entitled to withdraw his benefit under the fund in the following circumstances:

(a)   he has attained the age of 55;
(b)   he has become mentally incapacitated and is unable to continue in any employment;
(c)   death;
(d)   the member of the fund is not a Malaysian national and is about to leave the country with no intention of returning.

Under the same Amendment Act, the EPF Board may authorise the partial withdrawal of the outstanding credit of a member if it is satisfied that the member:

(a)   has attained the age of 50;
(b)   has either purchased or built a house;
(c)   has either purchased or built a house and has taken a loan made on the security of a charge upon the house for its purchase or construction;
(d)   has either purchased or built a house and has taken a loan provided by the fund for its purchase or construction;
(e)   or any person approved by the Board requires medical financing.

A point of importance to all employers is that the definition of 'wages' under the EPF Act is extremely wide. It includes all remuneration in money under the employee's contract of service or apprenticeship and includes any bonus or allowance payable whether such bonus or allowance is payable under his contract of service, apprenticeship or otherwise. The only excluded items are service charge, overtime payment, gratuity, retirement benefits, retrenchment benefits, lay-off benefits, termination benefits, travelling allowance or value of travelling allowance or concession and any other payment exempted by the Minister.

Many employers fail to realise that extra payments over and above the basic wage attract EPF contributions and fail to contribute on these extra payments. This has inevitably caused trouble for many employers with the EPF authorities who will not hesitate to institute criminal proceedings against errant employers. Furthermore, if arrears are payable, the employer will be liable to contribute both the employer's and employees' contributions, without having any recourse to recover the employees' portion, unless the conditions of s 48(4)(a) and (b) of the Act are satisfied.

EMPLOYEES' SOCIAL SECURITY ACT 1969 (ESSA)

This scheme provides an employee with protection for industrial accidents that occur at the employee's workplace and while travelling on a route between his residence and workplace. The scheme also provides coverage for occupational diseases. The employer and the employee are liable to make monthly contributions based on a schedule set out in the Act which in turn is dependent on the employee's wages. This liability to contribute is only in respect of employees who earn up to RM2000 per month. However, once an employee is covered under the Act, he will continue to enjoy SOCSO coverage irrespective of his monthly salary even if he eventually changes his employer. This is in accordance with the principle 'once a contributor, always a contributor'.

This Act is only applicable to employees who are Malaysian citizens and non-citizens who are permanently resident in Malaysia. Domestic servants do not fall within the scope of this Act.

WORKMAN'S COMPENSATION ACT 1952 (WCA)

The objectives of the WCA as stated in the preamble are as follows:

> an Act to provide for the payment of compensation to workmen for injury suffered in the course of employment.

This legislation is to provide for compensation to employees who meet with accidents arising out of and in the course of employment. However, with the extension of the Employees Social Security Act 1969 to cover all employees employed under a contract of service, the scope of this Act is limited to cover only foreign workers who are not permanently resident in Malaysia. This Act only applies to foreign workers engaged in a manual capacity irrespective of the wages earned and to foreign workers engaged in a non-manual capacity, whose wages do not exceed RM500 per month. Domestic servants do not fall within the scope of this Act. Currently, under the provisions of this Act every employer is required to insure his employees for coverage.

WORKER'S MINIMUM STANDARDS OF HOUSING AND AMENITIES ACT 1990

An employer is not required to provide accommodation or housing to his employees under any legislation. However, if the employer chooses to provide accommodation or housing to his employees in an area which is situated outside the city council, municipal council or Federal Territory, he is required to provide housing and amenities such as gas, water, electricity and community halls in accordance with the specifications of this Act.

OCCUPATIONAL SAFETY AND HEALTH ACT 1994

The objectives of this Act as set out in its preamble are as follows:

> An Act to make further provisions for securing the safety, health and welfare of persons at work for protecting others against risks to safety or health in connection with the activities of persons at work, to establish the National Council for Occupational Safety and Health, and for matters connected therewith.

This Act imposes obligations on employers to ensure a safe system of work, a safe and healthy environment for employees to work in and for employers to provide information, instructions, training and supervision to ensure safety and health in the workplace.

It also imposes obligations on workers to take reasonable care for the safety and health of themselves and other persons, to cooperate with their employers in the discharge of their duties, to wear protective equipment and clothing provided by employers and to comply with the instructions of employers on matters relating to health and safety.

CHILDREN AND YOUNG PERSONS (EMPLOYMENT) ACT 1966

This Act provides for protection of children and young persons in employment. It specifies the conditions under which a child or a young person may be employed. A child is defined in the Act as any person who has not attained the age of 14 years and a young person is defined as a person who has not attained the age of 16 years. Under this Act, a child below the age of 14 may only be engaged in light work in any undertaking carried on by his family. He may, however, be employed in public entertainment, as an apprentice or in work carried on in any school or training institution. A young person below the age of 16 may be engaged as domestic help or employed in non-industrial undertakings. If it is an industrial undertaking, the employment must be suitable to his capacity.

WAGES COUNCIL ACT 1947

This Act provides for the establishment of wages councils which in turn submit proposals to the Minister of Human Resources to regulate the remuneration and conditions of employment of workers in specific sectors of industry where there is a need or requirement to regulate wages of workers. The Minister of Human Resources may make various regulations and orders pursuant to the proposals submitted by the wages council. There are currently four such orders in existence. These are:

(1) Wages Council (Shops) Order 1967.

(2) Wages Regulation (Catering and Hotel) Order 1967.

(3) Wages Regulation (Cinema Workers) Order 1967.

(4) Wages Regulation (Penang Stevedores and Cargo-Handlers) Order 1967.

THE HUMAN RESOURCES DEVELOPMENT ACT 1992

The objectives of the Act are set out in the preamble as follows:

> An Act to provide for the imposition and collection of a human resources development levy for the purpose of promoting the training of employees, the establishment of a Human Resources Development Council and Fund and for matters connected therewith.

The Act provides for the imposition of a levy in respect of each employee at the rate of 1% of the employee's monthly wage. Employers are also required to register with the council as prescribed by the Act.

Any employer who has paid the applicable levy upon registration and has continued to do so for a period of five months will be eligible to receive financial assistance or other benefits under the Act for the purposes of promoting the training of his employees.

CONCLUSION

There is currently widespread speculation about the need to make labour laws in Malaysia more dynamic in order to provide the correct atmosphere to achieve the government's targets of Vision 2020. The increase in the use of foreign labour will at the same time compound the problems of human resource management. Protection of employees from non-payment of termination benefits and other contractual and statutory benefits due to winding up of companies is also likely. Skill training to provide a viable labour force is being given attention.

Thus, the labour scene seems ready for significant changes in the approach and attitude of employers, employees and the government. The state of the law referred to in this chapter may therefore be altered over the next decade by statutory amendments as well as decisions of the courts. Readers would be well advised to keep abreast of such developments.

1 *Turner v Goldsmith* [1891] 1 QB 544.
2 *Herbert Clayton and Jack Waller Ltd v Oliver* [1930] AC 209.
3 *KV Pillai v Power Foam Rubber Products (Mfg) Co Ltd* (1963) 29 *MLJ* 268.
4 *Kian Huat Lorry Transport v Kamardin Bin Adan & Anor* (1980) 1 *MLJ* 280.
5 *Paris v Stepney Borough Council* [1951] 1 All ER 42 per Lord Oaksey.
6 *Oasis Milk Bar v Lim Teng & Ors* (1962) 28 *MLJ* 306.
7 *Boston Deep Sea Fishing & Ice Co Ltd v Ansell* (1888) 39 Ch D 339.
8 *Reading v Attorney-General* [1951] 1 All ER 617.
9 *Robb v Green* [1895] 2 QB 315.
10 *Manager, Scudai Estate, Johore Bahru v Narayanan* (1960) 26 *MLJ* 162.
11 *Hoh Kiang Ngan v Mahkamah Perusahaan Malaysia & Anor* (1995) 3 *MLJ* 369.
12 *Good Kwee Phoy v J & P Coats (M) Bhd* (1981) 2 *MLJ* 129.
13 *Dreamland Corporation (M) Sdn Bhd v Choong Chin Sooi & Anor* (1988) 1 *MLJ* 111; *Wong Yuen Hock v Syarikat Hong Leong Assurance Sdn Bhd & Anor (appeal)* (1995) 2 *MLJ* 753.
14 *Stanley Ng Peng Hon v AAF Pte Ltd* (1979) 1 *MLJ* 57.
15 *Wong Chee Hong v Cathay Organisation (M) Sdn Bhd* (1988) 1 *MLJ* 92.
16 *Han Chiang High School / Penang Han Chiang Associated Chinese Schools Association v National Union of Teachers in Independent Schools, W M'sia* (1988) 2 ILR 611 [Award 306/88].
17 *Stevedore Employers' Association, Penang v G Raymond* (1987) ILR 150 [Award 48/87].

CHAPTER 6
MARKETING AND DISTRIBUTION ISSUES
by Lim Meng Seng

INTRODUCTION

It is axiomatic that each market is different and presents a set of conditions that is unique. Thus it is impossible for a foreign company seeking entry into a new market to apply its experience in another market to the present one.

An unsolicited or 'accidental' order does not constitute successful market entry in the context of this article as the ability to secure a firm niche in a particular market must be sustainable over the long term.

The problems facing a foreign company seeking a firm foothold in a new market are aggravated by rapid changes in the particular market, whether these are political, economic, social or regulatory. This is particularly true in Malaysia as the economic landscape today is entirely different from that 20 to 25 years ago because of the introduction of the New Economic Policy, privatisation and the profound structural economic changes that have taken place.

The dynamics of nation-building, culture and the aspirations of a nation and its people interfuse and are translated into national ideologies, economic policies and business practices which make it a nation distinctively its own. It is not possible for even the most perceptive and discerning foreigner to have an in-depth understanding of the local scene, as one would really need to be in the country for a fairly long time to become an 'insider' or expert on the country. Understanding conditions in a foreign market calls for much humility and the foreign company must be willing to discard preconceived notions or prejudices when it plans to enter the market.

Some suggestions on how to achieve successful entry into the Malaysian market follow for the benefit of the foreign company seeking to launch itself into the market.

'The foreign marketer' in this article refers to any foreign company planning to penetrate the Malaysian market, and includes all firms involved in international marketing: the multinational, the transnational, the small or medium-sized company irrespective of whether it is in manufacturing, trading or services. Where it is necessary to be explicit, the type of firm will be specifically mentioned.

MALAYSIA: A BOOMING MARKET

Malaysia, with a per capita income of US$3860 (RM9646), is classified by the World Bank as an 'upper middle income country' and as among the higher performance Asian economies whose other members include China, the Four Asian Tigers (Taiwan, Hong Kong, South Korea and Singapore), Thailand and Indonesia. Malaysia, Indonesia and Thailand have been labelled as newly industrialising countries.

Nineteen ninety-four marked Malaysia's seventh consecutive year of growth. The nation recorded a growth of 8.5% in 1994 and is projecting a growth of 8.9% for 1995. Malaysia's Gross Domestic Product (GDP) in 1995 (at constant 1978 prices) is estimated at RM119 billion.

Malaysia has a population of almost 20 million, with a growth of 2.3% a year. Its savings (34% of GDP) are third highest in the Third World.

It is a staggering fact that, despite its relatively small population, Malaysia ranks 19th in world trade. Gross exports totalled RM153.7 billion in 1994 and gross imports RM156 billion.

Significant structural economic changes over the 1980s and 1990s, particularly following the emphasis on heavy industries, have led to marked changes in the pattern of Malaysia's imports.

In 1994, out of gross imports of RM156 billion, RM67.902 billion (43.5%) constituted intermediate goods, RM64.384 billion (41.3%) investment goods and RM22.871 billion (14.7%) consumption goods. Imports for re-export accounted for RM843 million or 0.5%.

In the same year, importation of intermediate goods rose by 35.5%, investment goods by 35% and consumption goods by 20%.

Intermediate goods for manufacturing accounted for 36.3% of total imports in 1994, machinery 10.7%, transport equipment 6.5%, metal products 5.4%, consumer durables 3.6% and food 2.7%.

The upsurge in importation of intermediate goods in 1994 was the result of strong demand by local industries for semi-manufactured gold; electronic components; textile yarn and fabrics; CKD parts for motor assembly; pulp and paper; chemicals; building and construction materials, and feedstuffs and fertilisers.

On the other hand, the importation of investment goods in 1994 was encouraged by strong demand from infrastructure projects and public utilities, as well as by private investment in the manufacturing and oil sectors.

It is estimated that a sum of RM5.153 billion of capital expenditure was incurred by the manufacturing sector in 1994, compared with RM5.107 billion in 1993.

In 1994, 4844 industrial projects were approved by the Malaysian Government with a total investment of RM13.29 billion.

Value-added in manufacturing is estimated to have grown by 13.6% in 1994 compared with 12.9% in 1993.

Malaysia has 13 States—11 in Peninsular Malaysia and two in East Malaysia (Sabah and Sarawak). Kuala Lumpur (the Federal Territory) has the highest per capita GDP, followed by Terengganu, Selangor, Penang, Sabah, Johor and Sarawak in that order.

The country has been witnessing a consumer boom with rising disposable incomes and growing affluence. In 1994 private consumption expenditure grew by 12% compared with 9% in 1993. Wholesale and retail trade, hotels and restaurants recorded a growth of 11.5% in 1994 compared with 10% in 1993.

Malaysia's population consists mainly of young people who comprise 63% of the country's population.

THE ATTRACTIVENESS OF THE ASEAN AND ASIAN MARKETS

The Malaysian market itself is attractive enough to the foreign marketer. However, for certain multinationals, transnationals or substantial foreign marketers, the attractiveness of Malaysia lies in its strategic position in the region which could be used as a springboard for launching into the Association of South-East Asian Nations (ASEAN) and Asian markets.

ASEAN, created 25 years ago, has a population of 403 million with the recent entry of Vietnam (population 72 million) as a member, compared with 368 million of the North American Free Trade Area (NAFTA) and 334 million of the Economic Union (EU). ASEAN now has seven members: Malaysia, Singapore, Thailand, Indonesia, the Philippines, Brunei and Vietnam. It is a dynamic institution which is well respected by the world community.

ASEAN is expected to record an average growth of 7.9% in 1995. Singapore and Malaysia are each expected to record a growth of 8.9%, Thailand 8.5%, Indonesia 7.6% and the Philippines 6%. The impetus to growth in the region is from strong domestic consumption and investment, as well as exports.

In 1994, total imports into ASEAN rose by US$43.9 billion to US$262 billion and recorded an aggregate growth of 21%.

Singapore was the largest trading nation in ASEAN in 1994 followed by Malaysia which had imports of US$11.77 billion, up 25% over 1993's figure of US$9.36 billion. In 1994, Malaysia's exports to ASEAN rose by 23.8% to US$16.85 billion from US$13.62 billion in 1993.

ASEAN member countries are working closely towards the creation of an ASEAN Free Trade Area (AFTA) by 2003 involving 10,761 items. The materialisation of ASEAN will see tariffs at a maximum of 5% for the region.

Malaysia's emergence as a strong exporter of manufactured goods can be seen from its exports of such goods totalling US$3.9 billion to ASEAN members in 1994.

More and more multinationals are setting up their regional headquarters in Malaysia to take advantage of fiscal incentives and to launch their businesses into ASEAN and Asia. The existence of such a huge market in ASEAN makes it compelling for multinationals to consider locating their manufacturing bases in Malaysia.

Asia has a population of 3.1 billion taking into account the Indian sub-continent and Australia and New Zealand. Of Asia's population, 50% is under 25, opening up a gigantic youth market in the region.

By the year 2000, it is envisaged that 50% of the goods produced in the Asia-Pacific region will be sold within Asia, with a significant proportion of such goods being produced in the region by multinationals from the United States, Europe and Japan.

REGULATORY FRAMEWORK

Malaysia is an ardent advocate of free trade. Being a trade-oriented nation, it has always adopted an open economy policy. It is a member of the World Trade Organisation and strongly supports trade liberalisation, both regionally and internationally. Its determination to forge ahead with member countries of ASEAN to create AFTA clearly confirms this.

Malaysia's import policies are very liberal. Almost all goods can be freely imported. Malaysia is a member of the World Customs Organisation based in Brussels and its tariff codes are based on the Harmonised Commodity Description and Coding System.

In the 1995 budget, import duties on 2600 items of food were removed to combat inflation. Import duties range from nil (musical instruments, cameras, calculators) to over 200% (cars), but typically fall within the range of 5%–20%. The importation of certain items is completely prohibited (eg pornographic literature) while certain items can be conditionally imported under import licences (plants (agricultural), electrical products, guns and ammunition, and meat).

Certain products are subject to price control and are referred to as 'controlled items' (sugar, flour, steel bars and petroleum products).

Under the Sales Tax Act 1972, a sales tax at the rate of 5%, 10% or 15% is levied on imported goods and locally manufactured products, except for items that are exempted under the Act.

A service tax, which was introduced in 1975 at 5%, is levied on prescribed services and goods provided by or sold in certain establishments.

The Ministry of Domestic Trade and Consumer Affairs was set up in 1990. Apart from administering the Companies Act 1965, it has jurisdiction over the pricing of essential commodities; licensing, control of manufacturing and distribution of controlled items; registration of companies and businesses; copyright, trade marks and patents; sales and distribution of petroleum and petroleum products; protection of consumer interests, and prevention of unhealthy trade practices. Malaysia is a member of the World Intellectual Property Organisation.

There is no legislation in Malaysia relating to anti-trust, unfair competition, price discrimination or unfair business practices.

Under the Companies Act 1965, a locally incorporated company must have two individual shareholders subscribing to at least one share and there must be two resident directors and a secretary who must be a Malaysian.

Foreign companies desirous of doing business in Malaysia should set up a locally incorporated company or a branch, by registering with the Registrar of Companies, and must comply with the provisions of the Companies Act. The approving authority is the Ministry of Domestic Trade and Consumer Affairs.

A foreign incorporated company must file annually, within one month of its Annual General Meeting, a copy of the Annual Return and within two months a copy of the Balance Sheet of its head office, including an audited Statement of Assets used in and liabilities arising from its operations in Malaysia, as well as its audited financial statements.

Trading companies, unlike manufacturing companies, do not enjoy fiscal and other incentives but can qualify for Operational Headquarters incentives. They must seek approval from the Ministry of International Trade and Industry and must carry out qualifying services for their offices or related companies outside Malaysia. The qualifying services are management and administrative services; treasury and fund management services; other financial services; research and development (R&D); training and personnel management, and sourcing of raw materials, component parts and finished products for use of their offices outside Malaysia or their related companies outside Malaysia.

Companies desirous of selling their products or services to the government have to register with the relevant local authorities. To do this they must have the requisite Bumiputra (Malay) equity content. The usual quantum is 30% but there are many cases where foreign companies prefer to hold stakes of less than 51%. This is in compliance with the New Economic Policy (NEP), which aims to grant the Bumiputra population a larger stake in business, and in the interests of an equitable distribution of wealth among the races.

As a result of a recent policy change, all new wholesale and retail companies with foreign participation must be incorporated under the Companies Act. Prior to this change, introduced in November 1995, such companies were only required to be registered with the Registrar of Companies.

Companies with foreign participation venturing into the wholesale and retail trade must also meet minimum capital investment requirements set by the government, as follows: RM10 million for companies setting up department stores, mega-malls and hypermarkets; RM5 million for companies setting up supermarkets; RM1 million for companies setting up speciality stores, and RM500,000 for direct selling companies.

Under this new ruling any company in the wholesale and retail trade which has foreign participation and requires the services of expatriates will only be given one expatriate key post. The maximum tenure by the expatriate shall be limited to 10 years, each duration for a maximum of five years, depending on the amount of capital investment and the expertise to be contributed by the expatriate.

It is apparent that these changes were introduced to enable Malaysian entrepreneurs to have a larger share of the distributive trade and to tighten control over this segment of the economy.

WHAT IS THE MARKET PLACE LIKE?

The Malaysian marketing environment is characterised by intense competition with major players from all over the world vying for a share of the market. Over 3000 international companies from more than 50 countries have invested in Malaysia. However, this competition has not eroded overall market prospects because of the rapid growth of the market for both industrial and consumer products.

Multinationals operating in Malaysia include Esso, Shell, Mobil, CONOCO, BP, Unilever, Nestle, BHP, Dow Chemical, Du Pont, Sony, Sanyo, Procter and Gamble, ICI, Guinness, Acer, Texas Instruments, Harris Corporation, Hewlett Packard, Monsanto, Mattel, Otis, Ansell, Asea Brown Boveri, Matsushita, NEC, General Electric, AEG, Siemens, Ericsson, Carrefour, Makro, Philips, IBM, Bayer and BASF. All the leading Japanese trading companies (Sogo Shoshas) including Mitsui & Co, Marubeni, Sumitomo and Mitsubishi have a presence in Malaysia, while the South Korean *chaebol* (conglomerates)—Daewoo, Hyundai, Ssangyong, Lucky-Goldstar and Samsung—have also recently entered the market.

The Crown Agents and British trading companies that flourished during the pre-Independence years have given way to Malaysian-owned concerns. Many no longer operate in the market, while the business of some of them has been absorbed by Malaysian institutions.

The Malaysian market is characterised by brand consciousness. Imported products, especially those which are leading brands, find ready acceptance and command premium prices, with the young as the main buyers. Very aggressive advertising techniques are pursued in promoting consumer products.

Local manufacture has resulted in a high degree of self-sufficiency in consumer products. However, it is difficult for Malaysia at this point to replace imported capital, investment and intermediate goods with local manufacture because it still lags behind the developed nations in these areas with its limited R&D base. It is true that Malaysia has laid some of the foundations for heavy industry, but much remains to be done to enable the country to gain self-sustaining industrial growth. The indications are that the demand for imported technology will continue with sustained growth of the country's manufacturing sector, a feature that Malaysia shares with the other newly industrialising countries. Malaysia's long-term industrial strategies are articulated in its Industrial Master Plan.

Malaysia is considered as an ideal country for private investment and also as one of the most competitive nations in the world. That is why it becomes a natural target for foreign investors seeking expansion overseas. Malaysia has political and economic stability, a solid judicial system based on English principles of law, good infrastructure, a productive and adaptive labour force, and dynamic and innovative entrepreneurs. English is used in practically all business transactions.

It is true to some extent that geographical proximity confers strategic advantages on Asian marketers seeking to sell to Malaysia. The flying time from the following Asian cities to Kuala Lumpur (Melbourne and Sydney included) is provided below:

Place of Departure	Flying time to Kuala Lumpur (approximate only)
Bangkok	2 hours
Beijing	6 hours
Hong Kong	3 hours 30 minutes
Jakarta	2 hours
Manila	4 hours
Melbourne	7 hours 30 minutes
Seoul	5 hours
Singapore	55 minutes
Sydney	8 hours 30 minutes
Taipei	4 hours 15 minutes
Tokyo	6 hours 15 minutes

In an intensely competitive market such as Malaysia, being first in the market and being close to the market place are vital determinants of business success, and Asian marketers exploit this advantage over their rivals from North America, Europe, Africa, Latin America and other areas.

Physical proximity to the market place confers a more subtle advantage in the form of easier access to market intelligence, which enables Asian firms to respond much more quickly to the needs of the market. Timeliness, to say the least, is certainly of essence in business, particularly when very substantial deals are involved. That there are time and cost savings is obvious. Where very frequent visits are made necessary by business circumstances and opportunities, the overall advantages of physical proximity to the market cannot be over-emphasised.

Marketers outside Asia are not totally disadvantaged, thanks to the efficiency of modern telecommunications. Companies already having a presence in Malaysia would be in a position to compete effectively with companies located in the Asian region.

The growing 'Look East' outlook among countries in the Asian region tends to favour Asian companies in certain respects, apart from the advantage of geographical proximity. There is no longer the obsession that products from the West are best, and this growing Asian self-assurance and confidence have sparked off much entrepreneurial initiative and have driven Asian companies to venture into a number of new business areas in competition with the West. This newly created self-reliance is manifest in the desire of Asian companies to venture abroad. Malaysia's foray into Vietnam, Cambodia, China, India, Sri Lanka, Africa and Eastern European countries is evidence of this. A growing number of Asian companies have become conglomerates and have been very active all over Asia. Chinese-owned businesses abound in the region and some Chinese transnationals or very large corporations have set up offices in a number of countries in Asia and have been able to build up sizeable businesses there before the arrival of competitors from America or Europe, a process accelerated by common cultural ties.

Outside China, Mandarin is widely spoken in Malaysia, Singapore, Hong Kong and Taiwan, and is a powerful incentive for Chinese companies to work together in business, facilitated by a common language. China's emergence as an industrial power and open espousal of free enterprise have far reaching implications.

Companies in ASEAN are preparing themselves for the materialisation of the ASEAN Free Trade Area (AFTA) which will create a free market by the year 2003.

The Economic Union, ASEAN, the United States, Japan and East Asia constitute the main exporters to Malaysia. Japan is Malaysia's largest supplier and accounted for RM41.62 billion (26.7%) of its imports in 1994, followed by the United States (RM26.016 billion or 16.7%), ASEAN (RM29.183 billion or 18.7%, with Singapore accounting for RM21.943 billion or 14.1%), Taiwan (RM7.959 billion or 5.1%), South Korea (RM4.962 billion or 3.2%), Thailand (RM3.865 billion or 2.5%), China (RM3.569 billion or 2.3%) and Hong Kong (RM3.105 billion or 2%).

EMERGENCE OF MEGA-CORPORATIONS AND MEGA-BUYERS

If a large traditional foreign marketer that has been exporting to Malaysia for a long time was asked, 'What is the biggest change your company finds today in the Malaysian market compared with conditions (say) 20 years ago?' the typical reply would perhaps be: 'We are amazed at the size of the order value nowadays. In the past we would have considered an order size of US$1–2 million as exceptional, but today we are dealing with order values 10 or 20 times those of the past.'

The above illustration reflects the current market situation in Malaysia where large ticket imports are very common with the emergence of a number of mega-corporations, especially privatised entities, in the country.

The government's drive for privatisation is guided by the criteria of growth, efficiency and the necessity to unburden itself from having to finance a number of capital-intensive projects in view of its limited financial resources. This policy has scored remarkable success. Major government entities that have been privatised include electricity, telecommunications, shipping, airlines, petroleum production, ports, railways and heavy industries. The successors to those entities include corporations, bearing the names of Telekoms Malaysia (telecommunications), Tenaga Nasional (electricity generation), Malaysia International Shipping Corporation, Malaysia Airlines, KCT (container terminal operator in Port Kelang), Malaysia Airports, KTM (the former Malayan Railway) and HICOM (the entity involved in heavy industries). These are not only growth catalysts, but also enjoy huge market capitalisation, some being billion ringgit corporations. At the same time they are very substantial buyers of capital goods and technical services from overseas, and are potential customers of the foreign marketer.

The government still retains a strategic stake in most of these concerns, although a significant proportion is now in private hands.

Following the phenomenal success of the projects privatised up to now, many more are about to be privatised and the names of such entities have been announced, reflecting the government's desire to expand the privatisation process even further.

Such privatised corporations are still referred to as being part of the government's Non-Financial Public Enterprises (NFPE). There are now 41 NFPEs in Malaysia. Their size may be gauged from the fact that their revenue in 1994 totalled RM46.605 billion, their capital expenditure standing at RM12.181 billion and their retained income at RM10.576 billion.

The NFPEs whose activities are in the utilities, transportation, manufacturing and commodities sectors are poised for rapid expansion. Telekoms Malaysia intends to invest RM4.138 billion to upgrade its telecommunications facilities; Tenaga Nasional is expected to invest RM3.114 billion to increase its power generation capacity and improve its distribution and transmission network, while PETRONAS (the national petroleum company) is expected to spend RM7.4 billion on upstream and downstream activities.

Huge opportunities are open to the foreign marketer as many capital goods are only available from overseas, while most technical services have also to be sourced from abroad. This has led to the setting up of a number of consortia with Bumiputra participation to bid for and jointly undertake massive projects. Major consortia that have been awarded large projects are those associated with Kuala Lumpur International Airport, Kuala Lumpur City Centre and the light rail transit project. Recently Taylor Woodrow, a leading British engineering and construction group, was awarded an RM1.638 billion project in connection with Phase Two of the light rail transit project in Kuala Lumpur. It will be working jointly with AEG of Germany in implementing the project. There are many consortium projects underway in the country.

As such projects are massive in nature and call for a host of sophisticated engineering, construction, architectural and technical skills, it is hardly surprising that so many international firms providing these services should be vying for a piece of this gigantic cake. For most of them, initial entry could open up a lot of possibilities in the future, as there is always the likelihood of their being awarded repeat jobs.

The 13 State governments have their own investment arms, usually referred to as State Economic Development Corporations (SEDC), which also undertake huge projects either on their own or usually in collaboration with the private sector. Such collaboration has generally yielded good results and the private sector is keen to have tie-ups with SEDCs. The Johor State Economic Development Corporation is an outstanding success, having built up a diversified range of business activities within Malaysia, and has ventured abroad following its rapid expansion and diversification.

Some companies listed on the Kuala Lumpur Stock Exchange are very substantial concerns. Among these are companies owned or controlled by Bumiputra individuals or Malay corporations associated directly or indirectly with the government, its agencies or State government bodies. Clearly there are potential business opportunities for the foreign marketer from these companies.

It is difficult, if not impossible, for medium-sized Malaysian firms to participate in the mammoth projects mentioned above because they are constrained by size, financial resources and technical know-how. As such, they would have to seek their niches elsewhere.

THE UBIQUITOUS CHINESE TRADER

The emergence of mega-corporations has not reduced the role of the traditional Chinese trading firm which is involved in importing, wholesaling and retailing. While it is true that such Chinese companies are unable to compete with mega-corporations in the supply of products to utilities, in infrastructure, or in massive construction and engineering projects because of their limited resources, they are still dominant players in the market.

Some of these set-ups are very large, enjoying annual turnovers of RM50 million or more. However, most of them tend of be medium-sized or small. A firm with an annual turnover of up to RM10 million may be considered medium-sized, while small firms would have an annual turnover of RM500,000 to RM1 million. In general, these firms have built up strong market niches either within a particular State or nationally. They have strong agency lines, which they have held for many years, and such products have been well received. Some of these companies are very well-established, having been in the business for 20, 30 or even 50 years. They deal in a host of imported items, including electrical accessories, household appliances, food items, agricultural products, building materials, chemicals, paper, furniture, liquor, machinery, motor vehicle spare parts, textiles, gold and jewellery. They really form the backbone of the country's marketing and distribution system. Several have expanded their product range and diversified into new areas, while others have ventured into local manufacture, or assembly of traditionally imported products, to strengthen or to preserve their market niches as necessitated by market changes and the forces of competition. Some have grown to a size necessitating going public to tap capital for future growth.

The proportion of consumer items, including food, imported by these Chinese companies has declined significantly with the introduction of local manufacture, but they still depend on importation of many items.

With the setting up of many import-substitution industries, such companies are handling an increasing number of locally produced items. There are still ample opportunities for growth in the business because of strong economic growth and changes in the import mix brought about by structural economic changes, rising consumer expenditure and changes in consumer tastes.

Such companies exist in every major town. Very often the business has been handed down from one generation to another and continues to thrive with the firm market niches that have been built up. It is common for the present generation to introduce modern management techniques in the companies it has inherited, and a new corporate culture emerges which appears to be a hybrid of traditional conservatism and modern dynamism.

Importers sell to wholesalers or retailers or directly to end-users. Whatever the case, extension of credit is the rule. Credit terms up to 120 days are not unusual, and collection can stretch up to 150, or even 180, days. Business rests on goodwill, and personal relationships are very important.

The larger Chinese trading companies have warehouses and also own transportation fleets. Such companies tend to have a fairly large capital base and are fiercely competitive.

A number of foreign marketers have been able to gain successful market entry by appointing Chinese intermediaries. In some cases, joint ventures in manufacturing have materialised between the foreign marketer and the Malaysian agent after a certain sales volume has been achieved in the market.

Since the mid-1970s, more Bumiputra-owned trading companies have ventured into the distributive trade, largely through encouragement of the government. These companies are able to obtain distributorship rights from local manufacturers through government intervention and are usually engaged in the distribution of building materials and food. The average outfit tends to be very small and most of them are retailers. The principal problems faced by such companies are lack of capital and experience, absence of storage and transportation facilities, limited market access and lack of economies of scale. For this reason, the government is seeking to consolidate small Malay-owned wholesale and retail outfits into more viable units and is providing management training to such organisations to integrate them into the distributive trade.

There are a few exceptions. For example, PERNAS Edar, a well-established trading company owned by the government, is a substantial concern. It handles both imported and locally made products and is a major player in the distributive trade. There are also Bumiputra-owned or controlled trading companies which are major importers and distributors among the publicly-listed companies.

On the whole, the impact of Malay-owned firms on the distributive trade is very slight. According to official statistics, out of 152,000 licences granted by local authorities to companies in the wholesale and retail trade in 1990, only 28% were Malay concerns, of which 46% constituted firms which were in petty trading.

Indian firms are active as importers, wholesalers and retailers but their activities are mainly in commodities, groceries and pharmaceuticals, textiles, food, paper, gold and jewellery. Their share of the distributive trade is also small vis-à-vis the Chinese sector.

THE VITAL ROLE OF EXPORT CREDIT

A major factor contributing to Japan's export success is availability of government-sponsored export credit at very favourable rates. This facility has enabled Japanese exporters to win world markets through price competitiveness.

It has been mentioned above that the Malaysian market is characterised by intense competition. The foreign marketer needs the support of export credit to gain a competitive edge in world markets.

Malaysian importers are now very well informed and have a wide choice of suppliers before them. They are inundated by product information supplied by intending foreign exporters, each offering different terms and conditions of sale. For large deals, the competition is even fiercer, with foreign exporters knocking repeatedly at the doors of potential buyers, hoping to wrap up the deals at hand before their competitors can do so.

All other factors being equal, availability of favourable credit will decide whether a particular deal will succeed or fall through.

Payment by letters of credit is no longer the rule in the game of winning international markets. It is not to say that the interested Malaysian importer is not financially sound just because it is seeking credit terms. The realities are that the astute foreign marketer desiring to sell to a Malaysian buyer must be able to structure the most acceptable deal for the potential customer because it realises that its competitor would be only too eager to edge it out of the deal by offering something better.

Availability of credit is cheaper to the potential buyer and administratively convenient, particularly when an 'open account' is made available to it by the foreign marketer.

Credit terms such as CAD (cash against documents), DP (documents against payment), DA (documents against acceptance) and 'open account' are all looked upon favourably by the intending buyer. DA terms of 90–180 days are considered very useful to the intending Malaysian importer.

It is a well-known fact that Chinese trading companies have a tendency to over-trade and sometimes have sales/equity ratios as high as 20:1 or even higher. Another reason credit terms are so important to the intending buyer is that, under Malaysian market conditions, receivables stretching up to 150 or 180 days are quite common, for example, as experienced in the hardware and building materials trade.

The popularity of British confirming houses in Malaysia with local importers 20–30 years ago testifies to the usefulness of credit. Confirming houses provide short-term import facilities (up to 180 days) to their clients without security, and undertake to pay the suppliers selling to the Malaysian buyers. The facility was found by Chinese trading companies to be a most useful one: it enabled them to expand their business and helped them to have a better cash flow, as settlement of the draft presented by the confirming house did not take place until 180 days later. In fact, it was confirming which helped a very large number of British exporters to secure a foothold in the Malaysian market. Confirming was a British invention, although it logically evolved from Britain's position as a leading exporter to the world in earlier years, particularly to its colonies. Confirming was a great boon to Malaysian companies in the 1950s up to the 1970s and it is a well-known fact that a number of companies which are now either very substantial concerns or large publicly-listed companies have at one time or another made use of confirming and owe their present success to confirming. It is somewhat regrettable that confirming began to lose its grip in Malaysia after the 1980s, largely because of its inability to compete with local banks and financial institutions which were able to offer much more competitive rates. It has since ceased to be a force in Malaysia and other parts of the world.

The exclusive purpose of export credit is to finance international trade, and medium-term export credit facilities finance the export of capital goods.

For mega-projects such as those related to infrastructure, telecommunications, engineering, construction, and oil and gas among others, export credit at subsidised rates provided by government-sponsored export credit insurance institutions of the exporting countries is a major factor determining the competitiveness of their exporters. That is why all governments vigorously encourage their top exporting firms to use export credit facilities when they bid for mammoth projects overseas. A wide range of services is made available by export credit insurance agencies in each country in competition with their counterparts in other parts of the world. Export credit has become a *sine qua non* for success in bidding for mega-projects in the intensely competitive overseas market.

Credit insurance agencies insure exporters and institutions financing export credits against political and exchange transfer risks as well as commercial (insolvency or default) risks.

Credit insurance policies take various forms such as insurance for supplier credit; guarantees for buyer credit financing; guarantees for supplier credit financing; insurance covering cost-escalation and consortium projects, and performance bonds.

The world's leader in export credit insurance is the Export Credits Guarantee Department (ECGD) of the British government. However, ECGD has disposed of its short-term insurance cover business to the Dutch group known as NCM Credit Insurance.

Both NCM Credit Insurance and ECGD are very active in the Malaysian market. Other credit insurance agencies providing insurance cover for their nationals doing business include ECICS Credit Insurance Ltd (Singapore), Export-Import Bank of the United States, Hermes Kreditverscherung-AG (Germany), Companie Francaise d'Assurance pour le Commerce Exterieur (COFACE, France), Export Finance and Insurance Corporation (Australia), Canadian International Development Agency, Exports Guarantee Office (New Zealand), Export Credit and Guarantee Corporation Ltd (India), Hong Kong Export Credit Insurance, the Export-Import Bank of the Republic of China and Compania Espanola de Seguros de Credito a la Exportacion (CESCE, Spain).

MARKETING METHODS AND DISTRIBUTION CHANNELS

The traditional and most prevalent method of selling to the Malaysian market is for the exporter to appoint an agent in Malaysia as the marketing intermediary. The intermediary is usually a Chinese concern. In most cases, the agent itself would be the wholesaler, although there are instances where it would work through a wholesaler or wholesalers. For consumer products, the wholesalers would sell to retailers who in turn would serve the individual consumers. For industrial goods, the agent would be selling to dealers or directly to end-users. It is common for the agent to appoint agents or dealers at State or district level to cater for regional needs. As industrial goods usually require after-sales service, the appointed agents or dealers would need to have back-up facilities and adequate manpower to be able to service the customers effectively.

The use of commission agents, indenters or manufacturers' representatives is not popular nowadays as such firms do not have the capacity to hold stocks, are too small and are not able to project the image required of them by their overseas principals or local clients. However, such institutions still exist and usually handle industrial products such as machinery, hardware, chemicals, paper, spare parts and engineering merchandise among other things. Such firms were able, in the first instance, to persuade exporters to appoint them in such capacities because the individuals behind the firms had previously been involved in marketing these products while working as employees in firms that had originally been the agents of such exporters. These individuals were usually marketing managers, executives or sales personnel who in their previous jobs had been able to build up good connections with Malaysian clients who are still willing to buy the same products through such commission agents, indenters or manufacturers' representatives. However, the use of such firms to handle consumer products is rare. For small exporters selling limited quantities in a number of markets, the appointment of commission agents, indenters or manufacturers' representatives is an inexpensive way of securing market entry. The volume of business handled by such outfits is very small compared with that of importers or distributors which are stockists. It is interesting to observe in Malaysia that several commission agents, indenters or manufacturers' representatives eventually turned importers or distributors in their own right after having achieved certain sales volumes. In this sense it is rewarding for exporters to have worked with such firms in the past.

It is possible for exporters to sell directly to small individual buyers in Malaysia, such as small wholesalers or retailers, and some exporters still do. This applies to both consumer and industrial products. In such instances, the exporters have known the Malaysian buyers as a result of past connections, and business relationships subsist without the intervention of a marketing intermediary. This has been the case with a number of British exporters who have been selling to Malaysia for a number of years, going back to pre-Independence days or even earlier. However, without a local presence either through the appointment of a local marketing intermediary or the setting-up of a local office in the country, market penetration is not likely to be significant and there is always the danger that valuable business opportunities will be lost to competitors with a strong local presence.

Where the exporter is a manufacturer, market entry via a Malaysian joint-venture manufacturing company has proved to be very effective, particularly after certain sales volumes have been achieved. This has certainly been one of the most successful methods of market entry in Malaysia—the success stories of many import-substitution industries since the introduction of the country's industrialisation program after Independence in 1957 bear testimony to this. Local manufacturing companies are given preference in government tenders over pure trading companies.

There is a growing tendency for exporters desirous of selling to the government or its agencies to appoint Bumiputra (Malay) agents or to enter into local joint ventures with Bumiputra individuals or corporations for this purpose, as this is a basic requirement and such collaboration facilitates success. Participation in consortia with Bumiputra interests to tender for large projects, especially in the public sector, has enabled many foreign exporters to gain successful market entry and this trend will certainly persist as such collaboration has brought tangible results to all parties concerned and is looked upon by the Malaysian government with favour.

More and more exporters are entering into joint ventures with State government agencies, such as State Economic Development Corporations, public enterprise bodies or corporations related to the government or its agencies, or well-connected Bumiputri corporations, to bid for large public sector contracts as well as substantial private sector contracts as the official policy is to award such contracts to these joint ventures provided they have the requisite know-how and are of sound standing.

Market entry via licensing is gaining popularity in Malaysia. A number of consumer products, such as apparel, leather, tourist goods and luxury items, are now successfully marketed in Malaysia through licensing. This has been the result of sustained demand for such items by the youth market which is a major source of buying power in the country.

Licensing in the industrial sector has also seen a sharp upturn with technology-based manufacturing companies seeking competitive edges over their rivals and greater efficiency and technological superiority. In several cases, the launching of projects at hand was entirely dependent upon the availability of the technical know-how or patent of the foreign principal. More and more foreign companies have gained market entry through licensing. Up to 1994, the number of major technical agreements concluded between Malaysian and foreign interests was 705. Tremendous opportunities still exist in this area.

The incidence of contract manufacturing through a local manufacturer as a vehicle of market entry is very low. Some foreign marketers have gained market entry under management contracts. There were 158 such cases up to 1994.

Up to 1994, there were 35 turnkey and engineering agreements between Malaysian and foreign interests.

Franchising has worked very well in Malaysia as exemplified by the spectacular success of fast-food and ice-cream chains, as well as retail store chains. The Malaysian Franchise Association was recently set up and the government has a special unit to educate and assist Bumiputras who want to enter the industry. The indications are that there is still plenty of scope in the industry for aspiring newcomers.

Direct marketing, inspired by the leader Amway of the United States, has recorded much success, but the industry only captured the imagination of Malaysian sponsors some 15 years ago. There is in existence the Direct Sales Association of Malaysia and the business is governed by the Direct Sales Act 1993. The combined turnover of such companies is very substantial and direct marketing has already created an impact on the local marketing scene. The success of direct marketing in Malaysia has largely been due to the aggressiveness and imagination of its sponsors, the dedication of its members and sustained consumer spending.

In Malaysia, the products of direct marketing companies are sourced principally from overseas and their core products are usually associated with leading brands in the countries of origin. However, such companies, in their quest for a diversified range of products, have introduced locally made products under their brands. 'Pyramid sales' are prohibited.

Mail order marketing has been introduced and seems to be growing, with the key players being the credit card companies, which are in a strategic position to exploit the potential market of their members. There seems to be scope for the expansion of such business, if properly promoted.

Cooperatives are closely regulated in Malaysia. Up to July 1995, there were 3500 cooperatives with 3 million members, a capital of RM2.3 billion and total assets of RM9 billion. The two leading cooperatives are the Armed Forces Fund Board (Lembaga Tabung AngKatan Tentera) and the Police Cooperative (Koperasi Polis

Berhad) whose activities are diversified and whose investments in private sector projects are huge, making them a very visible force in the local business scene. MOCCIS (a cooperative whose members consist of government employees) is one of the most successful cooperatives and is a large purchaser of consumer goods.

The pattern of marketing and distribution of consumer products in Malaysia has been affected to a great degree by the emergence of large supermarket chains and the recent introduction of hyper-markets. Such institutions are in a phase of very rapid expansion in the face of the current consumer boom. Strategically located in areas of high traffic and dense population with strong purchasing power, they have displaced traditional retailers and convenience stores. They have generally done well despite severe competition between themselves, with annual turnover running into billions. Because of the size of their purchases, they are in a strong bargaining position vis-à-vis their suppliers and are able to source their products at the best prices and on the most favourable terms. While most of their products are sourced locally from manufacturers, suppliers or agents handling imported products, some import part of their requirements themselves, particularly those items with very high turnovers. This tendency is expected to grow. It is also likely that some of the supermarket chains will aim at vertical integration by setting up their own manufacturing facilities or by acquiring existing manufacturing concerns. The experience of Western countries shows that supermarket chains and hyper-markets exert tremendous economic power and have a growing tendency to deal directly with suppliers overseas in order to by-pass local suppliers and marketing intermediaries. A vast opportunity is open to foreign marketers looking at this segment of the market.

This section concludes with a brief examination of the involvement of Japanese trading companies (Sogo Shoshas) in Malaysia. All the leading Japanese trading companies are represented in Malaysia: Mitsui & Co, Marubeni, Nichimen, Sumitomo, Mitsubishi, C Itoh, Nissho Iwai and Tomen. They have a strong presence, some having been in the country for a long time. They handle a wide range of industrial products, raw materials and primary commodities, and are major suppliers to both Malaysian commercial and industrial users. They are hard to replace with their strong niches in a number of areas. They have built up an excellent name in the market over the years and Malaysian buyers have complete faith in their ability to fulfil contracts, deliver their products on time and provide the types of after-sales service they have promised. As the leading Japanese trading companies are huge concerns and are part of very substantial multinational groups back home, with a multitude of related companies, the range of products they handle is very impressive. For example, Mitsui & Co has over 500 companies within its group and Marubeni has almost 380 companies. Their strength is further enhanced through their representation of the products of other multinationals which do not have a presence in the country. It is a well-known fact that the internationalisation of the businesses of Japanese multinationals has been due to the efforts of Sogo Shoshas spread all over the world. The Sogo Shoshas not only assist multinationals back home to sell to or purchase from overseas countries, but also help them to set up joint ventures abroad. The same situation applies to Malaysia. For example, Mitsui & Co in Malaysia has a management service unit within its trading office to service Japanese companies not represented in the country and also to assist existing Japanese companies operating in Malaysia. The position of Sogo Shoshas in Malaysia is therefore unique, and the indications are that Japanese companies keen to do business in Malaysia will continue to use them to secure market entry.

SERVICES: A VAST POTENTIAL

In 1994, services constituted 44.5% (RM48.8 billion) of Malaysia's GDP (at 1978 prices) compared with manufacturing's of 31.6% (RM34.7 billion) and agriculture's of 14.5% (RM15.9 billion). The services sector grew by 9% in 1994 compared with 10% in 1993. The slight moderation in growth in 1994 was due to a slower increase in government services and also in finance, insurance, real estate and business services. Other services recorded strong growth: wholesale, retail, hotels and restaurants grew by 11.5%; transport, storage and communication by 10% and electricity, gas and water by 13% for the year.

In tandem with structural economic changes, the role of the services sector is expected to expand in the future.

Malaysia, despite its spectacular growth, is still a technology-deficient nation. In its aspiration to become a fully developed nation by the year 2020, it has quickly to build up its R&D base which is still very small. The nation's strategy is not only to widen and deepen its technology base, but also to accelerate industrial inter-sectoral links to secure as high a degree of industrial self-sufficiency as is technologically feasible. Labour-intensive industries are now accorded low priority as emphasis has shifted to high-tech industries with high value-added content and selected medium-sized industries.

Malaysia welcomes technology transfer, as is exemplified in the manufacture of the national car (Proton) which is based on technology of the Mitsubishi Corporation.

According to statistics of the Ministry of International Trade and Industry (MITI), 1744 technology agreements were approved by 1994. Out of 705 major technology transfer agreements approved by MITI, 456 (65%) are from Japan, 112 (16%) from the United States, 70 (9.3%) from the United Kingdom, 35 (4.7%) from Germany and 32 (4.5%) from South Korea.

Malaysia Technology Development Corporation (a government sponsored institution) was recently set up to act as a catalyst for the development of a joint venture capital market for research and development projects. It has participated in several local technology-based ventures.

The government has recently set up technology parks to promote and nurture technology-based projects in the country.

Under the Fifth (1985–90) and Sixth (1991–95) Malaysia Plans, the Malaysian government allocated RM1 billion for Intensification of Research in Priority Areas. The Ministry of Science, Technology and Environment is seeking a larger allocation under the Seventh Malaysia Plan (1996–2000) in view of the vital role of research in accelerating national development.

The demand for technology and services is felt in a number of sectors and has received a tremendous response from both local and foreign companies. Major examples are:

(1) The RM15 billion Bakun hydro-electric project in Sarawak which has attracted 23 applications from consulting and service firms from Brazil, Canada, China, Italy, Japan, Sweden and Switzerland, with an American international consulting group (Herza Engineering) as the principal adviser to the government on economic, technical and financial aspects of the project.

(2) The giant British construction group, Taylor Woodrow, was recently awarded a contract worth RM1.638 billion in connection with Phase Two of the light transit system in Kuala Lumpur with AEG of Germany as its technical partner.

(3) Kuala Lumpur International Airport Bhd awarded contracts to several consortia made up of local, Japanese, British and German interests.

(4) Kuala Lumpur City Centre which will house the 88 Tower—the highest in the world—is being constructed by Japanese and Korean interests.

(5) Twelve nucleus hospitals were recently built in Malaysia by a leading Malaysian construction firm in collaboration with a leading British firm.

(6) KTM Bhd (the privatised entity of the former Malayan Railway) awarded contracts to firms from Japan, Korea and India among others.

There appears still to be more scope for a wide range of services as the economy forges ahead into self-sustaining growth, but the interested foreign marketer has to conduct its own market research to determine the specific demand for the types of services it seeks to provide in the market:

- engineering and construction services;
- technical support services to telecommunications, electronics, utilities, oil and gas, infrastructure, aerospace and aviation, and heavy industries;
- architectural design and landscaping services;
- health care services (hospital construction, planning, management);
- tertiary and technical educational services (twinning between local and foreign educational institutions);
- international banking and financial services (setting up of offshore banking/financial services in Labuan, Malaysia's international offshore financial centre; underwriting; syndicated loans participation; subscription to bond issues; private placement; guarantees; performance bonds etc);
- securities broking;
- investment banking, investment analysis and advisory services;
- fund and portfolio management;
- reinsurance;
- cross-border legal, management consulting, strategic planning, accounting and taxation services;
- air and freight services;
- logistics and warehousing services;
- consortium services.

The above list is not an exhaustive one and is intended to illustrate the scope that still exists for various types of services.

MARKETING AND DISTRIBUTION INFRASTRUCTURE

As one of the most prosperous nations in Asia, Malaysia's marketing and distribution infrastructure is well developed and sophisticated and generally has been able to meet the major demands of trade, but serious bottlenecks still exist. The government is deeply

125

conscious that sustaining growth depends on further strengthening of such infrastructure.

During the Sixth Malaysia Plan (1991–95), the transport, storage and communications sectors received a total allocation of RM10,832 million from the Federal Government, equivalent to 10.7% of the total development allocation to meet the nation's burgeoning demand for infrastructural facilities. Of this allocation, RM7585 (70%) was set aside for expansion and upgrading of the nation's road system. Malayan Railway (since privatised under KTM Bhd) received RM1368 million (12.6%) mainly for the purchase of rolling stock, construction of the double tracking system and modernisation of signalling and communications facilities. A sum of RM997 million (9.2%) was provided for the development and improvement of existing and new airports of which RM176 million (1.6%) was for upgrading of the Subang International Airport. Development of ports received RM758 million (7%).

The share of the transport, storage and communication sectors was expected to rise to 8% of GDP in 1995 compared with 6.9% in 1990 and was expected to record an annual growth of 10.5% during the Sixth Malaysia Plan compared with 8.6% during the Fifth Malaysia Plan.

The Malaysian Government expects the private sector to play a complementary role in developing the country's transportation and communications infrastructure. Priority is given to the privatisation of such facilities, while growing emphasis has been placed on upgrading information technology to accelerate growth and enable these sectors to serve international needs.

Some 90% of Malaysia's freight and passenger movement is by road. Efforts are being made to expand major road networks and upgrade existing roads and bridges. The roads sub-sector received RM6011 million or almost 75% of the total allocation for transport and communications under the Sixth Malaysia Plan.

The north-south highway is a major achievement. This stretch of express highway covers 844 km and has contributed much to the efficiency of the domestic distributive trade. The travel time from Johor in the south to Penang is about seven hours. The 'Second Crossing' linking Singapore to Johor is under way.

In the rail sub-sector, the emphasis is on speeding up services and on better commuter services. Development programs include the setting up of Inland Container Depots (ICD) to promote intermodal and improved services.

The rapid expansion of local trade and industries has led to increased demand for port facilities and maritime services. The government is seeking to improve port operations to enhance the use of Malaysian ports. Domestic shipping has been given positive encouragement.

Following the recommendations of the National Trade Facilitation Committee, exchange control formalities have been simplified and the number of forms and documents used for shipping and cargo clearance has been reduced. At the same time, documents relating to foreign trade have been standardised.

Of Malaysia's foreign trade, 80% is handled by its ports. It is projected that in 1995 total cargo throughput will be in the region of 125 million tonnes compared with 80 million tonnes in 1990. During the Sixth Malaysia Plan, the annual growth of cargo throughput was estimated at 9.3% compared with 8.9% in the Fifth Malaysia Plan. The government privatised the container terminal in Port Kelang in 1986.

The government has introduced the Electronic Data Interchange (EDI) network which has made possible automated processing of trade documents and the linking of ports with other relevant government agencies.

Civil aviation received an allocation of RM4932.1 million under the Sixth Malaysia Plan compared with RM2957.7 million during the Fifth Malaysia Plan. Air cargo has recorded strong growth. The volume of freight handled by Malaysian airports is expected to increase by 13% a year for the international sector and 8% for the domestic sector during the 1991–95 period.

Malaysia Airlines has been expanding and now flies to new destinations such as Africa and Latin America, as well as increasing its flights to traditional destinations. It is embarking on a massive plan, in view of current constraints, to expand its cargo throughput capacity.

Work on the airport in Sepang managed by Kuala Lumpur International Airport Bhd (KLIAB) is on schedule and expected to cost between RM8 and RM9 billion. The airport is designed to handle 25 million passengers initially, but its capacity will be stepped up to 60 million by the year 2020. The technology used by KLIAB will include the installation of a multi-use communications system with a 'backbone' allowing integration of all airport communications and computer services.

Malaysia Airports Bhd has been established under a privatisation program to own and manage the various airports in the country, but is a separate body from KLIAB.

Free Zones enable manufacturing establishments producing or assembling products for export to operate with minimum customs control and formalities, and are available in several areas. Bayan Lepas (Penang), Ampang Hulu Kelang (Kuala Lumpur) and Johor Port are examples. Licensed Manufacturing Warehouses offer the same facilities as Free Zones and are available in several areas.

Both Free Zones and Licensed Manufacturing Warehouses are very popular with export-oriented industries, and their contribution to the process of industrialisation has been immense as is evident from Malaysia's status as the world's leading exporter of electronics and air-conditioners.

The private sector has responded eagerly to the growing demand for transportation (including inland haulage and refrigerated trucking), warehousing and total logistics facilities. There are several companies (including publicly-listed ones) operating in the industry and, despite growing competition, interest in such business has not abated. Large distribution parks have recently been set up in the country and offer a wide range of services to exporters and importers.

The modernisation and upgrading of the nation's transport, storage and communications sectors must extend indefinitely into the future as greater demands will be made on such facilities as the nation moves closer to achieving its Vision 2020, by which time hopefully it will have joined the ranks of the developed nations.

Much remains to be done. Serious problems were recently faced in clearance of goods in Port Kelang and Subang International Airport, causing the private sector much concern. Clearly the matching of supply of infrastructural facilities to demand is a key policy issue concerning development planners, and the introduction of corrective measures cannot be delayed.

Traffic congestion in Kuala Lumpur and the Klang Valley (the two major growth areas) is reaching unmanageable proportions and is creating a serious bottleneck that has affected the efficiency of the distributive trade. A similar problem is being faced by other major towns. Infrastructural constraints affect Malaysia in the same way as they affect the other High-Performance Asian Economies and loom as serious problems that compel urgent solution.

The relocation of the Federal Government's administrative centre in Putra Jaya (25 km from Kuala Lumpur) is expected to take place in 1998, a project expected to cost RM20 billion. This move reflects the government's determination to overcome the traffic congestion problem in the federal capital and the Klang Valley.

KEY SUCCESS FACTORS

It is recommended that the foreign marketer focuses on the following, which are the key success factors in seeking entry into the Malaysian market:

(1) *Commitment.* It has to be truly committed to the project, as feeble and poorly planned efforts are bound to fail.

(2) *Budget.* It must have a sufficient and flexible budget for this purpose and should not seek to cut corners.

(3) *Market research.* Most foreign marketers have not tapped the services of market research or management consulting firms which can provide in-depth knowledge of, and valuable insight into, the particular products or services intended to be sold in the Malaysian market. In today's competitive market place, market entry can be considerably facilitated by access to reliable market studies and valuable recommendations of Malaysian consultants. Costly mistakes can thereby be avoided.

(4) *Always seek sound advice.* Apart from consultants, the expertise and knowledge of commercial divisions of Embassies and High Commissions should be tapped, as often what they can offer is valuable. Chambers of Commerce, trade associations, business councils and other related bodies should also be contacted to gain an insight into the issues at hand.

(5) *Value introductions.* Take introductions seriously. Within Malaysia, there persists a business culture which values introductions by persons or corporations of influence.

(6) *Be open to possibilities.* Some foreign marketers make the mistake of being too restricted in their approach and concentrate their efforts on only a handful of potential partners or agents. They should meet as many parties as possible to obtain a clearer and broader view of the market place in order to make better business decisions.

(7) *Avoid making hasty decisions.* Some foreign marketers make the mistake of too hasty decisions. As a rule, avoid making major business decisions while in Malaysia. Make copious notes of meetings and jot down on-the-spot perceptions. Review your notes when you return to your country and then decide. Mistakes mean loss of business opportunities and precious time, they could jeopardise your reputation and usually cause much frustration.

(8) *Study and evaluate your potential partner/agent.* Is the Malaysian party financially sound? What are its capabilities? Does it have the requisite experience? Is it likely to be fully committed or would

129

it be just 'trying its luck' with your product? Can it produce trade references? What has its track record been like? What is its reputation? Is its style likely to fit with your corporate culture? Can it provide a business plan for your consideration? How many staff does it have?

(9) *Use credit reports.* Credit reports are inexpensive and it is surprising how few foreign marketers make use of such reports, which are provided by credit research and business information firms. These reports, being independently written and assessed, usually provide valuable information on the financial standing and reputation of the companies concerned. As foreign marketers usually find it difficult to ask certain questions that could be deemed sensitive by the Malaysian party, access to reliable credit reports is most useful and revealing

(10) *Respect local culture and sensitivity.* The basis of enduring business relationships is mutual trust and respect. Avoid arrogance and insensitivity. Do not give the Malaysian party the impression, 'I am here to teach', but rather the impression, 'Let us work together for our mutual benefit. We respect your Malaysian culture and your way of doing things.' Be a good listener. Be polite. Do not be critical and too outspoken. If you need to disagree, do so with tact and friendliness. Do not rush your potential partner or agent into making decisions. Give the Malaysian party adequate time to reply to you. It is unfortunate that there are practically no firms in Malaysia specialising in offering advice and guidance on Malaysian culture to foreign businessmen entering the market for the first time. At the same time, there is a paucity of published literature on this subject in the country.

(11) *Create genuine and lasting partnerships.* Aim long-term. After having put so much effort into finding the Malaysian partner or agent, it would not make sound business sense to aim at short-term gains. Foreign marketers thinking only of short-term gains would be losing bigger profit opportunities that could be generated through deeper market penetration. Be content with initial small gains. Support your local partner or agent. Treat the Malaysian party as 'a member of your family'. Be fair—your Malaysian counterpart must make a reasonable return from the collaboration, and the terms and conditions of the deal must make this possible.

(12) *Exercise flexibility.* Business partnerships, like marriages, do not enjoy 'fair weather' conditions all the time. More often than not, partnerships are full of problems and conflicts. Be flexible and supportive when 'rough weather' conditions are faced. Turn business

problems into real opportunities and challenges. Every time a major business obstacle is overcome, resilience, mutual goodwill and solidarity are created which lay the foundations of enduring business relationships.

(13) *Seek sound legal advice.* Do not attempt to draft your own legal agreements even though you may have at your disposal agreements drawn up in other markets. World markets are not homogeneous and conditions in each country are different. It is surprising to observe that there are foreign marketers who try to draft their own legal agreements. Seek sound legal advice. Mistakes of such a nature could be very costly indeed, particularly with very large deals.

(14) *Explicitness is necessary.* Experience shows that some partnerships run into serious problems because the parameters of the collaboration have not been spelt out explicitly and there is a number of grey areas in the legal agreements. The result is entirely predictable: ultimately conflicts, disagreements and friction ensue. Often this awkward situation arises because both parties had not thought through the key issues thoroughly in the first instance and had not devoted adequate time to this matter. They usually give the excuse that they were too busy at that time.

(15) *Training and broadening the vision of your partner/agent.* Invite your Malaysian counterpart to your home office to get a thorough understanding of your products, your organisational set-up and your corporate culture. This is very effective if partners or agents from other countries are present at the same time, as sharing of experiences would be very useful and rewarding to all participants.

(16) *Participate in Malaysian trade exhibitions/trade missions.* Malaysia has become a very popular trade exhibition and convention centre and hosts a number of such events every year. The largest trade exhibition-cum-exhibition hall is the Putra World Trade Centre located in Kuala Lumpur. Major international trade exhibitions held regularly in Malaysia include those pertaining to electronics, computers, building materials, office equipment and furniture, printing and packaging, plastics, machinery, motor vehicles and spare parts, power generation, oil and gas, laboratory and medical equipment, health care, rubber products, materials handling equipment, education, books, food, footwear and many more.

A number of foreign marketers have gained successful market entry via participation in such exhibitions, which is still regarded as one of the most effective methods of achieving entry.

Trade missions are also a very effective means of selling to the Malaysian market by bringing together potential partners or agents and foreign marketers. The British High Commission in Kuala Lumpur every year handles a number of trade missions which are widely publicised. It has been officially announced that participants often achieve tangible results from such missions. Other Embassies and High Commissions are also active in this area of investment and trade promotion. A major attraction with trade missions is that the gestation time could be reduced substantially because of immediate contacts between principals and potential agents/partners.

(17) *Be Focused.* Are you selling to the government and its agencies or is your market the private sector? If your products or services are intended for government or its agencies, you would be optimising your prospects of success by dealing with respectable and well-connected Bumiputra individuals, corporations or entities with government or public sector equity participation.

CONCLUSION

A word of warning is necessary here. Do not underestimate the difficulties of the Malaysian market. As it is intensely competitive, and as quite often the foreign marketers are late entrants, it would be out of keeping with market realities to underestimate the difficulties of market entry. While Malaysia is a promising market, much is required of the foreign marketer before success comes its way. In a nutshell, total commitment and preparedness, appreciation of local culture, finding the right Malaysian counterpart and striking the right deal with that counterpart, and a genuine desire to seek long-term business relationships constitute the key winning streaks.

Kenichi Ohmae in *The Borderless World: Power and Strategy in the Interlinked Economy* (William Collins & Co Ltd, London, 1990) remarks (at pp 105–6):

> Once your business horizons are no longer constrained by national borders, you will probably find that many of the things that made you a first-rate competitor at home will not apply elsewhere—at least, not quite the same way. The local infrastructure may well be different: likewise, the nature and extent of government influence, the tax codes, the expectations of customers, and so on. Each national market has its own rules for determining success and failure, and there is no guarantee that those rules will be the one you know best.

He speaks of the fundamental need for the foreign businessperson to know the local counterpart and its psychology, not superficially, but really well and to work towards building up mutual confidence, a process that is time-consuming but essential for the success of the collaboration. Although writing for an international readership, and although he is truly a consultant with a global vision, Kenichi is foremost an Asian at heart and feels the international business environment very much from the viewpoint of an Asian who believes that culture and business are inextricably interwoven. The Malaysian experience confirms the veracity of his basic argument.

CHAPTER 7

TAXATION OF CORPORATIONS AND INDIVIDUALS
by Chooi Tat Chew

INTRODUCTION

Income tax is levied by the Federal Government. Income tax collected from corporations and individuals accounts for 34.5% of the Federal Government's total revenue in 1996. States derive their revenue mainly from the collection of licence fees, property taxes and royalties from the exploitation of mineral resources onshore and offshore.

Malaysia operates a territorial basis of income taxation. Corporations, whether resident or non-resident, are taxed on income accruing in or derived from Malaysia. The exception is when the corporation is resident and carries on banking, insurance or air or sea transport operations, in which case tax is levied on world income scope. Resident individuals and other non-corporate entities (such as trusts) are taxed on income accruing in or derived from Malaysia and on foreign-sourced income received in Malaysia. Foreign-sourced income in Malaysia is not, however, taxed on non-residents.

The principal classes of domestic and foreign taxpayers covered by the income tax legislation are companies, individuals, trade associations, cooperative societies, trusts and deceased estates. Partnerships are not taxable entities, since they are treated as conduits, with the partners and not the partnership being taxed on the partnership income.

The sources of income subject to tax include, but are not restricted to:

(1) Gains or profits from any trade, business, profession or vocation.

(2) Gains or profits from employment, including allowances and benefits-in-kind.

(3) Dividends, interest and discounts.

(4) Rents, royalties and premiums.

(5) Pensions, annuities and other periodic payments.

(6) Net annual value of land and improvements used by the owner (or occupied rent-free) for residential purposes, except that the

net annual value of any one owner-occupied residential property is exempt from tax.

(7) Amounts received by a non-resident for provision of technical advice, assistance or services; or the provision of services in respect of the installation or operation of any apparatus or plant.

(8) Rent or other payments for the use of movable property received by a non-resident.

There is no tax on capital gains other than the tax on gains arising from the sale of real property (including shares in companies owning real property) in Malaysia. Capital gains may be subject to income tax instead of real property gains tax where there is a series of transactions giving rise to these gains. The tax authorities may take the view that a business is being carried on and tax the recipient accordingly.

Each tax year is referred to as the 'year of assessment'. The year of assessment follows the calendar year beginning on 1 January. Tax is assessed for a year of assessment on all income arising in the immediately preceding calendar year (the basis year). However, the income from a business source is generally assessed to tax on its accounting year ending in the basis year.

ADMINISTRATION OF THE TAX SYSTEM

The administration of the tax legislation comes under the Director-General of Inland Revenue with the Inland Revenue Board acting as the agent of the government vested with the responsibility for the assessment and collection of taxes and other related administrative matters. The head office of the Inland Revenue Board is located in Kuala Lumpur and major technical issues are referred to it, while policy issues are referred to the Minister of Finance. The two other main sections are the Assessment Branch and the Collections Branch.

Assessment Branch

The Assessment Branch is responsible for ascertaining the tax liability of taxpayers and issuing notices of assessment to them. Assessment branches are located in every State in Malaysia.

Collections Branch

The Collections Branch receives copies of the notices of assessment issued by the Assessment Branch and is responsible for ensuring the collection of the tax stated in the notices. Collection of tax is centrally administered in Kuala Lumpur for West Malaysian residents, in Kota Kinabalu for Sabah residents and in Kuching for Sarawak residents.

The Collections Branch will impose late payment penalties and institute legal proceedings for the recovery of unpaid taxes.

Corporate Taxpayers

There is no distinction between resident and non-resident corporate taxpayers, since both are subject to income tax at the rate of 30%. The system for corporate taxpayers is one of information filing. A tax return is filed for each year and an assessment is made. The tax authorities may require further information for the purpose of making the assessment.

Tax returns

Every company subject to tax is required to file an annual return of income. Tax returns are issued by the tax authorities in February/March of each year. Any company liable to tax which has not received a return by 31 March in any year must notify the Director-General within 14 days from that date. Failure to file a return or to give notice of chargeability is a punishable offence.

Normally a tax return is required to be filed within 30 days from the date of its service. However, in practice, the tax authorities do not penalise a company if its returns are filed on or before 31 May of each year. Applications for extension of time beyond 31 May (up to 31 August) to file tax returns are normally granted to companies whose financial year ends on or after 1 October of the preceding year, on condition that the company has already been paying its tax under a tax-deduction scheme. Further extension beyond 31 August is granted only on a case-by-case basis.

The tax return must be accompanied by a copy of the audited financial statements, together with statements of taxable profits and other relevant information to facilitate agreement of the tax position. Companies frequently appoint a firm of public accountants or a tax agent to deal with the preparation and submission of the tax computation and to obtain agreement of tax liabilities with the authorities.

Assessments

Assessments are issued after review of the returns by the tax authorities.

The Director-General has power to reject a return and to make an assessment based on his best judgment. He may also make an estimated assessment in the absence of a return.

Appeals

If a person is dissatisfied with an assessment, he has the right to file a written notice of appeal to the Director-General within 30 days of the service of the notice of assessment. Where agreement cannot be reached with the Director-General, the appeal will be forwarded for hearing by the Special Commissioners of Income Tax, who have all the powers of a Subordinate Court. Appeals may be made from the decisions of the Special Commissioners to the High Court, the Court of Appeal and finally to the Federal Court. Appeals to the Special Commissioners may be conducted by a tax agent or an advocate, but appeals to the courts are conducted by legal counsel. Generally, appeal hearings before the Special Commissioners are heard in camera.

Where a person contends that tax was overpaid by reason of an error in a return, an appeal may be filed to claim relief within six years from the date of service of the notice of assessment. Appeals to the competent authority under a double taxation treaty are rare.

Payment and collection

Assessed tax is payable within 30 days from the date of service of a notice of assessment, whether or not a notice of appeal has been filed.

Companies are subject to a compulsory tax-deduction scheme requiring advance payment of tax by instalments for each assessment year. Under the scheme, companies are issued notices requiring payment of an estimated amount of tax in five bimonthly instalments, beginning from the month of January or February. Payment of each instalment must be made within 30 days of the due date for payment as stated in the notice. The estimates of tax payable are usually based on the tax assessed for the preceding year. Any downward variation of the instalment payments must be submitted to the tax authorities on or before 15 April of each year of assessment.

Where the actual tax payable in an assessment notice exceeds the amount paid by instalments, the excess must be settled in the month subsequent to the date the final instalment falls due or within one month from the date of service of the notice of assessment, whichever is later.

Withholding taxes

Withholding taxes on royalties, interest, technical fees and contract payments made to non-residents are due and payable to the tax authorities within one month after paying or crediting such payments.

As Malaysia operates on an imputation system, there is no withholding tax imposed on dividends. Dividends are franked with (deemed to be paid net of) the income tax deemed paid by companies. If any company has not paid sufficient tax to cover the total tax deemed deducted from the dividends paid, it has to make good the shortfall to the tax authorities. The amount of the shortfall is due and payable as tax on the issue of a requisition order by the tax authorities.

Employees are subject to the schedular tax deduction scheme. Under the scheme, employers are required to make deductions on account of tax from the emoluments of their employees. The deductions, to be made monthly, are based on amounts specified in the gazetted schedules.

Tax audits

The tax authorities examine tax returns and computations submitted (in varying degrees of detail) and make inquiries as to any matter which may have a bearing on the tax liability. Tax investigations are carried out on an ad hoc basis and are usually very detailed. Tax agents normally act for companies in these matters and negotiate with the tax authorities. These negotiations generally lead to agreement on the tax liability.

Penalties

Various penalties, fines and/or periods of imprisonment may be imposed on taxpayers for late filing or non-filing of tax returns, filing of incorrect or fraudulent returns, late payment or non-payment of taxes, or late payment or non-payment of withholding tax. Fines range from RM200 to RM20,000 and penalties from 5% to 300% of the tax payable.

A penalty of 10% of the amount unpaid may be added to any tax that is overdue. This penalty is increased by 5% on the balance of any unpaid tax at the end of 60 days after the imposition of the first penalty of 10%. No further late payment penalties are imposed after this period.

In the case of a default in submitting true and complete tax returns without reasonable excuse, the penalty may be up to 300% of the tax payable.

Statute of limitations

The tax authorities have up to 12 years to issue additional assessments. There is no limitation period where fraud, wilful default or negligence is proved.

Individual Taxpayers

The procedures for taxing individuals under employment are similar to those applicable to companies. The individual is subject to similar filing requirements to a company but extension of time for the filing of the tax return will not be granted beyond 31 May of each tax year. Appropriate documentation should also be submitted to support their tax returns.

Employees are subject to a tax-deduction scheme whereby their employers are required to make a monthly deduction of tax from their salaries. The deduction of tax will be based on schedules establishing the amount of tax to be deducted. The amount is predetermined, based on certain standard circumstances pertaining to the taxpayer.

Spouse

The general rule is that a married woman is required to declare her income from all sources in her husband's tax return. There is provision in the law for a wife living together with her husband to be separately assessed on her income from all sources without an election being made. The advantages of a separate assessment are the availability of higher personal relief and generally lower marginal tax rates. Alternatively, the law also provides for a wife to make an election in writing for her income to be jointly assessed with her husband's.

Employees leaving Malaysia

Employers of foreign personnel are required to notify the Inland Revenue Board at least one month before the date of departure. Additionally, the Inland Revenue Board would also need to be notified if an employee is about to leave Malaysia for a period exceeding three months. In such an instance, the employer is required to retain all moneys due to the employee until 90 days after the receipt of such notification by the Inland Revenue Board except where such departures from Malaysia at frequent intervals are in the course of employment.

Exit permits

The Director-General has power to prevent any person from leaving Malaysia until all tax assessed has been paid or security for payment has been furnished. In practice, such power is rarely exercised, since the Act requires an employer to withhold moneys due to a departing employee until tax clearance is given.

Trusts, Partnerships and Joint Ventures

Trusts

Trustees are responsible for filing returns of all income received by them in their fiduciary capacity as well as paying the tax assessed on the trust. Compliance requirements and penalties are similar to those applicable to companies.

Partnerships

A partnership is required to make a return of the total partnership income annually. Filing requirements are similar to those applicable to companies. No assessment is made on a partnership; partners are assessed separately in respect of their share of the partnership income.

Joint ventures

An unincorporated joint venture is treated in the same way as a partnership.

TAXATION OF CORPORATIONS

Corporate Tax System

Taxable entities

Tax on corporations is payable by 'companies', a term defined to mean a corporate body, including any body of persons established with a separate legal identity by or under the laws of a territory outside Malaysia but excluding a partnership. A partner which is a company of a partnership is, however, subject to tax on its share of the partnership profits.

Territoriality

Both resident and non-resident companies are assessed on any income accruing in or derived from Malaysia. Foreign-sourced income of a company is not liable to tax, except resident companies carrying on the business of banking, insurance, shipping and air transport operations. Resident companies carrying on such operations are assessable on their world-wide income, notwithstanding that the foreign-sourced income is not remitted to Malaysia.

A company is considered to be resident in Malaysia if its control and management are exercised in Malaysia at any time during the year. Control and management are normally considered to be exercised at the place where directors' meetings are held, so that tax residence could be deemed to arise out of a single directors' meeting being held in Malaysia unless no significant decision was made at that meeting. Once it has been established that the company is resident, it is presumed to remain resident for subsequent years until the contrary is proved.

Corporations and shareholders

Malaysia operates an imputation system of taxation whereby resident companies are subject to income tax at the flat rate of 30% on their net profits, whether distributed or not. Shareholders (resident and non-resident) are deemed to have paid income tax at 30% on the Malaysian-sourced dividends received through the mechanism of the tax credit system.

Dividends paid by companies resident in Malaysia are deemed to be derived from Malaysia. The company is entitled to deduct tax at the corporate income tax rate (currently 30%) when paying dividends, and is then required to account to the tax authorities for the tax deducted or deemed to be deducted. The accountability is regarded as having been satisfied to the extent that the company has been charged to tax by direct assessment on its profits. Where the tax deducted or deemed to be deducted from the dividends exceeds the tax paid by direct assessment, the shortfall becomes a debt due to the tax authorities and an amount equivalent to the shortfall is payable by the company to the tax authorities.

The tax charged by direct assessment for this purpose is the tax up to and including the year of assessment following the calendar year in which the dividend is paid.

All shareholders (resident or non-resident, corporate or individual) are entitled to the tax credit attached to the dividends received from Malaysian companies. Where the Malaysian tax liability of a shareholder for a year of assessment is less than the tax credit on the dividends received, the balance of tax credit will be refunded by the tax authorities to the shareholder.

Gross Income

Gross income subject to income tax is generally based on the audited financial statements of the company.

Accounting period

Generally, the basis period for a year of assessment is the calendar year immediately preceding that year of assessment. This means that the basis year is always the 12 months up to 31 December. However, in respect of income from a business where the accounts of that business are made up to some day other than 31 December, the income basis for the year of assessment is that of the accounting period ending in the calendar year immediately preceding that year of assessment. Other non-business income, such as that derived from rental interest and dividends, is assessed to tax on the preceding calendar-year basis.

If there is a failure to make up accounts of a business for a period of 12 months (ie, change of accounting year-end date) the tax authorities have the power to determine the basis period of the following two years of assessment. In certain instances, this would result in an overlap of basis periods, resulting in income being charged to tax twice over two assessment years. However, a change of accounting year end by reason of a company law requirement would not result in overlapping basis periods.

From a tax planning point of view, a company that has an accounting year-end early in the calendar year would effectively enjoy a deferred filing date of its tax return measured from the end of its accounting year. This could result in significant cash flow advantages over another company having an accounting year-end nearer the end of the calendar year.

Accounting methods

The accrual method of accounting prepared on a historical-cost basis in accordance with generally accepted accounting principles applies in Malaysia. The percentage-of-completion method for contract accounts is acceptable, provided it is applied consistently. The completed-contract method is acceptable only for short-duration contracts and on a case-by-case basis. A cash basis of accounting for a company's financial affairs is not acceptable for taxation purposes.

Business profits and intercompany transactions

Business profits are computed on the basis of the audited accounts adjusted for non-taxable and non-tax-deductible items, such as profits on sale of fixed assets and depreciation. There are no specific regulations on intercompany pricing levels, although the Director-General has wide powers to disregard transactions that have the effect of avoiding or altering the incidence of tax that may otherwise have been imposed.

Inventory valuation

Inventories (stock-in-trade) must be valued at market value unless the items are physically tangible, in which case an election may be made to value them at original cost, including carrying costs and such other expenses incurred on any work or process done to the original inventory. In practice, the election will be regarded as having been made where the accounts submitted to the tax authorities indicate that inventories have been valued at the lower of cost or net realisable value.

Reserves against inventories are not tax deductible unless they represent specific write-downs against the cost value of inventories in order to reduce the cost to net realisable value. The LIFO basis for determining inventory flows may be used for book reporting but it is not regarded as acceptable by the tax authorities for tax reporting.

Capital gains

Capital gains are not regarded as income and are not taxable as such. However, a capital gains tax known as real property gains tax is imposed on capital gains arising from the sale of real property or shares in a real property company.

Rental, interest and dividend income

Rental, interest and dividend income are taxable. The basis period for assessing interest and dividend income is the calendar year in which such income is received. In the case of a company carrying on a business and also deriving rental interest or dividend income, the tax authorities, as a concession, accept the assessment of such income by reference to the company's financial year-end. This concession is not extended to investment holding companies.

Dividends paid out of tax-exempt income are not taxable in the hands of shareholders. Dividends received from companies in a group are not distinguished from other dividends for taxation purposes.

Bonus issues of shares are regarded as capital receipts and are not subject to tax. Dividend-in-kind is not common in Malaysia, but would be regarded as distribution of dividends when made. Generally the net amount of the dividends is equal to the market value of the assets distributed.

Royalties

Royalties are taxable as trading income.

Exchange gains and losses

A gain on foreign exchange is subject to tax and a loss is deductible only where the gain or loss arises from revenue account, ie, in the course of trading. Profits from regular speculation in foreign exchange are similarly taxable if these are deemed to arise from the carrying on of a business.

Non-taxable income

Capital receipts are non-taxable. Dividends paid out of tax-exempt income received by a corporation are exempt from tax.

Deductions

Business expenses

Deductions are allowed for all outgoings and expenses wholly and exclusively incurred in producing taxable income, unless specifically disallowed. Deductions are not allowed for domestic or private expenses, income or similar taxes, pre-incorporation, preliminary or start-up expenses, capital withdrawn, or capital expended on improvements.

Expenses that are expressly deductible by legislation include:

(1)   Interest paid on borrowed money and employed in acquiring the income.

(2)   Rent payable in respect of any land or building occupied for the purpose of producing the income.

(3)   Repairs to premises, plant, machinery, or fixtures used in the production of income.

(4)   Trade debts that are reasonably estimated to be irrecoverable.

(5)   Contributions to approved funds or schemes in respect of an employee, subject to a maximum of 17% of the employee's remuneration.

(6)   Qualifying abortive prospecting expenditure incurred in the searching for minerals.

(7)   Scientific research expenses.

(8)   Plantation replanting expenditure.

(9)   Cost of equipment provided to disabled employees.

(10) Expenditure incurred in the provision of library facilities that are accessible to the public and contributions to public libraries, subject to a maximum of RM100,000 each year.

Depreciation

The depreciation charged in the books in arriving at the accounting profit is not deductible for tax purposes. The law, however, provides for corresponding deductions to be allowed in respect of capital expenditure incurred on certain fixed assets, such as factory buildings and plant and machinery, used for the purposes of the business in the form of capital allowances calculated at prescribed rates.

Generally, no allowance is granted for expenditure incurred for the acquisition of goodwill and leases.

Capital allowances deduction

Capital allowances for a business source are deductible against the adjusted income of the same business source and are not deductible against income from another business or against other non-business sources.

Where there is insufficient adjusted income to absorb the full amount of capital allowances available, the unused amount would be carried forward indefinitely for deduction against future business income from the same source. Capital allowances would not increase a business loss.

Depreciation recapture on disposal of assets

Balancing adjustments will arise on the disposal of assets for which capital allowances have been claimed. A balancing charge/allowance is the excess/shortfall of the sale proceeds over the tax written down value of the asset disposed of. Balancing charge, however, is restricted to the amount of allowances previously claimed.

No balancing adjustments will be made where assets are sold or transferred between companies under common control. In such cases, the actual consideration for the transfer of the assets is disregarded and the disposer/acquirer is deemed to have disposed of/acquired the assets at their tax-written-down values.

In the case of an asset sold within two years of purchase, the tax authorities may direct that capital allowances previously granted be clawed back unless there is commercial justification in the disposal.

Interest

Interest on money borrowed and employed in producing income is a tax-deductible expense. However, if part of the borrowed money is used to finance other non-business loans or investments, the portion of interest attributable to the non-business loans or investments is not tax deductible against business income. That portion of interest would, however, be tax deductible against the income (if any) from the non-business loans or investments. There are no thin capitalisation rules in the tax legislation.

Interest paid to a non-resident person (other than interest attributable to a business carried on by that person in Malaysia) requires a withholding tax deduction to be paid to the tax authorities within one month after the payment or crediting of the interest to the non-resident. The deduction of interest payments is conditional upon payment of the withholding tax.

Other than interest derived from funds required for the purpose of maintaining net working funds of a bank, interest paid to a non-resident person by commercial or merchant banks operating in Malaysia is also exempt from withholding tax.

Royalties, technical service fees, management fees and rental of movable properties

Royalties, technical service fees, management fees and rental of movable properties are deductible expenses. However, such payments made to a non-resident person require withholding tax deductions, which must be paid to the tax authorities within one month after paying or crediting the payments. The deduction of these payments to a non-resident as expenses of the paying company is conditional upon payment of the withholding tax. The Ministry of International Trade and Industry would require companies issued with manufacturing licences to submit draft agreements for prior approval for the payment of royalties, technical service fees or management fees to non-residents. The current policy on royalties is to approve the rate of payment to between 2% and 5% of net sales.

Approved industrial royalties under particular treaty provisions are exempt from withholding tax.

Services under contract

Payments made to a non-resident contractor in respect of services under a contract are subject to deduction of tax at the rate of 20%, unless expressly reduced or waived by the Director-General. Where the requirement in respect of the deduction of tax (which is similar to the withholding tax on interest payments) has not been complied with, the contract payments will not be allowed as a tax deduction. The 20% deduction of tax comprises 15% on account of the non-resident contractor's tax liability and 5% on account of the employees' tax liability. This deduction of tax at source does not represent a final tax, which is determined on the filing of the annual tax returns. Any excess of credit over the actual tax liability will be refunded to the non-resident contractor, while any shortfall must be paid to the tax authorities.

Other deductions

Travelling expenses are deductible but are normally subject to scrutiny by the tax authorities. Proper records and receipts should be maintained to avoid disallowance of claims. Leave passage provided to employees is not an allowable expense.

Donations to approved institutions are deductible. Trade debts that are reasonably estimated to be irrecoverable are tax deductible, as are research and development costs.

Non-deductible items

The following are the principal items not deductible in computing trading profits:

(1) Domestic or private expenditure.
(2) Expenses not wholly and exclusively laid out for the purpose of producing gross income.
(3) Capital withdrawn or any sum employed or intended to be employed as capital.
(4) Contributions to non-approved provident, savings, pension, widows' and orphans', or other similar funds.
(5) Interest, royalty or technical fees, rental of movable properties, or contract payments paid to non-resident persons where withholding tax has not been paid.
(6) Sums paid for rental of non-commercial motor vehicles in excess of RM50,000.
(7) Leave passage provided to employees.
(8) Business entertainment expenses.
(9) General provisions, as opposed to specific provisions of bad debts.
(10) Fines and penalties.
(11) Depreciation and amortisation.
(12) Non-approved donations.

Losses

Current year business losses arrived at after adjustment for tax purposes can be utilised against income from all sources. Any excess business losses may be carried forward for set-off against future business income from all business sources. These unutilised tax losses can be carried forward indefinitely, notwithstanding a change in ownership or business activity of the company unless it is part of a scheme to avoid or reduce the incidence of tax. There is no provision for loss carryback. Tax losses cannot be offset by the grouping of profitable and unprofitable affiliates.

Tax Computation

Net income

Net business income is adjusted for tax purposes by adding to accounting profits any non-deductible expenses (including depreciation charged in the accounts) and deducting non-taxable receipts to arrive at the adjusted income. Capital allowances and donations are deducted from this adjusted income to arrive at the net business income. However, if there is insufficient adjusted income to utilise the full amount of capital allowances available, the excess capital allowances are available for carry forward for deduction against future business income from the same source. Capital allowances will not increase a business loss.

Net business income is then aggregated with the taxable income from other sources, eg, dividends, rental or interest income, to arrive at the total taxable income.

Tax rates

Generally, all companies (resident or non-resident) are subject to income tax at a flat rate of 30%. However, certain income received from Malaysia by a non-resident which is not attributable to a business carried on by that non-resident in Malaysia is subject to withholding tax at the following rates, unless a double taxation agreement prescribes otherwise.

Tax category	%
Interest	15
Royalties	10
Technical and management fees	10
Rental of movable properties	10

Tax credits

Companies resident in Malaysia are entitled to claim a credit against Malaysian tax in respect of foreign taxes paid on foreign-sourced income either under a double taxation agreement or by way of unilateral relief. The credit/relief is restricted to the lower of Malaysian tax payable on the foreign income or foreign tax paid under a double tax treaty or one-half of the foreign tax paid otherwise.

Consolidation

Although the accounts of groups of affiliated companies are consolidated to reflect the overall financial position and trading results of the group, each company in the group is taxed as a separate legal entity. There are no provisions in the tax legislation for offsetting losses of one company against the profits of another company.

Special Industries

Banks

Banking income of a tax resident is subject to tax on a world-wide basis. Banking income of a non-resident is taxed only on the income accruing in or derived from Malaysia. There are no special regulations or rules on the taxation of banks and the general rules affecting trading income would apply. Other income received by a bank, such as leasing or investment income, would fall outside the 'world-wide' scope.

Investment companies

Income of investment holding companies is taxed as investment income. No capital allowance claims are allowed, and only a fraction of management charges, computed based on a prescribed formula, is allowed as a deduction. Any excess direct expenses and charges on income over taxable profits are not available for set-off against other income or for carry forward for set-off against future investment income. Companies trading in stocks and shares are treated as trading companies.

Insurance companies

Income from an insurance business of a tax resident is subject to tax on a world-wide basis, whereas a non-resident is taxed on income accruing in or derived from Malaysia.

There are special rules for determining the profits assessable on resident and non-resident insurance companies, depending on the type of insurance business transacted in Malaysia. Re-insurance must be placed with companies having branches or doing business in Malaysia; otherwise, only 95% of re-insurance premiums are allowable. A person carrying on inward or offshore re-insurance business is regarded as carrying on a separate general insurance business. The income from these activities is subject to a reduced income tax rate of 5% provided certain conditions are met. The whole of such income, less the 5% tax, is credited to an exempt account, which is available for distribution as tax exempt dividends in the hands of the shareholders.

With effect from the year of assessment 1995, new rules have been formulated for the taxation of a life insurance business. In essence, the income derived from a life insurance business is distinguished between the income of the life fund and the shareholders' fund. The income from the life fund is taxed at a concessionary rate of 8%, while income of the shareholders' fund is taxed at the normal corporate rate of 30%.

Leasing industry

There are special rules and regulations regarding the determination of taxable profits of a leasing business. Under the rules, certain types of lease agreements are deemed to be sales agreements.

Petroleum industry

Companies carrying on petroleum operations in Malaysia are taxed under the Petroleum Income Tax Act 1967. Petroleum operations exclude the transportation of petroleum outside Malaysia, the process of refining or liquefying of petroleum, dealings in petroleum products, or services involving the supply of rigs, derricks, ocean tankers and barges.

In 1990 Malaysia and Thailand signed an agreement relating to the establishment of the Malaysia-Thailand Joint Authority (MTJA) for the development of the resources of the seabed in the defined area of the continental shelf of the two countries in the Gulf of Thailand. The MTJA was created upon the subsequent enactment of the MTJA Act 1990. Income derived from petroleum operations carried out in the joint development area would fall within the ambit of the Petroleum Income Tax Act 1967.

Petroleum income tax is chargeable at the rate of 40%. Income derived from petroleum operations in the Malaysia-Thailand joint development area will be chargeable to petroleum income tax as follows:

Petroleum income tax	%
For the first eight years of production	0
For the next seven years of production	10
For subsequent years of production	20

The income from petroleum operations is not subject to income tax. Dividends paid out of petroleum income will not be chargeable to any further taxes.

The non-petroleum income of a petroleum company is taxed according to the general income tax rules. For a non-resident petroleum company, interest, dividends and royalties will be taxed as follows:

Tax category	%
Interest	15
Dividends	Nil*
Royalties	10

* Imputation system.

Resident oil companies pay tax at the rate of 30% on all non-petroleum income.

Chargeable persons include PETRONAS (the government-owned national petroleum corporation), MTJA and any company, partnership, body of persons or corporate sole (corporate body) carrying on petroleum operations under a petroleum agreement. A person who carries on petroleum operations under more than one petroleum agreement will be regarded as a separate chargeable person in respect of each of those agreements. A partnership includes joint ventures, syndicates etc, where the parties have agreed to combine their rights, powers, property, skill or labour for the purpose of carrying on petroleum operations and sharing production or profits.

Deductions allowable against taxable income include the following items:

(1)   Depletion of exploration expenditure incurred.
(2)   Intangible drilling costs.
(3)   Depreciation of machinery and equipment used in the petroleum operations.

Resident shipping companies

Resident companies carrying on a shipping business are exempt from tax on income derived from the operation of Malaysian ships. The tax exempt income of such companies is available for distribution as tax exempt dividends to their shareholders.

Income derived by residents from the operation of non-Malaysian ships is subject to tax on a world-scope basis. The term "Malaysian ships" is defined to mean a sea-going ship registered under the Merchant Shipping Ordinance 1952, other than a ferry, barge, tugboat, supply vessel, crew boat, lighter, dredger, fishing boat or other similar vessel.

Non-resident shipping companies

A non-resident person carrying on a sea transport business in international traffic would be assessable to Malaysian tax on profits derived from the carriage of passengers, mails, livestock, or goods embarked or loaded in Malaysia (other than on trans-shipment). The taxable income of a non-resident shipping operator is determined based on either the 5% method or the acceptable certificate method. Income ascertained under either method would be subject to normal corporate income tax.

(1) 5% method: Under this method, statutory income is deemed to be 5% of the shipping charges received from the embarkation of passengers or cargo loaded from Malaysia.

(2) Acceptable certificate method: The acceptable certificate method may be used if the ratio certificate issued by a foreign tax authority is regarded by the Malaysian tax authorities as an acceptable certificate.

The tax authorities would accept ratio certificates issued by the tax authorities of countries whose basis of computation of the taxable profits of shipping operators does not substantially differ from the basis adopted in Malaysia. These countries include Australia, Brunei, Denmark, Germany, India, Japan, the Republic of Korea, Myanmar, the Netherlands, Norway, the Philippines, Singapore, Sri Lanka, Sweden, Thailand and the United Kingdom.

Where such an acceptable certificate is provided, the statutory income is computed by using the following formula:

$$\frac{\text{Gross income derived from Malaysia}}{\substack{\text{Gross world income as shown} \\ \text{in acceptable certificate}}} \times \text{World income/World loss}$$

A loss arising as a result of using this method would be allowable against future Malaysian freight income.

There is no tax liability on income derived by a ship making a casual call, but there must be no intention to call again for a period of two years.

Non-resident airline companies

Rules similar to those for determining the liability of non-resident shipping companies would apply to non-resident airline operators.

Operational headquarters company

The income derived by an approved operational headquarters company from the provision of qualifying services is taxed at the reduced rate of 10% for a period of 5–10 years. The after-tax income may be distributed to shareholders as tax-exempt dividends.

Resident airline companies

Income derived by resident airline companies is also subject to tax on a world scope basis. Non-residents engaged in air transport operations are taxed in the same manner as that applicable to non-resident shipping companies.

Venture capital company

Gains derived by an approved venture capital company in respect of the disposal of shares in a venture company are exempt from tax. Gains from the disposal of shares of venture companies which are listed on the Kuala Lumpur Stock Exchange are also exempt if the disposal takes place within three years from the date of listing of those shares. The tax exempt gains arising from the disposal of venture company shares are available for distribution to shareholders as tax exempt dividends. Losses incurred on the disposal of shares in a venture company or on liquidation of a venture company are deductible against any sources of income of a venture capital company. Any unutilised losses are available for carry forward for set-off against future income from business sources only.

A venture company is a Malaysian incorporated company involved in high risk ventures.

Unit trusts

Similarly, gains from the disposal of investments are exempt from tax in the hands of a unit trust. Distributions from these gains are tax exempt in the hands of unit holders.

Closed-end fund company

A closed-end fund company is a public limited company incorporated in Malaysia and approved by the Securities Commission to engage wholly in the investment of funds in securities.

To encourage the development of close-end funds and to provide a comparable tax treatment with unit trusts, gains arising from the realisation of investments are exempt from tax and are available for distribution to shareholders as tax-exempt dividends.

Foreign fund management company

The chargeable income of a foreign fund management company from the provision of fund management services to foreign investors is subject to a concessionary tax rate of 10%. Local fund management companies are also eligible for this concessionary tax rate in respect of services rendered to foreign investors.

International Procurement Centre (IPC)

An IPC refers to a locally incorporated company, whether local or foreign owned which carries on a business in Malaysia to undertake procurement and sale of raw materials, components and finished products to its group of related and unrelated companies in Malaysia or abroad. It includes procurement and sales from Malaysia or from a third country. Upon meeting certain criteria, an approved IPC would be eligible for various incentives, such as no limit imposed on expatriate posts, exemption from customs duties on raw materials, components and finished products, and exemption from equity requirements imposed by the Ministry of Domestic Trade and Consumer Affairs.

Multimedia Super Corridor (MSC)

The MSC is a regional launch site for companies developing or using leading multimedia technology by integrating ground-breaking cyberlaws and outstanding information infrastructure in a green environment.

The MSC is a 15 km by 50 km zone spreading south of Kuala Lumpur. Putrajaya and Cyberjaya, the seat of electronic government and IT city respectively, are located in the centre of the MSC. Developers or heavy users of multimedia or information technology products and services satisfying certain criteria can qualify for MSC status.

To ensure that the MSC achieves its objectives, the Multimedia Development Corporation (MDC) was established. It is a "one-stop super shop" with functions including permit and licensing approvals for companies setting up operations in the MSC.

Companies with approved MSC status will enjoy full exemption of their profits for a period of five to ten years, subject to level of technology transfer. Alternatively, these companies may be granted investment tax allowance (ITA) of 100% on new investments made in MSC-designated cybercities. The ITA is given as a deduction against the MSC companies' income without any restriction.

Approved MSC companies are also exempt from import duties on multimedia equipment used directly in facilitating their operational process. Other significant non-fiscal incentives available are unrestricted employment of foreign knowledge workers, exemption from equity conditions and exchange control requirements, intellectual property protection, the world's first comprehensive framework of cyberlaws and a world-class physical and IT infrastructure.

Additionally, research and development grants are available on application to the MDC for local small and medium-size enterprises (SME) within the MSC. However, these SMEs should be at least 51% Malaysian-owned.

Tax Incentives

Malaysia offers investors attractive investment incentives which are generally available to resident companies. Among the more significant incentives are pioneer status, investment tax allowance, reinvestment allowance and incentives for research and development activities. A summary of these incentives is given below.

Pioneer status

Corporations in the manufacturing, agricultural, hotel or tourist sectors, or any other industrial or commercial sector, that participate in a promoted activity or produce promoted products may be granted pioneer status incentive. The incentive is given by way of an abatement of 70% of the profits after deduction of capital allowances for five years. The remaining 30% of the profits will be taxed at the prevailing corporate tax rate. The profits abated are exempt from tax and will be available for distribution as tax-free dividends.

However, the general rule of tax abatement and the period of incentive are varied under the following circumstances:

(a) A corporation carrying out a project of national and strategic importance involving heavy capital investment and high technology will be granted full exemption on its profits after deduction of capital allowances, and the tax-relief period may be extended for a further five years.

(b) A high-technology company granted pioneer status for engaging in a promoted activity or in the production of a promoted product in areas of new and emerging technologies will be fully exempt from tax on its profits after deduction of capital allowances for a period of five years.

(c) Corporations with projects eligible for pioneer status that are located in the Eastern Corridor States of Peninsular Malaysia, Sabah and Sarawak will be granted an abatement of 85% of their profits after deduction of capital allowances for five years. An existing pioneer or ex-pioneer corporation that undertakes an expansion program through a subsidiary or controlled company in the Eastern Corridor States of Peninsular Malaysia, Sabah or Sarawak that involves the same promoted activities or promoted products is eligible for a second round of pioneer status or investment tax allowance if certain conditions are satisfied. The Eastern Corridor States include Kelantan, Terengganu and certain designated areas in the States of Pahang and Johor.

Investment tax allowance

As an alternative to pioneer status, a corporation may be granted an investment tax allowance (ITA) of 60% of capital expenditure incurred on a factory or plant and machinery used for the purposes of an approved manufacturing, agricultural, hotel, tourist or other industrial or commercial activity. ITA is granted on capital expenditure incurred for a period of five years; for an intergrated agricultural activity, ITA may be granted in respect of the agricultural activity for five years and to the processing activity for five years. ITA is granted in addition to the normal capital allowances.

The amount of ITA granted will be used for offset against the profits derived from that promoted activity or promoted product, after deduction of capital allowances. However, the amount to be utilised each year is restricted to a maximum of 70% of such profits. The balance of 30% will be taxed at the prevailing corporate tax rate. Unutilised ITA may be carried forward indefinitely for set-off against future profits derived from that promoted activity or promoted product, after deduction of capital allowances of the business. Dividends paid out of exempt profits are not liable to tax in the hands of shareholders.

The ITA incentive is enhanced for the following types of projects:

(a) A corporation carrying out a project of national and strategic importance may be granted ITA at a rate of 100%. The ITA is available for set-off against its profits after deduction of capital allowances each year without restriction.

(b) A high-technology company may be granted ITA at the rate of 60% and the amount of ITA would be available for set-off against its profits after deduction of capital allowances without restriction.

(c) A company granted ITA in respect of a project located in the Eastern Corridor States of Peninsular Malaysia, Sabah or Sarawak would be granted ITA at a rate of 80% and the amount of ITA that could be utilised for each year would be restricted to a maximum of 85% of the profits after deduction of capital allowances. An existing or ex-ITA company that undertakes an expansion program through a subsidiary or controlled company in the Eastern Corridor States of Peninsular Malaysia, Sabah or Sarawak involving the same promoted activity or promoted product is eligible for a second round of ITA or pioneer status if certain conditions are satisfied.

(d) A company that provides technical and vocational training in Malaysia may be granted ITA of 100% of qualifying capital expenditure incurred within a period of 10 years, and the maximum amount of ITA that could be utilised each year would be restricted to 70% of profits after deduction of capital allowances.

Reinvestment allowance

A corporation that embarks on a program to expand, modernise or diversify its existing manufacturing or processing business, in participating in an approved industrial adjustment program or in undertaking an agricultural project is entitled to a reinvestment allowance (RIA) of 60% of qualifying capital expenditure incurred on factory or plant and machinery used for the expansion, modernisation or diversification activity. Similar to the ITA incentive, the RIA is given in addition to the normal capital allowances.

Utilisation of RIA is resticted to 70% of profits after deduction of capital allowances. The remaining 30% is taxed at normal corporate tax rate. The 70% restriction on utilisation of RIA will not apply to projects located in the Eastern Corridor States of Peninsular Malaysia, Sabah or Sarawak.

The amount of profits after deduction of capital allowances equal to the RIA granted is exempt from tax. Unutilised RIA may be carried forward indefinitely for set-off against future profits of the business. Dividends paid out of exempt profits are not liable to tax in the hands of shareholders.

The RIA incentive for any project would not be granted during the period in which the companies are enjoying pioneer status or ITA incentive for that period.

Incentives for research and development activity

Companies that provide research and development (R&D) services to third parties are eligible for pioneer status with full exemption of their profits for a period of five years. As an alternative, such companies may be granted ITA at the rate of 100% of qualifying capital expenditure incurred within a period of 10 years. The ITA incentives may also be granted to companies undertaking R&D for their group companies.

Companies undertaking in-house R&D projects would be eligible for ITA at the rate of 50% of the qualifying capital expenditure incurred within a period of 10 years. In all cases, the ITA which can be utilised in each year is restricted to 70% of profits after deduction of capital allowances.

Double deduction is granted for revenue expenses incurred on approved R&D projects, as well as payments for services made to R&D companies, contract R&D companies and approved research institutes.

Labuan—An International Offshore Financial Centre

Labuan, which is a federal territory of Malaysia, was established in October 1990 as an international offshore financial centre (IOFC). It is a free port island off the coast of Sabah on the north-west side of Borneo. Its location is in the centre of the ASEAN countries, being 1300 km from Singapore and within 1550 km of all other ASEAN capitals except Bangkok. It is in the same time zone as Singapore and Hong Kong and is accessible by air from Kuala Lumpur. There are 57 offshore banks and more than 1000 offshore companies registered with the Labuan Offshore Financial Services Authority (LOFSA) operating in Labuan.

LOFSA was established on 15 February 1996 under the Labuan Offshore Financial Services Authority Act 1996 as part of the government's efforts to streamline and rationalise the administrative machinery for offshore financial activities in Labuan.

LOFSA is a one-stop agency and its primary functions are to administer, enforce, carry out and give effect to the provisions of the various pieces of offshore legislation.

As an IOFC, Labuan offers a package of tax and non-tax incentives for multinational companies undertaking offshore activities. Entities which are incorporated or registered under the Labuan legislation (known as offshore companies) undertaking offshore

159

activities are not subject to any exchange control restrictions, and are able to enjoy preferential tax treatment.

Offshore activities are broadly categorised into offshore trading and non-trading activities. Offshore trading activities include banking, insurance, trading, management and licensing, but exclude shipping operations. Offshore non-trading activities refer to the holding of offshore investments in securities, stocks, loans or immovable properties belonging to the offshore companies. Such activities must be carried out with non-residents and in foreign currencies, although there are some exceptions for banks and insurance companies. Also, an offshore company carrying on both offshore trading and non-trading activities is deemed to be carrying on offshore trading activities.

An offshore company carrying on offshore trading activities is subject to tax at a rate of 3% of net profits as reflected in the audited accounts of the company or, upon election, at a fixed rate of RM20,000. The option to pay the RM20,000 tax may be exercised annually. The income of an offshore company from an offshore non-trading activity will not be subject to tax.

Under specific preferential tax treatment, royalties, interest and technical or management fees paid by an offshore company to a non-resident or another offshore company would be exempt from income tax and hence not subject to withholding tax. Dividends distributed by an offshore company are not subject to any withholding tax.

TAXATION OF SHAREHOLDERS

Dividends

Malaysian sourced dividends received by corporate and individual shareholders are deemed to have had tax deducted at the corporate tax rate (currently 30%) by the paying company, except where dividends are paid out of tax-exempt profits. Dividends paid out of tax-exempt profits are not subject to tax in the hands of shareholders. The dividend income is subject to tax at the grossed-up amount prior to deduction of tax by the paying company. Under the imputation system, the tax deducted by the company on payment of the dividend is credited in full against the shareholder's final income tax liability. If there is an excess of tax credit, a refund will be made to the shareholder.

Foreign-sourced dividend income is taxable when remitted into Malaysia by resident individuals and companies carrying on the business of banking, insurance, shipping and air transport operations. The dividend income is subject to tax at an amount grossed-up for any foreign tax incurred at source. Such resident shareholders are entitled to claim foreign tax credit/relief.

The rules discussed above also apply to non-resident shareholders. There is no withholding tax on dividends paid to non-residents. Foreign-sourced dividends received by non-residents are not subject to tax.

Capital gains

There is no tax on capital gains arising from the disposal of shares other than shares in a real property company. See the section on real property gains tax.

TAXATION OF FOREIGN CORPORATIONS

Foreign corporations are taxed on income accruing in or derived from Malaysia. A broad basis for determining whether or not business profits are derived from Malaysia is to determine whether the foreign corporation is 'trading within' (taxable) or 'trading with' (non-taxable) Malaysia.

Where a double tax agreement exists with the home country of the foreign corporation, the taxation of business profits derived by the foreign corporation is limited to the profits that are attributable to the permanent establishment of the foreign corporation in Malaysia.

In respect of income that is not attributable to a business carried on in Malaysia, such as royalties, interest or service fees, the tax liability of the non-resident is settled by way of withholding tax deducted by the paying entity.

The transfer of branch profits to the head office is not subject to any tax. Branch operations are subject to similar income tax to resident companies.

PARTNERSHIPS AND JOINT VENTURES

Partnerships, which are defined to include unincorporated joint ventures, are treated as conduits in Malaysia and the income of a partnership is divided among its partners, who are taxed in their own names. A partnership is nevertheless required to file a tax return on the partnership income.

Partnership income is computed according to the ordinary rules applicable to business income (taking into account all deductions, etc). The income and capital allowances so computed are then apportioned among the partners according to the profit-sharing ratio. Partners are assessed individually on their share of the partnership income, on which income tax is levied.

Non-resident partners (including corporate partners) are subject to income tax on their share of the partnership income at the rate of 30%.

TAXATION OF INDIVIDUALS

Territoriality and Residence

Income tax is chargeable on the income of a resident person accruing in or derived from Malaysia or received in Malaysia from outside Malaysia. The resident individual is subject to income tax at graduated rates after deducting personal relief.

A non-resident individual is not entitled to personal relief and is taxed only on income accruing in or derived from Malaysia at a flat rate of 30%. Income received in Malaysia from outside Malaysia is not subject to Malaysian tax in the hands of the non-resident.

Residence

For any year of assessment, residence status is determined in relation to the preceding calendar year. Individuals are resident under any of the circumstances described below:
(1) They are in Malaysia for at least 182 days in a calendar year.
(2) They are in Malaysia for a period of less than 182 days but that period is linked to a period of physical presence of at least 182 consecutive days in an adjoining year. In determining the qualifying period, absences from Malaysia for business and health reasons, as well as social visits not exceeding 14 days in aggregate, are ignored.
(3) They are in Malaysia for 90 days or more during the year and were in Malaysia for at least 90 days or were resident in any three of the four immediately preceding years.
(4) They are resident for the immediately following year and were also resident for each of the three immediately preceding years.

For purposes of determining resident status, being present in Malaysia for a part of the day counts as a day in Malaysia.

From a tax planning point of view, in order to take advantage of the graduated tax rates and personal relief, expatriates should time their arrival/departure in such a manner as to ensure that they are tax residents in the year of arrival/departure.

Special provisions

There are no special provisions applicable to foreign nationals working in Malaysia apart from the concession granted to a non-citizen employed in Labuan in a managerial capacity with an offshore company.

Employment Income

Employment income is regarded as being derived from Malaysia and subject to Malaysian tax where the employment is exercised in Malaysia. This is notwithstanding that the income may be wholly or partly paid outside Malaysia. Employment income also includes income in respect of duties performed outside Malaysia which are incidental to the Malaysian employment.

Gross employment income includes wages, salary, leave pay, fees, commissions, bonuses, gratuities, perquisites or allowances (whether in money or otherwise), and benefits-in-kind in respect of having or exercising the employment.

Entertainment allowances are also assessable on the employee unless it can be demonstrated that the amounts have been expended solely in connection with the employer's business. Proper records must be maintained by the employee for submission to the tax authorities in support of this claim.

The tax of the employee borne by the employer would constitute a taxable benefit to the employee.

Benefits-in-kind

The following benefits-in-kind provided by an employer constitute taxable benefits:

(1) Household utilities, domestic servants and gardener. The employee is taxable on the actual cost to the employer in providing these benefits.

163

(2) Household effects: The value of the benefit attributable to the use of household furnishings, equipment and appliances is based on values specified by the tax authorities. See Appendix II.

(3) Company car: The value of the benefit attributed to the use of a company car and chauffeur is based on the tax authorities' valuation. See Appendix II.

Certain benefits-in-kind are specifically exempt from tax in the hands of employees as follows:

(1) Leave passage: Leave passage provided to the employee and members of his immediate family are exempt from tax but this is restricted to one overseas trip and three local trips in a calendar year.

(2) Medical, dental and hospitalisation: Medical, dental and hospitalisation provided to the employee and members of his immediate family are also tax exempt.

(3) Child care: A benefit for child care provided to the employee is a non-taxable benefit.

Value of living accommodation

The employee is taxed on accommodation provided by his employer, the taxable value being the lower of the actual rental paid for the unfurnished accommodation or 30% of the gross cash remuneration for the proportionate period of occupation. The benefit of accommodation provided in a hotel is taxable at 3% of the gross cash remuneration for the proportionate period of stay.

Retirement gratuity

A gratuity received by an individual on retirement from employment due to ill health or on reaching the age of 55 after completing 10 years' service with the same employer or group of companies is exempt from tax. Where these conditions are not satisfied, the gratuity is assessable on the basis of the amount being spread back over the period of employment or last 10 years, whichever is shorter.

Compensation for loss of employment

Compensation received for loss of employment is exempt from tax up to RM4000 for each completed year of service with the same employer or group of companies. The balance is assessable as income in the year of receipt.

However, if the payment is made on account of loss of employment due to ill health, the full sum received is tax exempt.

Pensions

Pensions received upon retirement at the age of 55 or on reaching the compulsory age of retirement or due to ill health are exempt from tax. Where a person receives more than one pension, the exemption will only apply to the highest pension.

Prize money

Prize money received by both local and foreign professional athletes is exempt from income tax.

Short-term visitors

A short-term visiting non-resident employee, other than a public entertainer, is exempt from tax in respect of income from employment exercised in Malaysia for not more than 60 days in a calendar year. If any period of stay straddles two calendar years, then the non-resident employee is exempt if the total period of stay over the two years does not exceed 60 days.

Capital gains

There is no capital gains tax apart from the tax on real property gains.

Other income

Residents are subject to income tax on all classes of income accruing in or derived from Malaysia or received in Malaysia from outside Malaysia. Non-residents are taxed only on income accruing in or derived from Malaysia.

Amounts received from a non-approved pension or provident fund to which the employer makes the contributions are taxable.

The net annual value of land and improvements used by the owner or occupied rent-free for residential purposes is taxable (but the net annual value of one owner-occupied residential property is exempt).

Closely-held companies

For Malaysian tax purposes, a controlled (closely-held) company is one having less than 50 shareholders and controlled by not more than five persons. Where directors (other than service directors) are provided with rent-free living accommodation by the company, the actual value of the living accommodation is taxed without restriction.

Deductions

Business-related expenses

Employees are allowed a deduction for any expenditure wholly and exclusively incurred in the performance of their duties, but no allowance is given for tax depreciation (capital allowances), eg, on a vehicle used in the performance of duties.

Where an allowance is given by an employer for business purposes, such as for entertaining customers, the expenditure incurred by the employee is deductible up to the amount of the allowance received.

Non-business expenses

Non-business expenses, such as medical expenses and taxes, are not deductible. Expenses of a private or domestic nature are expressly excluded from deduction. For example, the cost of travelling from home to a place of employment and vice versa is not deductible. Mortgage interest incurred to finance the purchase of a house is deductible only to the extent of any rental income derived from the house. Donations to approved funds and professional subscriptions to an association related to the individual's profession are tax deductible.

Personal allowances

After the total income of a resident individual has been calculated on a basis similar to that for companies, taxable income is determined by deducting from the total income certain personal allowances determined by reference to the individual's personal circumstances prevailing in the year preceding the year of assessment.

Personal relief is only granted to resident individuals. See Appendix III.

The income of a wife living together with her husband is assessed separately from the income of her husband.

The wife is entitled to a personal relief of RM5000, or RM10,000 if she is disabled, as well as relief for parents' medical expenses of up to RM5000, deduction for life insurance premiums and Employees' Provident Fund contributions of up to RM5000, insurance premiums for education and medical benefits of up to RM2000 and medical expenses for self, spouse or child on treatment of serious illnesses up to RM5000.

Where a wife elects for all her income to be jointly assessed with the income of her husband, she will be regarded as having no income and the husband is entitled to claim wife relief of RM3000.

Child relief can be claimed by either husband or wife. The normal child relief of RM800 is granted in respect of:

(a) unmarried children not exceeding 18 years of age; and

(b) unmarried children over 18 years of age who are undergoing full time education at a university, college or school.

If the child is over 18 years of age and receiving higher education at a university or college or serving under articles or indentures, the relief granted is increased up to the amount expended but restricted to:

(a) 4 times the normal child relief if the higher education is received in Malaysia; and

(b) 2 times the normal child relief if the higher education is received overseas.

Tax Computation

Taxable income

Taxable income is arrived at after deducting personal relief and approved donations made from the total income of an individual. See Appendix I for a sample tax computation.

Tax rates

Residents

The rates of tax range from 0% on taxable income under RM2500 to 30% on taxable income in excess of RM150,000. Interest from financial institutions in Malaysia received by a resident is taxed separately at a rate of 5% by deduction at source. Any other interest will be aggregated with the individual's other income on which tax is levied at the graduated tax rates.

A resident individual whose taxable income does not exceed RM10,000 is granted a rebate of RM110. An additional RM60 is available in respect of a wife who has elected to be jointly assessed with her husband. Both husband and wife who are separately assessed are entitled to a rebate of RM110 each.

Non-residents

Taxable income of non-resident individuals is taxed at a rate of 30%. Royalties, rent and technical service fees received by a non-resident are taxed at the rate of 10%. Malaysian income of a non-resident public entertainer is taxed at the rate of 15%. Interest from financial institutions in Malaysia received by a non-resident is exempt from tax. Any other interest will be taxed at 15%, or less if reduced by a relevant tax treaty provision.

Tax credits

A non-resident individual can claim foreign tax credits against Malaysian tax. Where a treaty exists, the credit is the lesser of the foreign tax paid or the Malaysian tax payable. In the absence of a treaty, the credit is restricted to one-half the foreign tax paid.

OTHER TAXES

Provident Fund Contributions

It is compulsory for Malaysian employees to contribute to the government-established Employees Provident Fund (EPF). The statutory rates of contribution for the employee and employer are 11% and 12% of the employee's salary respectively. Non-Malaysians are not required to be members of the EPF but they may elect to be. The employer's contributions are not taxable on the employee.

Local Taxes on Income

There are no local taxes on income.

Wealth Tax and Gift Tax

There is no wealth tax or gift tax in Malaysia.

Inheritance Tax

Inheritance tax (estate duty), which was levied on all property passing on death, was abolished as from 1 November 1991.

Capital Gains

There is no capital gains tax apart from the tax on gains arising from the sale of real property situated in Malaysia.

REAL PROPERTY GAINS TAX

Basic Principles

Real property gains tax (RPGT) is charged on gains arising from the disposal of real property situated in Malaysia and shares in a real property company. Real property means land, buildings and crops standing on land as well as an interest, option or other rights in or over land and shares in real property companies.

A real property company (RPC) is a controlled company that owns or acquires real property or RPC shares with a defined value of not less than 75% of its total tangible assets. Every method, scheme or arrangement by which the ownership of an asset is transferred from one person to another would constitute an acquisition and a disposal of a chargeable asset for RPGT purposes.

Taxable Persons

Every person, whether or not resident in Malaysia, is chargeable to RPGT in respect of any gain accruing on the disposal of real property in Malaysia or RPC shares.

Gains and Losses

A chargeable gain arises if the disposal price exceeds the acquisition price and an allowable loss is incurred if the disposal price is less than the acquisition price. The loss arising from the disposal of RPC shares does not qualify as an allowable loss.

Tax relief available on an allowable loss is arrived at by multiplying the appropriate rate of RPGT applicable to the category of disposal giving rise to the loss. The amount so arrived at is allowed as a deduction from the total tax assessed on all chargeable gains in the same year. Unutilised losses are available for carry forward for relief against future RPGT gains.

Tax rates

RPGT rates are dependent on the period of ownership of the real property, as shown in the following table:

Category of disposal	Company %	Other persons %
Within two years	30	30
In third year	20	20
In fourth year	15	15
In fifth year	5	5
In sixth and subsequent years	5	Nil

Gains from the disposal of real property derived by an individual who is a non-citizen and a non-permanent resident is assessed to RPGT at a flat rate of 30% regardless of the period of ownership of the real property.

Scheme of Reorganisation

Relief from RPGT may be available where assets are transferred for purposes of greater efficiency in operations or under a scheme of reconstruction or amalgamation of companies and where certain prescribed conditions are satisfied.

Exemptions

Exemption from RPGT is available under the following circumstances:

(1) An amount of RM5000 or 10% of the chargeable gain, whichever is greater, accruing to an individual.

(2) A gain accruing to the government, a State government or a local authority.

(3) A gain equal to the amount of estate tax payable on the estate of a deceased person accruing in respect of disposal of an asset by that estate for the purpose of paying the estate tax of a person who died before 1 November 1991.

(4) A gain accruing to an individual who is a citizen or a permanent resident in respect of the disposal of one private residence.

(5) A gain accruing to a wife who is a citizen or a permanent resident but whose husband is neither a citizen nor a perma-

nent resident, in respect of the disposal of one private residence owned by the wife.

(6) A gift to the government, State government, local authority or approved charity.

(7) A gain arising on the disposal as a result of a compulsory acquisition of property under the law.

INDIVIDUAL TAX COMPUTATION

Year of Assessment 1997

Assumptions

Resident employee, married with two children; wife does not
have any income during the year.

Tax computation

		RM
Employment income:		
Salary		200,000
Benefits-in-kind		20,000
Value of living accommodation (30% of RM200,000 or actual value of accommodation—RM72,000—whichever is lower)		60,000
		280,000
Interest*		
Dividend (tax deemed deducted RM3,000)		10,000
Total gross income		290,000
Less: Approved donations		10,000
		280,000

	RM	
Less: Personal relief		
Self	5,000	
Wife	3,000	
Child (over 18 and attending local university—4x)	3,200	
Child (below 18)	800	
Life insurance premiums and provident fund contributions (maximum)	5,000	
		17,000
Taxable income		263,000

	RM		
Income tax on first	150,000		31,250
Income tax on balance	113,000	@ 30%	33,900
	263,000		65,150
Less: Tax deemed deducted at source			3,000
Tax payable			62,150

* Interest received from banks and financial institutions is subject to a
  withholding tax of 5%. As this is a final tax, no further tax is payable.

Household furnishing, equipment and appliances

Semi-furnished with furniture in the lounge, dining room or bedrooms	RM50 per month

Semi-furnished with furniture plus one or more of the following:
    air conditioners
    curtains
    carpets   RM100 per month

Fully-furnished with furniture plus one or more of the following:
    kitchen equipment
    crockery
    utensils
    appliances   RM200 per month

Car benefits

Cost of car (when new)		Annual value of private usage	Fuel per annum
RM	RM	RM	RM
Up to -	40,000	1,200	600
40,001 -	75,000	2,400	900
75,001 -	100,000	3,600	1,200
100,001 -	150,000	4,800	1,500
150,001 -	200,000	6,000	1,800
200,001 -	250,000	7,800	2,100
250,001	and above	9,600	2,400

Where the car provided is more than five years old, the taxable benefit is halved but the value of fuel provided remains unchanged.

The value of driver provided is fixed at RM50 per month.

Where an employee feels that the prescribed rates are excessive, the annual value may be computed as follows:

$$\frac{\text{Cost of car}}{8\,\text{years}} \times 80\%$$

173

	RM
Self	5,000
Self-disabled person	10,000
Wife	3,000
Wife-disabled person	5,500
Each child (maximum of five)	800
Physically/mentally handicapped child	5,000
Parents' medical expenses (maximum)	5,000
Cost of disability support equipment (maximum)	5,000
Alimony to former wife	3,000
Life insurance premiums and Employees' Provident Fund contributions (maximum)	5,000
Fees expended for approved courses in Malaysia (maximum)	2,000
Insurance for education or medical benefits (maximum)	2,000
Medical expenses for self, spouse or child for treatment of serious illness (maximum)	5,000

CHAPTER 8

CUSTOMS (INDIRECT TAXES)
by Boon Oon Seang

ADMINISTRATION

Most indirect taxes, namely customs duties, excise duties, sales tax, service tax and goods vehicle levying, are administered by the Royal Customs and Excise Department, which is headed by the Director-General of Customs who has supervision of all matters relating to customs subject to the direction and control of the Minister of Finance. For the efficient administration of the various indirect tax laws, customs offices are set up in major towns in the States of Malaysia with a work-force of about 10,000.

CUSTOMS DUTIES

Customs Act 1967

The Customs Act 1967 is an Act relating to all customs matters, ie the levy and collection of customs duty, the prohibition of import and export of certain commodities (for economic, social and political reasons) and facilitation of industrial development by way of exemption.

The Act empowers the Minister by Order to fix and publish in the *Gazette* the rate of customs duty levied on goods imported into or exported from Malaysia. The rates can be found in the Customs Duties Order 1988.

The goods are classified by a coding system, the Harmonised Commodity Description and Coding System, commonly referred to as the 'Harmonised System' (HS). It is a system agreed upon at the International Convention on the Harmonised Commodity Description and Coding System in 1983. Malaysia is a signatory to this Convention and adopted the system in 1988. As a result, the first six digits of any goods to be classified by all countries adopting the HS should be the same.

Importation of goods is generally subject to customs duty. Customs duty means:

> import duty, export duty, surtax, surcharge or cess imposed under the Act, countervailing duty or anti-dumping duty imposed by or under the Countervailing and Anti-Dumping Duties Act 1993, and includes royalty payable in lieu of export duty under any written law, contract, lease or agreement to which the Federal Government or the Government of any State is a party or to which such Government has consented.

Customs duty in Malaysia is generally imposed for revenue purposes, and in some cases import duty rates are such that they are used to protect deserving local industries. Several factors are taken into consideration before protection is given, such as the industry's ability to produce a major portion of the goods which are of acceptable quality and price, and the degree of local added value. Most of the import duty levied is on an ad valorem basis and the rate ranges from 2% to 60%, with the exception of motor vehicles where the rate ranges from 140% to 200%. However, beer and spirits are still levied at a specific rate: beer at RM74 per decalitre, and brandy at RM489 per decalitre.

IMPORT DUTY

Value

For the purpose of levying import duty, under the Act 'value':

> in relation to imported goods means the price which an importer would give for the goods on a purchase in the open market if the goods were delivered to him at the place of payment of customs duty and if freight, insurance, commission and all other costs, charges and expenses (except any customs duties) incidental to the purchase and delivery at such place had been paid.

From the definition it is obvious that customs authorities adopt the notional concept to arrive at the value for levying import duty. Simply put, the value for import duty purposes is the arm's length price between two independent persons.

Machinery and Equipment

Machinery and equipment which are not produced locally are generally not subject to import duty or sales tax. If they are dutiable or taxable and are directly used to manufacture a product, exemption can be obtained subject to certain conditions and criteria being fulfilled.

Raw Materials

Exemption from import duty can be granted for raw materials and components used in the manufacturing process, but the level of exemption given depends largely on whether the finished products are for export or are for sale in the domestic market.

(a) Manufacture of goods for export: Full exemption is given if the raw materials are not manufactured locally or, if they are manufactured locally, they are not of acceptable quality and price.

(b) Manufacture of goods for the domestic market: Exemption of import duty can be considered if the manufacturing company has complied with the equity conditions stipulated in the manufacturing licence issued under the Industrial Coordination Act 1975 or if it has been granted an extension of time to comply with the equity conditions.

Full exemption is normally given if the raw materials are not manufactured locally and the finished goods made from dutiable raw materials and components are not subject to import duty.

In all other cases, partial exemption is given, and manufacturers are required to pay only 2% or 3% import duty. However, if the raw material is subject to a rate of import duty of 2% or 3%, no exemption will be given.

Drawback on Import Duty on Raw Materials, Components and Packaging Materials by a Manufacturer

If, for some reason, an exemption is not obtained for raw materials, components and packaging materials used in the manufacture of finished goods for export, a full drawback of import duty may be given to the manufacturer when the finished goods are exported, subject to the following conditions:

(a) The finished goods for export are manufactured in the premises approved by the Director-General.
(b) The manufacturer keeps such books and accounts as required by the Director-General for the purpose of checking and accountability.

Licensed Manufacturing Warehouse

Basically, the purpose of setting up Licensed Manufacturing Warehouses is to encourage export-oriented industries to be set up in rural areas. Manufacturing operations in a Licensed Manufacturing Warehouse will only be subject to minimal customs procedures. Equipment and machinery used in the manufacturing process may be taken into the premises without payment of duties and taxes.

Raw materials and components for use in the manufacturing process are entitled to the same treatment. As stated earlier, the objective of setting up Licensed Manufacturing Warehouses is to encourage export-oriented industries. However, permission may be obtained from the authorities to sell a percentage (normally not more than 20%) of the finished goods domestically. Payment of whatever customs duty and sales tax are leviable has to be made before the goods can be released for the domestic market.

Any dutiable waste or refuse resulting from the manufacturing process may be destroyed with the approval and supervision of the customs authorities. The customs duty payable will be remitted automatically. However, if the dutiable waste or refuse is sold, customs duty must be paid before removal of the goods from the licensed premises.

Prohibition of Imports and Exports

For economic, social and political reasons, certain classes of goods may be prohibited on import or export. Some may be totally, while others are conditionally, prohibited. It is possible to import and export goods which are conditionally prohibited, provided permission from the relevant authorities is obtained. This permission is usually in the form of an import or export licence.

Refunds

The Act empowers the Director-General of Customs to give a refund for overpayment or erroneous payment of customs duty, if the claim is made within one year from the date of overpayment or erroneous payment. The Minister, however, is not restricted in time and can order a refund to be given in part or in full, subject to certain conditions.

Appeals

Any person who is aggrieved by the decision of the Director-General on any matter can appeal to the Minister of Finance, whose decision is final. Where it is provided in the Act that the matter rests specifically at the absolute discretion of the Director-General, then the decision of the Director-General is final and there is no avenue of appeal to the Minister.

EXCISE DUTIES

Excise Act 1976

The collection of excise duty is governed by the Excise Act 1976 which is the main law. There are no less than nine pieces of subsidiary legislation enacted under this Act. The subsidiary legislation mainly involves the licensing provisions under the Act; for example, any person who intends to sell liquor by wholesale or retail is required to obtain a licence. The Director-General of Customs has supervision of all matters relating to excise, subject to the control of the Minister of Finance.

Scope of Tax

Excise duty is levied on domestically manufactured goods which are gazetted under the Excise Duties (Order) 1991, as follows:

- aerated and non-aerated beverages
- beer and stout
- intoxicating liquor
- cigarettes, tobacco
- petroleum products
- air-conditioning machines, refrigerators and freezers
- televisions
- motor vehicles
- playing cards and mahjong tiles

Rate of Tax

The rate of tax varies. It can either be specific or ad valorem or both. The specific rate varies from 3 sen per litre to RM37 per decalitre and, at ad valorem, it ranges from 4% to 65%.

Licensing

Before any person is permitted to manufacture goods that are subject to excise duty, a licence in a prescribed form must be applied for (s 20). A licence will then be issued by the Director-General. Depending on the goods to be manufactured, a fee, which can be found in the Third Schedule of the Excise Regulation 1977, must be paid. The licence is renewable annually.

It is also possible for a person other than a licensed manufacturer to obtain a warehouse licence (s 25) to keep 'dutiable goods', ie goods subject to payment of excise duty and on which duty has not been paid. However, if a licence has been obtained under s 20, there is no need to apply for a licence under s 25 of the Act.

Payment of Duty

Generally, no goods can be released from the licensed premises unless excise duty has been paid. However, goods on which duty has not been paid can be moved from one licensed premises to another, subject to certain conditions being complied with. Relevant forms must be completed, and submitted to the customs authorities.

Value

Under the Act, 'value' is defined as the price which a buyer would give for the goods in the open market at the time when duty is payable, but will exclude any excise duty, costs, charges and expenses of transportation and storage immediately after removal from the place of manufacture. It is clear that a notional concept is used to determine the value for the purpose of levying excise duty, which, simply put, is an arm's length price.

Refunds

The Act empowers the Director-General of Customs to give refunds for overpayment or erroneous payment of excise duty or other moneys if the claim is made within one year from the date of overpayment or erroneous payment. The Minister, however, is not restricted by time and can direct that a refund be given in full or in part of any excise duty paid.

Exports

Dutiable goods, when exported, are not subject to excise duty. A claim for drawback is allowed for goods which are exported as components of other goods, manufactured in the country, on which excise duty has been paid.

Appeals

Under the provisions of the Act, any person aggrieved by a decision of an excise officer can appeal to the Director-General of Customs. A further appeal can be made to the Minister within 30 days of being notified of the decision, and this decision is final.

SALES TAX

Sales Tax Act 1972

Sales tax in Malaysia was introduced in 1972 by the Sales Tax Act 1972. This tax is a single-stage tax levied at the manufacturer's level on taxable goods manufactured, and at the importer's level on taxable goods imported for home consumption. In order to maintain the single-stage tax concept, a manufacturer of taxable goods is allowed to acquire his raw materials and components used in the manufacture of the finished goods free from sales tax, which will only be paid when the finished goods are sold or disposed of. As the tax is only levied at the manufacturer's level, there will not be any more imposition of tax at the wholesaler's and retailer's level. To maintain equity, sales tax is also imposed on similar goods imported into the country for home consumption.

Scope of Tax

The tax only covers taxable goods either manufactured in or imported into the country. 'Taxable goods' are defined in the Act as 'goods of a class or kind not for the time being exempted from sales tax'. The Act defines 'goods' as 'all kinds of movable property'.

Rate of Tax

At present there are three rates of sales tax. The general rate is 10%, luxury goods such as liquor and cigarettes carry a rate of 15%, and semi-processed goods a rate of 5%.

Licensing

Any person who manufactures taxable goods is required to apply for a licence under the Act. Once the person is a licensed manufacturer (taxable person), he will be able to acquire all raw materials and components used in the manufacturing of finished goods free from sales tax. The licence is issued free of charge. Any manufacturer of taxable goods whose annual turnover is less than RM100,000 is exempted from licensing. The exemption is not automatic. It must be applied for and is renewable annually.

Acquisition of Tax-Free Raw Materials and Components Used in the Manufacturing Process

At present there are three methods whereby a licensed manufacturer can acquire tax-free raw materials and components for use in the manufacturing process of his finished goods.

Ring system

Under this system, also referred to as the Suspension System, the payment of tax is suspended. A licensed manufacturer is able to acquire, free from tax, for use in the manufacturing process, taxable raw materials and components from other licensed manufacturers, or to import them free of tax, provided prior approval from the customs authorities has been obtained. Approval is obtained by using the prescribed form, Sales Tax No 5 (ST No 5).

Refund system

By this method, a licensed manufacturer who possesses an ST No 5 is able to buy from a vendor, without sales tax, raw materials and components on which sales tax has already been paid. The vendor can then make a claim from the customs authorities for refund of sales tax paid by submitting the claim in the prescribed form, JKED 2.

Credit system

This system is mainly used by licensed manufacturers who, for one reason or another, are not able to use the ring system or refund system to obtain their tax-free components. Under this system, licensed manufacturers can deduct from the total sales tax payable a sum of tax equivalent to either $\frac{1}{25}$, $\frac{1}{13}$ or $\frac{1}{9}$ of the total value of the raw materials and components purchased, depending on the rate of tax applicable.

Payment of Tax; Taxable Period

Every licensed manufacturer is required to charge and levy sales tax on taxable goods sold or disposed of otherwise than by sale. The sales tax payable must be remitted to the customs authorities within 28 days of the expiration of the taxable period, irrespective of whether the sales tax has been collected. If the sales tax is not remitted to the customs authorities within the stipulated time, a mandatory penalty of 10% will be imposed on the outstanding sum. If the sum remains unpaid, the penalty will be increased by a further 2% for every succeeding period of 30 days or part thereof, subject to a maximum of 50% for as long as the sales tax remains unpaid.

A 'taxable period' is defined as 'two calendar months', and would, therefore, depend on when a person is registered as a licensed manufacturer.

Sale Value

Unlike the Customs Act 1967 and the Excise Act 1976, where 'value' is defined, the Sales Tax Act 1972 does not define 'value', but provides for the 'determination of value'. Basically, 'value' for charging and levying sales tax is:

(a) in the case of goods sold by a taxable person to a person independent of him, the price for which the goods are actually sold (positive concept); and

(b) in the case of goods sold otherwise by a taxable person, the price at which such goods would have been sold, if they had been sold in the ordinary course of business to a person independent of the taxable person (notional concept).

However, in the case of goods imported for home consumption, it is the sum total of the value of such goods for the purpose of customs duty and the amount of customs duty, if any, payable on such goods.

Export

All taxable goods manufactured locally and exported are exempt from sales tax. This is provided for in the sales tax legislation. Furthermore, subject to certain conditions, a full drawback of sales tax paid in respect of goods (raw material, components or finished goods) exported is also allowed under the Act.

Refunds

The Act empowers the Director-General of Customs to give refunds for overpayment or erroneous payment of sales tax, if the claim is made within one year from the date of overpayment or erroneous payment. The Minister, however, is not restricted by time and can order a refund to be given in part or in full, subject to certain conditions.

Appeals

If any person is aggrieved by a decision of a sales tax officer, appeal can be made to the Director-General of Customs. A further appeal can be made to the Minister of Finance if the person is still aggrieved by the decision of the Director-General, provided the appeal is lodged within 30 days from the date of notification of the Director-General's decision. The Minister's decision is final and not subject to review in any court.

SERVICE TAX

Service Tax Act 1975

Service tax was introduced in Malaysia in 1975. The tax, when it was first introduced, was a simple tax, meant only to cover certain services and goods provided at the retail stage. Being a consumption tax, it is revenue oriented. With the passing of time it has become complex, professional services being brought within its ambit.

Scope of Tax

Basically, the tax is levied and charged on prescribed services provided in or by prescribed establishments, or professional prescribed establishments, and prescribed goods sold or provided by prescribed establishments. The scope does not extend to exported taxable service, provided the service supplied is not in connection with goods or land situated in Malaysia and the person is not in Malaysia at the time the service is performed.

Licensing, Taxable Person

Any person who carries on the business of providing prescribed services (taxable services) by or in any prescribed establishment, or any prescribed professional establishment, must apply for a licence to carry on the business. Likewise any person who sells or provides goods (taxable goods) either in or by a prescribed establishment will have to apply for a licence to carry on the business. The person referred to above is a taxable person, and includes an individual, a firm, an association of persons, a company and every other juridical person. There is no fee charged for the licence.

Prescribed Establishment, Professional Establishment, Services and Goods

A complete list of prescribed establishments, prescribed professional establishments, prescribed services and prescribed goods can be found in the Second Schedule of the Service Tax Regulation 1975, as follows:

Prescribed establishment

(1) Hotels, excluding
(a)   Hotels having not more than 25 rooms;
(b)   Hostels for pupils or students of educational institutions;
(c)   Hostels established and run or maintained by religious institutions or bodies.

(2) Restaurants, bars, snack bars and coffee houses located in hotels.

(3) Restaurants, bars, snack bars and coffee houses located outside hotels, but excluding restaurants, bars, snack bars and coffee houses

186

located outside hotels and having an annual sales turnover of less than RM500,000 of prescribed goods and prescribed services.

(4) Private clubs, excluding private clubs having an annual sales turnover of less than RM500,000 of prescribed goods and prescribed services.

(5) Nightclubs, dance halls and cabarets.

(6) Health centres and massage parlours which are approved by the appropriate local authorities or which are lawfully registered and, where applicable, which are approved by the appropriate local authorities and lawfully registered.

(7) All places licensed under s 35(1)(a) and (b) of the Excise Act 1976 as 1st Class Public House and 1st Class Beer House Licences.

(8) Motor vehicle service and or repair centres, excluding motor vehicle service and or repair centres having an annual sales turnover of less than RM150,000 of prescribed services.

Prescribed professional establishment

(1) Establishments of public accountants who are registered under the relevant laws for the time being in force, excluding public accountants having an annual sales turnover of less than RM300,000 of prescribed services.

(2) Establishments of advocates and solicitors who have practising certificates under the relevant laws for the time being in force, excluding advocates and solicitors having an annual sales turnover of less than RM300,000 of prescribed services.

(3) Establishments of professional engineers who are registered under the relevant laws for the time being in force, excluding professional engineers having an annual sales turnover of less than RM300,000 of prescribed services.

(4) Establishments of architects who are registered under the relevant laws for the time being in force, excluding architects having an annual sales turnover of less than RM300,000 of prescribed services.

(5) Establishments of licensed or registered surveyors including registered valuers, appraisers and estate agents, who are licensed or registered under the relevant laws for the time being in force, excluding licensed or registered surveyors including registered valuers, appraisers and estate agents having an annual sales turnover of less than RM300,000 of prescribed services.

(6) Establishments of forwarding agents given permission under the Customs Act 1967, excluding forwarding agents having an annual sales turnover of less than RM150,000 of prescribed services.

(7) Insurance companies registered under the relevant laws for the time being in force.

(8) Companies, firms, sole-proprietors, government and semi-government agencies, dealing in or providing advertising services excluding companies, firms, sole-proprietors, government and semi-government agencies, dealing in or providing advertising services and having an annual sales turnover of less than RM500,000 of prescribed services.

(9) Companies, firms and sole-proprietors providing consultancy services, excluding companies, firms and sole-proprietors providing consultancy services and having an annual sales turnover of less than RM300,000 of prescribed services.

(10) Private hospitals licensed under the Private Hospitals Act 1971, excluding private hospitals having an annual sales turnover of less than RM300,000 of prescribed services.

(11) Companies, firms and sole-proprietors, dealing in or providing telecommunication services.

(12) Private agencies licensed under the Private Agency Act 1971, excluding private agencies having an annual sales turnover of less than RM300,000 of prescribed services.

(13) Private veterinary clinics, excluding veterinary clinics having an annual sales turnover of less than RM300,000 of prescribed services.

(14) Companies, firms, sole-proprietors, government and semi-government agencies operating or providing parking space for motor vehicles, excluding companies, firms, sole-proprietors, government and semi-government agencies operating or providing parking space for motor vehicles and having an annual sales turnover of less than RM150,000 of prescribed services.

(15) Companies, firms and sole-proprietors providing courier services, excluding companies, firms and sole-proprietors having an annual sales turnover of less than RM150,000 of prescribed services.

Prescribed services

(1) Provision of rooms for lodging or sleeping accommodation.

(2) Provision of premises for meetings or for promotion of cultural or fashion shows, on an ad hoc basis.

(3) Provision of health services which are normally provided by health centres.

(4) Provision of massages, excluding massages provided in barber shops, hairdressing salons and beauty salons.

(5) Provision of dancing partners, social escorts and services on which cover charges are imposed.

(6) Provision of services in the form of 'corkage', 'towel charge' and 'cover charge'.

(7) Provision of all advertising services.

(8) Provision of hospitalisation services, including medical and health care services, consultancy and other services normally provided by private hospitals.

(9) Provision of general servicing, engine repair and tuning, changing, adjusting and fixing of parts, wheel balancing, wheel alignment, body repair including knocking, welding and repainting, of motor vehicles.

(10) Provision of all types of insurance policies to all business organisations.

(11) Provision of services for clearing of goods from customs control.

(12) Provision of accounting, auditing, bookkeeping, consultancy and other professional services normally provided by public accountants.

(13) Provision of legal services, including consultancy service on legal matters.

(14) Provision of engineering, consultancy and other professional services normally provided by professional engineers.

(15) Provision of architectural services normally provided by architects, including professional consultancy services.

(16) Provision of all types of surveying services normally provided by surveyors, including valuation, appraisal, estate agency and professional consultancy services.

(17) Provision of all types of consultancy services.

(18) Provision of sports and recreational services by private clubs, including the entitlement to use such services by club members for which membership subscription fees are charged.

(19) Provision of telecommunication services in the form of telephone, facsimile, telemail, paging, cellular phone and telex by companies, firms and sole-proprietors dealing in or providing telecommunication services.

(20) Provision of guards and protection for the personal safety and security of another person or for the safety and security of the property or business of such other person by private agencies licensed under the Private Agency Act 1971.

(21) Provision of veterinary services normally provided by veterinary surgeons.

(22) Provision of parking space for motor vehicles where a charge is imposed.

(23) Provision of courier delivery services for documents and parcels not exceeding 30 kg each.

Prescribed goods

These are foods, drinks and tobacco sold, or provided by or in, prescribed establishments.

Rate of Tax

There is only one rate of service tax of 5% for both taxable goods and services.

Charge, Premium and Value

In the case of taxable services, the charge, premium or value on which service tax is payable is the charge levied or collected. If no charge or premium is levied or collected, then it is the charge or premium which would have been levied or collected in the normal course of business provided by a taxable person independent of him.

In the case of taxable goods, it is the actual price for which the goods are sold and if no charge is made, it is the charge in providing the goods in the ordinary course of business between the taxable person and a person independent of him.

Payment of Tax, Taxable Period

The service tax collected by a taxable person is required to be remitted to the customs authorities within 28 days of the expiration of each taxable period, which is two calendar months. This provision is similar to the provision under the Sales Tax Act 1972.

To a certain extent, service tax is different from sales tax in that it allows leeway in the payment of tax to the customs authorities, ie, payment of service tax need only be made to the customs authorities when payment is received for services rendered. However, if the payment is not received within 12 calendar months from the date of issue of the invoices, payment of tax will have to be made to the customs authorities on the due date of the next taxable period.

If the service tax is not remitted to the customs authorities within the stipulated time, a mandatory penalty of 10% is imposed on the outstanding sum up to a maximum of 50%. If the sum remains unpaid, the penalty will be increased by a further 2% for every succeeding period of 30 days or part thereof.

Refunds

The Act empowers the Director-General of Customs to give refunds for overpayment or erroneous payment of service duty or moneys, if the claim is made within one year from the date of overpayment or erroneous payment. The Minister, however, is not restricted by time and can direct a refund be given in full or in part of any service tax paid.

Appeals

The appeal provisions under the Service Tax Act 1975 are similar to those under the Sales Tax Act 1972.

FREE ZONES

Another Act involving the Customs Department in Malaysia is the Free Zones Act 1990.

The objective of the establishment of Free Zones under the Free Zones Act 1990 is to promote the economic growth of the country and for other related purposes. Free Zones are administered by an Authority, which can be a statutory body, or a company or department of the Government of Malaysia or any State of Malaysia, appointed by the Minister of Finance.

For all intents and purposes, Free Zones are considered to be places outside the country, as far as customs laws are concerned. In fact, they are created to cater for export-oriented industries. Being places outside the country, they are subject to minimal customs procedures. The Free Zones are divided into two distinct zones: (a) Free Industrial Zone—for manufacturing activities and any other activities approved by the Minister; (b) Free Commercial Zone—for trading, breaking bulk, labelling, repacking and consolidation.

Free Industrial Zones

The Free Industrial Zones are: Bayan Lepas Free Zone, Penang; Perai Free Zone, Seberang Perai; Jelepang Free Zone, Ipoh, Perak; Sg Way Free Zone, Petaling Jaya, Selangor; Ulu Kelang Free Zone, Wilayah Persekutuan; Teluk Panglima Garang Free Zone, Selangor; Batu Berendam Free Zone, Melaka; Tanjung Keling Free Zone, Melaka, and Pasir Gudang Free Zone, Johor.

Free Commercial Zones

The Free Commercial Zones are: Port Kelang Free Zone, Selangor; Bukit Kayu Hitam Free Zone, Kedah; Pengkalan Kubur Free Zone, Kelantan, and Pasir Gudang Free Zone, Johor (excluding trading).

Equipment and Machinery Used in the Manufacturing Process

Equipment and machinery used in the manufacturing process can be taken into a Free Industrial Zone without any payment of customs duty, excise duty, sales tax and service tax.

Raw Materials

All raw materials and components used in the manufacturing process can be taken into a Free Zones without payment of duties and taxes.

Eligibility for Location in a Free Industrial Zone

A manufacturer whose products are only for export can be considered to be located in a Free Industrial Zone. In exceptional circumstances, a manufacturer who only exports 80% of his products may be allowed to be located in a Free Zone. This can only be done with permission from the Minister of International Trade and Industry.

Goods Permitted into a Free Commercial Zone

Goods of any description can be taken into a Free Commercial Zone for retail trade, breaking bulk, consolidation, labelling or repacking without payment of customs duty, excise duty or sales tax.

Responsibility of an Operator in a Free Zone

A manufacturer and an operator in the Free Zone must keep records in the proper manner for:

- (a) all goods received in the premises;
- (b) all goods taken to any part of the Principal Customs Area from a Free Zone;
- (c) all goods released for consumption or sale, or manufactured within a Free Zone or for export;
- (d) waste, stocks and their manner of disposal;
- (e) loss through spillage, evaporation and other causes, and
- (f) the balance of all goods stocked at the place or premises where the activities are carried out.

Movement of Goods

Goods may be moved to and from a Free Zone, after obtaining permission from the relevant authorities using the prescribed form.

Finished Goods

Finished goods are normally exported but, with special permission from the relevant authorities, may be released into the country for home consumption. The goods are then subject to the same treatment as similar goods imported for home consumption under the Customs Act.

GOODS VEHICLE LEVY

The Goods Vehicle Levy Act, which came into force in 1983, is an Act to provide for the imposition of a levy on all goods vehicles leaving Malaysia.

Levy

The levy charged on goods vehicles leaving the country is RM100. This means that every goods vehicle leaving the country, whether laden or empty, will have to pay this amount to the customs authorities, unless exempted.

Exemption

The Minister may by order exempt certain goods vehicles from paying this levy. Examples are goods vehicles, whether fully laden or unladen, leaving Malaysia for Thailand, specified goods vehicles unladen entering Singapore for the purpose of returning fully laden with cement belonging to Kedah Cement Sendirian Berhad. The full exemption list can be found in the Goods Vehicles Levy (Exemption) Order 1983.

CHAPTER 9

INTELLECTUAL PROPERTY
by Dato' V L Kandan

INTRODUCTION

Intellectual property law is essentially that branch of law that attempts to safeguard the rights of creators and other originators of intellectual property.

In Malaysia intellectual property is protected largely through statute. Statute law has traditionally followed English law so that English case law, although not binding, has much persuasive weight in Malaysian courts. The following are the statutes that presently govern the respective intellectual property rights in Malaysia:

(1) The Patents Act 1983, which came into force on 1 October 1986 and enabled patents to be registered directly in Malaysia. Prior to 1 October 1986, the only method of obtaining a patent in Malaysia was by first obtaining the grant of a United Kingdom patent or by obtaining a European patent designating the United Kingdom and then re-registering the United Kingdom or European patent in Malaysia.

(2) The United Kingdom Designs (Protection) Act 1949 by which a design registered in the United Kingdom enjoys like privileges and rights in Malaysia as though the Certificate of Registration granted in the United Kingdom has been issued with an extension to Malaysia. It is only in the case of registered designs that Malaysia is still dependent on United Kingdom laws for registration rights. The Industrial Designs Act 1996, which has been passed but not enforced as yet, provides for the registration of designs in Malaysia.

(3) The Trade Marks Act 1976 governs registered trade marks. Service marks are presently not registrable in Malaysia. The Trade Marks (Amendment) Act 1994, which is expected to come into force in 1997, provides for, inter alia, the registration of service marks.

(4) The Copyright Act 1987 as amended by the Copyright (Amendment) Act 1990 and the Copyright (Amendment) Act 1996 is the only law in Malaysia which governs copyright matters. It came into force on 1 December 1987 and expressly provides that no copyright shall subsist otherwise than by virtue of that Act.

There is also a body of law, non-statutory, but which can be classified as Malaysian common law (law established through judicial decisions) that gives protection against unfair trade practices generally, that recognises trade secrets and merchandising as property rights.

PATENTS

Patent law is designed to confer a monopoly on the creator of a novel invention. Monopoly and protection of the invention are secured by applying for and obtaining a Certificate of Registration of Patent from the Malaysian Patent Office, pursuant to the provisions of the Patents Act 1983.

Conditions of Patentability

An invention is patentable if it is new, involves an inventive step, and is industrially applicable, ie, solves a specific technological problem. The invention may be, or may relate to, a product or process, and is new if it is not anticipated by prior art, which basically consists of everything disclosed to the public in the world, by written publication, oral disclosure, or by use or in any other way, prior to the filing date.

The requirement of an 'inventive step' is intended to avoid obvious extensions to known products or processes. It must be a step which would not be obvious to a person having ordinary skill in the art, taking into consideration any matter which forms part of the prior art. As to industrial applicability, it is considered as such if it can be made or used in any kind of industry.

An invention is not patentable if it is any of the following:

(a) discoveries, scientific theories and mathematical methods;
(b) plant or animal varieties or essentially biological processes for the production of plants or animals, other than man-made living micro-organisms, micro-biological processes and the products of such micro-biological processes;
(c) schemes, rules or methods of doing business, performing purely mental acts or playing games;
(d) methods for the treatment of human or animal body by surgery or therapy, and diagnostic methods practised on the human or animal body, although products used in any such methods would be patentable.

Grant of Patent and Duration

The grant of a patent gives to the owner the exclusive rights to exploit, assign or transmit, and conclude licence contracts in relation to the patent. Exploitation of a patented invention means the making, importing, offering for sale, or sale of the invented product, or of the product obtained directly by means of the invented process. Performance of any of the acts within the exclusive rights of the patent owner without consent, during the subsistence of the patent, is an infringement.

A patent expires 15 years after the date of its grant, provided that, where a patentee intends, at the expiration of the second year from the date of grant of the patent, to keep the same in force, he must pay the prescribed annual fees 12 months before the date of expiration of the second and each succeeding year during the term of the patent.

Prior to the coming into force of the 1983 Act (on 1 October 1986), grant of a patent was first obtained in the United Kingdom or from the European Patent Office designating the United Kingdom and then re-registering the same in Malaysia. Such prior certificates of registration of patent issued remain in force under the 1983 Act as long as the original patent remains in force in the United Kingdom or until the expiration of 20 years from the date of application, whichever is the earlier.

Utility Innovations (Utility Model)

'Utility innovation' means any innovation which creates a new product or process, or any new improvement of a known product or process, which can be made or used in any kind of industry, and includes an invention.

For a certificate for utility innovation to be granted, absolute novelty is required as in an application for grant of patent. Thus, the novelty required is on a world-wide basis and is new if it has not been disclosed anywhere in the world. Nevertheless, by the definition in the 1983 Act of 'utility innovation' as given above, the requirement of inventive step is relatively low and more easily satisfied compared to that required for a grant of patent.

The definition of utility innovation also includes an invention and this allows for the conversion of a utility innovation application to a patent application, and vice versa, during the course of prosecuting the application. From the Examination and Search Report issued by the Examiner of the Patents Registry, applicants would be able to evaluate their chances of obtaining a grant depending on the novelty and inventive step requirements in either category of patent or utility innovation.

A certificate of utility innovation granted has a term of five years. Provided that the proprietor of the utility innovation certificate can show to the satisfaction of the Patent Office that the utility innovation is still in commercial or industrial use in Malaysia, the certificate can be extended for two further consecutive five-year terms, thus giving a total 15 years of possible protection from the date of grant.

Assignment and Transmission

Patents, utility innovation certificates and their respective applications may be assigned or transmitted.

Joint owners of a patent application or patent may, separately, assign or transmit their right in the patent application or patent, exploit the patented invention and take action against any person, unless there is an agreement to the contrary. However, the withdrawal of a patent application and the surrender of patent may only be effected jointly.

Any person entitled by assignment or transmission to a patent application or patent should apply to have such assignment or transmission recorded in the Register. Unless so recorded, the assignment or transmission has no effect against third parties.

Licence Contracts

A licence contract is any contract whereby the owner of the patent grants to another person the licence to exploit the patented invention. No special form of words is required for the grant of a licence, but a licence contract should be in writing and signed by or on behalf of the contracting parties.

The licensor cannot impose upon the licensee restrictions not derived from its rights to exploit the patented invention, or that are unnecessary for the safeguarding of such rights, by way of any clause or condition in the licence contract. Such clause or condition is invalid in so far as it has that effect.

Compulsory Licences

If after three years from the date of the grant of a patent there is no apparent exploitation of the patent without legitimate reason, or if the product produced under the patent for sale in Malaysia is sold at an unreasonably high price or does not meet public demand without any legitimate reason, any person may apply to the Registrar for a compulsory licence to exploit the said patent.

Infringement

The patent owner may institute civil proceedings against anyone who has infringed or is infringing the patent or who has performed acts which make it likely that an infringement of the patent will occur. However, no action can be taken after five years from the date of the infringing act. The plaintiff patentee must prove infringement or imminent infringement, as the case may be, and may be aided by the process of interrogatories or by obtaining an order for inspection and seizure. Where appropriate, an Anton Piller order or a pre-writ discovery order for seizure of infringing products may be applied for in the High Court.

Any beneficiary of a compulsory licence and any licensee, where the licence contract does not otherwise provide, may request the owner to institute proceedings for infringement. The beneficiary or the licensee may institute proceedings in his own name if he can prove that the owner refused or failed to file action within three months from the date of receipt of the request. The owner must, however, be given notice first and has the right to join in the proceedings. In cases of urgency, the appropriate reliefs may be applied for from the High Court by licensees, even though the three-month period has not lapsed. The forms of relief available in a patent infringement suit are:

(a) a declaration that the subject patent is valid and has been infringed;

(b) an injunction to restrain further infringement of the patent, or to prevent infringement if imminent infringement is proved;

(c) an order for delivery up for destruction upon oath of any patented product in relation to which the patent is infringed or an article to which the product is inextricably comprised;

(d) an inquiry as to damages, or alternatively, an account of profits;

(e) costs.

(c) The finished goods are re-exported within 12 months of the date upon which the import duty was paid or such further period as the Director-General may approve.

(d) Written notice is made on the export declaration that a claim for drawback will be made, and such claim is made in a prescribed form and established to the satisfaction of a senior officer of customs within six months of the date of re-export or such further period as the Director-General may approve.

In determining the amount of drawback of import duties paid, the Director-General may also allow drawback on wastage or refuse resulting from the manufacturing process, whether re-exported or otherwise.

For the purpose of using the drawback facility, a 'manufacturer' includes any person to whom manufactured goods have been sold or otherwise disposed of. However, the claim for drawback has to be made through the manufacturer.

EXPORT DUTY

For obvious reasons, generally there is no export duty on goods manufactured in the country. Export duty is levied on exported commodities for revenue purposes. Some of the commodities which attract export duty are petroleum oil (crude), rattan, palm oil, rubber stumps and rubber seedlings.

Free Zones, Labuan and Langkawi

Certain areas in Malaysia, for the purpose of collection of customs duty, are gazetted to be outside the country. They are the Free Zones, the islands of Labuan and Langkawi. Simply put, goods sent to these places are regarded as exports and goods entering these places are not subject to any customs duty.

Bonded Warehouse

The Act provides for goods to be stored in a 'bonded warehouse' without payment of import duty. Import duty is only payable when the goods are released from the customs control for home consumption. The bonded warehouse can be public or private. As the name suggests, a public warehouse is open for everyone's use, while in a private bonded warehouse only dutiable goods belonging to the owner can be kept.

himself to be so described or held out as a patent agent without being registered commits an offence. The penalty is the same as for the offences referred to above.

Since 1 January 1989, Malaysia has been a member of the Paris Convention for the Protection of Industrial Property. The main significance of such membership is that applicants can claim priority based on a patent application filed elsewhere in a Convention country. For example, an application subsequently filed in Malaysia can claim the same filing date as the first application filed in a Convention State, provided the claim is made within the specified period of 12 months from the date of first filing in the Convention country.

REGISTERED DESIGNS

The aim of industrial design law is to protect industrially exploited designs as opposed to inventions. At present, the proprietor registers his design in the United Kingdom to obtain protection in Malaysia. Any design registered in the United Kingdom is protected and enjoys like privileges and rights as though the United Kingdom Certificate of Registration had been issued with an extension to West Malaysia, Sabah and Sarawak.

Conditions for Protection—Registrable Designs

To be registrable, a design must be original or novel, and must not be the same as any design which, before the date of application for registration, has been registered or published (used), or is different only in immaterial details or in features which are variants commonly used in trade. It is necessary that the design shows some new effect clearly distinguishable by the eye from what has gone on before. The eye test is the sole test of the existence of a difference between designs although, in judging the importance of that difference, other factors may properly be taken into account, for example, increased utility.

A design must also be registered in respect of an article, and applied to an article by any industrial process or means. However, the article must perform some function other than merely carrying the design. Registration will also not be granted for a method of construction in itself, although a design may, in some instances, incidentally protect a mode of manufacture. If the design seeking registration has the requisites of novelty and originality, it is no objection that it could also have been protected or is in fact protected by a grant of patent.

Features of shape or configuration which are dictated solely by the function which the article to be made in that shape or configuration has to perform are not registrable. Where an article is purely functional, so that it has no consumer eye appeal, the shape is not an industrial design and hence not registrable.

Disclosure and Similarity to Previous Designs

Broadly, there is publication if the design has been disclosed to the public as opposed to being kept secret. Publication may be by way of prior documents or by prior user. It is not necessary that the design should have been actually used, for there will equally be publication if it is shown that it was known to the public, without ever having been actually put in use. A relevant question would be: Has the public knowledge of the design?

There will also be publication if articles to which the design is applied are manufactured and used in such a way that members of the public may see them.

Registration and Duration of Protection

Registration of a design is as of the date on which the application for registration was made. The protection at first instance lasts for a period of five years but, by paying extension fees, protection can be kept in force for (a) 15 years, if the application was filed prior to 1 August 1989; or (b) 25 years, if the application was filed on or after 1 August 1989. The different periods of protection are a result of the change in the design registration laws of the United Kingdom effected in 1988.

Registration confers on the proprietor the exclusive right to make or import for sale or for use for the purposes of any trade or business, or to sell, hire, or offer for sale or hire, any article in respect of which the design is registered, and extends to articles to which a design not substantially different from the registered design has been applied.

By the extension of protection to designs which are not substantially different, the question arising in infringement proceedings will almost always be whether the design alleged to be infringing is substantially different from the one registered, unless the case involves one of direct copying. In determining such questions, the eye is the sole test.

Infringement

The doing of any acts within the exclusive rights of the proprietor without consent, while the United Kingdom Certificate of Registration is valid and subsisting, constitute an infringement. Action for infringement is brought in the High Court and may be brought only by the registered proprietor. Relief available consists of injunctions, both interlocutory and permanent, damages, order for delivery up and costs. In appropriate cases, a registered owner of an industrial design, who also claims copyright under the Copyright Act 1987, would additionally be able to sue for copyright infringement.

Innocent infringement

Although knowledge of the registration of a design is in general immaterial to proving infringement, the proprietor of a registered design will not be entitled to damages in an action against an infringer who is able to prove that, at the time of the infringement, he was not aware, nor had any reasonable means of making himself aware, of the existence of the registration of the design. Once infringement has been proved, the onus would be upon the infringer to prove his ignorance of the registration of the design. It is therefore advisable that the fact of registration of the design in the United Kingdom be advertised in the *Government Gazette* and/or the press soon after the issuance of the Certificate of Registration. Alternatively, articles bearing the registered design may be marked accordingly to indicate the fact of registration.

It is to be noted that the registered proprietor is only prevented from recovering damages against an innocent infringer. His rights in proceedings for an injunction or other relief are not in any way affected.

Cancellation of Registration

Any person interested may apply for cancellation of a design registered in Malaysia, applying under the Registered Designs Act 1949 (UK legislation) on grounds that the design was not, at the date of registration, new or original or on any grounds upon which the

Registrar could have refused to register the design. Conditions of registrability have been discussed above.

Upon the application of any person who alleges that his interests have been prejudicially affected, the (Malaysian) High Court has the power to declare pursuant to the United Kingdom Designs (Protection) Act 1949 (Malaysian legislation) that exclusive rights and privileges in a design have not been acquired in West Malaysia, Sabah or Sarawak under the provisions of the respective governing Acts on any of the grounds upon which the United Kingdom registration might be cancelled under the law for the time being in force in the United Kingdom.

It is to be noted that the powers conferred by the United Kingdom Designs (Protection) Act 1949 on the Malaysian courts are of a declaratory nature in respect of the exclusive privileges and rights of the registered proprietor in Malaysia. Thus, Malaysian courts have no jurisdiction to cancel registration of a design in the United Kingdom. Cancellation can only be made by filing proceedings in the United Kingdom.

TRADE MARKS

Trade marks are designed to indicate the origin of goods, and service marks are similarly used to denote the source of the service concerned. With use, promotion and planned advertising, a mark will usually acquire reputation and goodwill. Trade mark law is intended, therefore, to regulate the use of marks to prevent customers and purchasers being deceived and confused. In particular, it makes it unlawful to imitate a mark or trade badge of another with impunity to get the benefit and advantage of whatever goodwill is associated with it.

Trade mark law in Malaysia is governed by the Trade Marks Act 1976. However, the Act only deals with registered marks. Where a mark is unregistered, there can be no infringement under the Act and legal relief would have to be obtained by way of the common law tort of passing-off.

Criteria of Protectabiilty—Registration

To be registrable, a 'mark', which is defined under the 1976 Act as including a device, brand, heading, label, ticket, name, signature, word, letter, numeral or any combination thereof, must be used or proposed to be used in relation to the goods for the purpose of indicating a connection in the course of trade between the goods and the owner. As the use must be in relation to goods, a mark which is used in relation to services would not be registrable. However, registration of service marks will soon be allowed under amending provisions to the 1976 Act, expected to come into force in the very near future.

For a trade mark to be registrable, it must be distinctive and must contain or consist of at least one of the following essential particulars:

(a) the name of an individual, company or firm represented in a special or particular manner;

(b) the signature of the applicant for registration or of some predecessor in his business;

(c) an invented word or words;

(d) a word or words having no direct reference to the character or quality of the goods, not being, according to its ordinary meaning, a geographical name or surname; or

(e) any other distinctive mark.

The effect of the legislation is to enable certain classes of marks to be registered if they are distinctive. Any name, signature or word which does not come within any of (a) to (d) above will not be registrable unless it is shown to be distinctive. The presence of any one of the essential particulars is sufficient, each of them being treated as separate and distinct. But even where all the conditions of the 1976 Act are complied with, the Registrar has some discretion whether to allow or refuse registration.

Requirement of distinctiveness

'Distinctive' within the meaning of the 1976 Act means that the mark must distinguish, or at least be capable of distinguishing, one person's goods from similar goods of his competitors. Thus, the Registrar, in considering an application to register a mark, must consider both its aptitude to distinguish and also the extent to which it is shown by evidence, if any, to be distinctive.

Distinctiveness is established by showing evidence of use of the mark in relation to the goods, including use by way of advertising and promotional efforts, use in invoices issued, catalogues, brochures, pamphlets, shipping documents, on cartons, packagings and wrapping materials.

Broadly, the right to registration very much depends on whether other traders are likely, in the ordinary course of their business and without any improper motive, to desire to use the same mark or some mark nearly resembling it, on or in connection with their own goods. Thus, descriptive words or words which have a direct reference to the character or quality of the goods are rarely registrable as such unless there is evidence of distinctiveness in fact by way of use.

Certification Trade Marks

These are marks adopted in relation to any goods to distinguish in the course of trade certified by any person in respect of origin, material, mode of manufacture, quality, accuracy or other characteristics from goods not so certified. By virtue of their definition, certification trade marks do not indicate trade origin. The difference between these and other ordinary marks is perhaps most clearly illustrated by the requirement, in the case of ordinary marks, of use or intended use by the proprietor and the opposite requirement in the case of certification trade marks, of no trade in the relevant goods by the proprietor.

These marks are usually owned by trade associations or semi-public bodies having dealings with a particular trade. For example, 'SIRIM' or 'Malaysian Standard' are typical certification trade marks.

Defensive Trade Marks

Where a trade mark consisting of an invented word or words has become so well known as regards any goods in respect of which it is registered and used and where its use in relation to other goods would likely be taken as indicating a connection in the course of trade between those goods and a person entitled to use the mark in relation to the first-mentioned goods, the proprietor may apply to register the mark as a defensive mark, even though he does not use or propose to use the mark in relation to the other goods. All the rights and incidents of an ordinary registered trade mark apply equally except that it is not liable to be removed or limited on the grounds of non-use.

Disclaimers

The Registrar or the court, in deciding whether a trade mark should be entered or remain on the Register, may require, as a condition of its being on the Register, that the proprietor:

(a) disclaim any right to the exclusive use of any such part or matter contained in the trade mark;

(b) make such other disclaimer as the Registrar or the court may consider necessary for the purpose of defining his rights under the registration.

The effect of a disclaimer is that the registered proprietor cannot claim any trade mark rights under the 1976 Act in respect of the parts of the mark to which the disclaimer relates. No action for infringement can lie in respect of use or imitation by others of the disclaimed parts.

The effect, however, is solely limited to rights given by registration. It will therefore still be open for the registered proprietor to sue under common law for passing-off in respect of use or imitation by others of the disclaimed parts.

Instead of disclaimers, the Registrar or the court has powers to impose conditions upon which registration will be granted, usually in order to overcome some potential deceptiveness. Breach of such a condition is not an offence or unlawful but may lead to rectification or removal of the registration.

Restrictions on Registration

There are certain prohibitions against registration under the 1976 Act. Registration would be refused where the use of the mark applied for is likely to deceive or cause confusion to the public having regard to the use of an earlier mark, or where the mark applied for is identical to or so nearly resembling another trade mark belonging to a different owner and already registered in respect of the same goods. The provisions of the Act are not limited to cases where the mark concerned would be deceptive by reason of prior use by a trade rival. Any deceptiveness arising from the use of the mark may be objected to, for example, deceptiveness as to the character or quality of the goods. Of course, any marks which would be illegal under the laws of Malaysia would not be registrable.

Any mark having the capacity to cause, or in the nature of causing, an occasion of offence or which is grossly disgraceful would not be allowed registration. The same applies to marks which are hurtful, injurious, insulting or which cause general unpleasantness.

Registration and Effect of Registration

The date of application is taken to be the date of registration and not the actual date of entry in the Register. On registration, the Registrar shall issue a Certificate of Registration under seal to the applicant. In all legal proceedings relating to a registered trade mark, the fact that a person is registered as proprietor is prima facie evidence of the validity of the original registration of the trade mark and all subsequent assignments and transmissions thereof. This, of course, is open to be rebutted by evidence showing the contrary.

Registration is for an initial period of seven years. On payment of the prescribed fee, it can be renewed from time to time for further periods of 14 years. Amendments to the Trade Marks Act 1976, to come into force shortly, make the duration of protection for a registered trade mark 10 years initially, and renewable for periods of 10 years thereafter. This would render the period of protection of registered marks in Malaysia similar to that of many other countries and would to an extent, make it easier for proprietors who have trade marks registered in countries around the world to maintain their records. Thus, as long as the mark has not been removed from the Register, the proprietor has the right to its use for an indeterminate duration. A valid registration gives the proprietor the exclusive right to use the mark in relation to the goods registered. The registered proprietor also has power to assign the same and give good discharges for any consideration for the assignment.

Infringement

A registered trade mark is infringed by a person who uses a mark, without consent of the owner, which is identical to or so nearly resembling the registered mark as is likely to deceive or cause confusion, in the course of trade, in relation to goods in respect of which the trade mark is registered. The question to be addressed in determining if there is infringement is, thus, whether the mark used by the defendant so nearly resembles the plaintiff's mark or comprises some of its essential features as to be calculated to cause goods to be taken by purchasers for the goods of the plaintiff.

A comparative use of the plaintiff's registered mark is also an infringement, as it is thought unfair that a trader should be allowed to sell his wares by reference to a well-known brand even if he does so in a completely non-descriptive manner.

Registered User

A person other than the registered proprietor may be registered as user of a trade mark for all or any of the goods in respect of which the trade mark is registered. The use by a registered user in compliance with any conditions or restrictions to which his registration is subject is known as 'permitted use'. The permitted use by a registered user is deemed to be use by the registered proprietor for purposes of provisions relating to actions for removal of a registration on the grounds of non-use, and for any other purposes for which use by the registered proprietor is material under the 1976 Act or the common law.

The registered user is entitled to call upon the registered proprietor to take proceedings for infringement. If the registered proprietor refuses or neglects to do so within two months after being so called upon, the registered user may institute proceedings in his own name, as if he were the registered proprietor, and make the registered proprietor a defendant. Unless he enters an appearance and takes part in the proceedings, the proprietor so added as defendant is not liable for costs. This is, however, subject to any agreement subsisting between the registered user and the registered proprietor of the trade mark.

A registered user is not entitled to assign or transmit the right to use the trade mark.

Civil Remedies

Proceedings for infringement are brought in the High Court. The plaintiff normally makes an application for an interim injunction to restrain further acts of infringement until trial of the main action. In appropriate instances, usually clear-cut cases where the offending mark used is identical to the registered mark, an application for summary judgment may be made. This would circumvent the necessity of proceeding with trial of the matter and would obtain judgment for the plaintiff summarily, upon grounds that the defendant has no real defence to the plaintiff's claims.

A pre-writ discovery order, commonly known as an Anton Piller order, is also available where it can be shown by the plaintiff that the defendant, if given notice of the plaintiff's action in court, would appropriate or destroy the evidence upon which the plaintiff would be relying to prove his case. An Anton Piller order allows the plaintiff to enter into specified premises to search and seize identified articles, documents or goods.

Criminal Remedies

The registered or common law proprietor's rights in a trade mark or get-up may also be enforced by way of criminal prosecution under the Trade Descriptions Act 1972. Under the 1972 Act, it is an offence for any person, in the course of his trade or business, to (a) apply a false trade description to any goods; or (b) supply or offer to supply any goods to which a false trade description has been applied.

The offence is punishable by a fine not exceeding RM100,000 or imprisonment not exceeding three years, or both. In the case of a body corporate, the fine is RM250,000.

Application to goods of a trade mark or get-up not belonging to the owner of the goods could constitute a false trade description as it would imply that the goods were manufactured or produced, processed or reconditioned by the trade mark owner when in fact they were not. The trade mark or get-up must be affixed to the goods so that if the marks are possessed in isolation and not affixed to the goods no offence is committed.

The 1972 Act is enforced by the Enforcement Division of the Ministry of Domestic Trade and Consumer Affairs. Although, under the 1972 Act, enforcement officers are empowered on their own initiative to receive complaints and to raid and seize products to which false descriptions have been applied, they act more expeditiously upon the production of a Trade Description Order obtainable from the High Court, declaring that the infringing or offending mark or get-up, as the case may be, is, for the purposes of the 1972 Act, deemed to be a false trade description in its application to such goods as may be specified in the order.

For a Trade Description Order to be granted, however, the 1972 Act requires that, in the case of a registered trade mark, the proprietor's rights in respect of such a trade mark are being infringed in the course of trade within the meaning of the written law and, in the case of an unregistered mark, that the acts complained of have given rise to an action for passing-off.

A Trade Description Order expires at the end of five years from the date on which it is made unless renewed upon application for such further period of time and upon such terms as the court thinks fit.

COPYRIGHT

Essentially, copyright law is concerned with protecting the various expressions of an idea. It does not protect the idea itself. It follows, therefore, that before protection can be conferred, the work must have been written down, recorded or otherwise reduced to material form.

The only law which governs copyright matters in Malaysia is the Copyright Act 1987 which came into force on 1 December 1987. This Act was amended in 1990 and further amendments are under consideration. No copyright in Malaysia subsists otherwise than by virtue of the Act. To be eligible for copyright protection, there is no requirement for registration. However, certain criteria under the Act need to be satisfied.

Criteria for Copyright Protection

Originality

Only works which are original qualify for copyright protection, which means that sufficient effort must have been expended by the author to make or create the work, so that it can be properly regarded as the original product of the author. It must not, however, be thought that only works of a high literary, artistic or musical standard can be protected by copyright. Works eligible to be protected under the 1987 Act will be protected irrespective of their quality and the purpose for which they were created.

Works

As to the type of works which may form the subject matter of copyright protection, this is stipulated and defined by the Act. They are (a) literary works; (b) musical works; (c) artistic works; (d) films; (e) sound recordings; and (f) broadcasts.

The 1987 Act also provides that copyright subsists in every published edition of any one or more literary, artistic or musical works in the case of which either the first publication of the edition took place in Malaysia or if the publisher of the edition was a qualified person at the date of the first publication. Copyright does not, however, subsist in an edition which reproduces the typographical arrangement of a previous edition of the same work or works. The exclusive right given to the owner (the publisher of the edition) is the right to control the reproduction of the typographical arrangement of the edition.

Derivative works, namely translations, adaptations, arrangements and other transformations of works eligible for copyright and collections of works eligible for copyright which, by reason of the selection and arrangement of their contents, constitute intellectual creation, are also protected as original works.

Qualified person

A further criterion is that the author or creator of the work must be a 'qualified person' at the time when the work is made. A 'qualified person' is a citizen of, or a permanent resident in, Malaysia, or a body incorporated in and vested with legal personality under the laws of Malaysia.

On 1 October 1990, Malaysia acceded to the Berne Convention for the Protection of Literary and Artistic Works 1886. Copyright protection in Malaysia is therefore extended to works of member countries after the date of accession. Thus, 'qualified person' would also include a national or a person who has his permanent residence in one of the countries of the Berne Convention, or a body incorporated in and vested with legal personality under the laws of any one of the countries that is a member of the Convention.

First publication

If the author is not a 'qualified person' at the time when the work was made but the work, being a literary, musical or artistic work or film or sound recording was first published in Malaysia or first published elsewhere but published in Malaysia within 30 days of such publication elsewhere, then copyright subsists in Malaysia. Similarly, if a work was first published in a Berne Convention State or published in a member State within 30 days of its publication in a non-member country, the work would be eligible to claim copyright protection in Malaysia, assuming all the criteria for protection mentioned above have been met.

A work is considered to be published if it is made available or accessible to the public with the consent of the copyright owner, in a manner sufficient to satisfy the reasonable requirements of the public. The performance of a literary or musical work and the exhibition of an artistic work do not constitute publication of the work.

Ownership of Copyright

The 'author' of a work is the first owner of the copyright therein. 'Author' in relation to:

(a) literary works, means the writer or the maker of the works;

(b) musical works, means the composer;

(c) artistic works other than photographs, means the artist;

(d) photographs, means the person by whom the arrangements for the taking of the photographs were undertaken;

(e) films or sound recordings, means the person by whom the arrangements for the making of the film or recording were undertaken;

(f) broadcasts transmitted from within any country, means the person by whom the arrangements for the making of the transmissions from within that country were undertaken;

(g) in relation to any other cases, means the person by whom the work was made.

Prima facie, the name on a work purporting to be the name of its author is taken as such, until the contrary is proved. Similarly, in the case of an anonymous or pseudonymous work, the name of the publisher as indicated in the work is taken as the legal representative of the anonymous or pseudonymous author.

Where a work:

(a) is commissioned by a person who is not the author's employer under a contract of service or apprenticeship; or

(b) not having been so commissioned, is made in the course of the author's employment,

copyright is deemed to be transferred to the person who commissioned the work or the author's employer, subject to any agreement between the parties excluding or limiting such transfer.

Duration of Copyright

Literary, musical or artistic works

The general rule is that copyright in such works will expire 50 years from the end of the calendar year in which the author dies. If the work is of unknown authorship, the copyright period is 50 years from the end of the year in which the work was first published and, if the identity of the author later becomes known, the general rule will apply. Copyright in a published edition of such works will expire 50 years from the end of the calendar year in which the edition was first published.

Other works

Copyright subsisting in a sound recording, photograph, film, works of the government, government organisations and international bodies will all expire 50 years from the end of the calendar year in which the respective works were first published. Copyright in a broadcast will similarly expire 50 years from the end of the calendar year in which the broadcast was first made.

Rights Comprised in Copyright

The nature of copyright in a literary, musical or artistic work, a film or a sound recording is defined by the 1987 Act and gives to the copyright owner the exclusive right to control in Malaysia the following acts in relation to the work:

(a) reproduction in any material form;
(b) performance, showing or playing to the public;
(c) broadcasting;
(d) communication by cable; and
(e) distribution of copies of the work to the public by sale, rental, lease or lending.

It follows therefore that copyright will be infringed if any person does or causes any other person to do without the permission or consent of the copyright owner any of the acts enumerated above in relation to his work.

Remedies for Infringement

Infringement of copyright is actionable at the suit of the copyright owner, and all such relief, by way of damages, injunction, account or otherwise as is available in corresponding proceedings in respect of infringement of other proprietary rights is available. Further, the normal rights of discovery of information and inspection of documents, whether against the parties to the action or third parties, including an Anton Piller order are similarly available.

Interlocutory injunctive relief is usually sought by the plaintiff to obtain temporary protection against injury by continuing violation of his rights for which he cannot be adequately compensated in damages in the action. The plaintiff's needs are weighed against the corresponding needs of the defendant against injury from being prevented from exercising his legal rights and for which he may not be adequately compensated under the plaintiff's cross-undertaking in damages.

An affidavit or statutory declaration made by the proprietor of the copyright pursuant to the 1987 Act is prima facie proof of the existence of copyright in the work under litigation.

Exclusive licensee

Where an exclusive licence has been granted and is in force at the time of the events to which the proceedings relate, the exclusive licensee will have, except against the owner of the copyright, the same rights of action and remedies under the 1987 Act as if the licence had been an assignment. The licence must, however, be wholly exclusive.

Where the action is brought whether by the owner or the exclusive licensee and the action, whether wholly or partly, relates to an infringement in respect of which they have concurrent rights of action under the Act, the owner or the licensee, as the case may be, will not be entitled except with the leave of the court to proceed with the action unless the other party is either joined as plaintiff or added as a defendant.

Criminal Offences Under the 1987 Act

A person is guilty of an offence under the Act if, at a time when copyright subsists in a work, he:

(a)   makes for sale or hire;

(b)   sells, lets for hire or by way of trade, exposes or offers for sale or hire;

(c)   distributes;

(d)   possesses otherwise than for his private and domestic use;

(e)   by way of trade, exhibits in public;

(f)   imports into Malaysia otherwise than for his private and domestic use, any infringing copy of a work; or

(g)   makes or has in his possession any contrivance used or intended to be used for the purpose of making infringing copies.

It is to be noted that the distribution of any infringing copies of a work suffices for the commission of an offence and it is not necessary that he distributes for the purposes of trade or for any other purpose to an extent that it will affect prejudicially the owner of the copyright.

The Act also provides a presumption whereby, if it is established that the accused has in his possession, custody or control three or more infringing copies of a work in the same form, the court shall presume that the possession or importation of such copies is for purposes otherwise than for his private and domestic use. Where the accused has in his possession or has imported into Malaysia less than three infringing copies of a work, it must be further positively established that they were otherwise than for the private and domestic use of the accused. The possession or importation of a single infringing copy by way of trade would be an offence under the Act.

Where a person makes or has in his possession any contrivance used or intended to be used for the purpose of making infringing copies, he will be liable on conviction to a fine not exceeding RM20,000 for each contrivance or to imprisonment for a term not exceeding 10 years or to both and for any subsequent offence to a fine not exceeding RM40,000 for each contrivance or to imprisonment for a term not exceeding 20 years or to both.

In the case of any other acts constituting an offence under the Act as enumerated above, the penalty on conviction is a fine not exceeding RM10,000 for each infringing copy or imprisonment for a term not exceeding five years or both and, for any subsequent offence, a fine not exceeding RM 20,000 for each infringing copy or imprisonment for a term not exceeding 10 years or both.

Innocence is always a defence. If the accused is able to prove that he acted in good faith and had no reasonable grounds for supposing that copyright would or might thereby be infringed, he is not guilty.

216

Offences under the 1987 Act are seizable offences, which means that the offender can be arrested. Criminal action is initiated by lodging a report with the Controller of Copyright, who is part of the Enforcement Unit of the Domestic Trade and Consumer Affairs, or the police. The Assistant Controller or the police will raid the premises of the offender, take into custody the infringing material and file charges in court. Prosecution in court for an offence under the 1987 Act may be conducted by an Assistant Controller or a police officer not below the rank of Inspector.

TRADE SECRETS

The common law of trade secrets or breach of confidence is not covered by legislation in Malaysia. This area of the law is based largely upon a broad and developing equitable doctrine, that a person who has received information in confidence should not take unfair advantage of it or profit from the wrongful use or publication of it.

To be entitled to protection, the information which is sought to be protected must, first, be of a confidential nature or secret, ie, that which a person of ordinary honesty and intelligence would recognise to be the property of another and not his own to do as he likes with. Secondly, the information in question must have been communicated in circumstances importing an obligation of confidence, and thirdly, there must be, or about to be, an unauthorised disclosure or use of that information.

Where there is shown to be a breach, permanent and interlocutory injunctions may be granted. However, if an injunction is granted, it must identify the particular items of information that the person restrained is not to use or disclose, since otherwise the person restrained would be placed in the difficult and embarrassing position of not knowing what he would have to avoid using or disclosing to keep clear of contempt of court. The injunction granted may also be of limited duration, usually confined to the period during which the information retains its confidential character. Once the secret information has been made public, there is no ground for intervention by the court.

In addition, the court can also make an order for delivery up of material containing confidential information. This may be ordered as an alternative to destruction of such material on oath and is useful where a defendant has shown, by his past conduct, that his oath is not to be relied upon. A person to whom confidential documents and information have been disclosed in breach of confidence may be ordered to disclose the identity of his informant to the person entitled to the benefit of the information.

A practical problem in cases of this nature is that the plaintiff may have to disclose the essential features of his secret information in pleadings or in affidavits in support of an application for interim relief. Where necessary, the court may require the defendant to give an undertaking that he will make no use of the information disclosed, although the sufficiency of such protection for the plaintiff's confidentiality is questionable.

UNFAIR COMPETITION

Malaysia does not yet have specific legislation against unfair competition. There is a proposal to enact a competition law. Presently, the common law action for passing-off is still largely relied upon against unfair competition such as unfair use of a trade name, symbol or get-up.

The principle of law in an action for passing-off may be very plainly stated—that nobody has any right to represent his goods as the goods of somebody else whether by direct statements or by using some of the badges by which the goods of the plaintiff are known. It is essential for the plaintiff in a passing-off action to show at least the following facts:

(a) that his business consists of, or includes, selling in Malaysia a class of goods to which the particular trade name (mark, get-up) applies;

(b) that the class of goods is clearly defined, and that in the minds of the public, or a section of the public, in Malaysia, the trade name (mark, get-up) distinguishes that class from other similar goods;

(c) that because of the reputation of the goods, there is goodwill attached to the name;

(d) that he has suffered, or is really likely to suffer, substantial damage to his property in the goodwill by reason of the defendant's selling goods which are falsely described by the trade name, mark or get-up to which the goodwill is attached.

Relief available is similar to that in cases of infringement.

LITIGATION

Competent Court

The lowest court with jurisdiction over anti-counterfeiting matters is the Sessions Court. These courts normally hear criminal prosecutions under the Copyright Act 1987 and the Trade Descriptions Act 1972.

The next tier is the High Court which has original as well as appellate jurisdiction in respect of appeals from lower courts or from the respective Trade Mark or Patent Registrar. For example, a person dissatisfied with the decision of the Registrar in an application for rectification of the Trade Mark Register or in refusing the grant of a patent may appeal to the High Court. In civil matters, anti-counterfeiting actions originate from the High Court which has jurisdiction to grant injunctions, Anton Piller orders or pre-writ discovery orders, declaratory orders and damages.

In 1993, an additional tier was added to Malaysia's legal structure, in the form of the Court of Appeal. All appeals from the High Court now lie to the Court of Appeal. An appellant may appeal from the whole or part of a judgement or order and the Court of Appeal has all the powers and duties, as to amendment or otherwise, of the appropriate High Court, together with full discretionary power to receive further evidence by oral examination, by affidavit or by deposition taken before an examiner or Commissioner. Three judges preside over a hearing at the Court of Appeal.

The Federal Court is the final appellate court in the country and hears appeals from the Court of Appeal. A hearing is also presided over by three judges.

Foreign Plaintiff

There is no restriction on jurisdiction where the plaintiff is a foreign company or individual. However, where the plaintiff is located or residing wholly out of jurisdiction, the defendant is entitled to make an application to the court that the plaintiff give security for his costs. Should he succeed in the litigation, security is usually given in the form of a bank guarantee.

Gatt TRIPS Agreement

Malaysia has signed the World Trade Organisation Agreement of which the Agreement on Trade-Related Aspects of Intellectual

Property Rights (TRIPS) is a part. Minimal changes are required to the existing intellectual property laws of Malaysia to meet with the requirements of TRIPS. The government has set up committees to study every aspect of intellectual property laws, to revise them well before the five-year time period.

Declaration of non-infringement

Any interested person has the right to request the court to make a declaration that the performance of a specific act does not constitute an infringement. The person interested in making the declaration is required to prove the same. Where the act in question is already the subject of infringement proceedings, the defendant in the infringement proceedings cannot then institute proceedings for a declaration of non-infringement. It is thought that the interest which a person must have before he qualifies to request the court for a declaration of non-infringement is akin to that of a person who wants to intervene in proceedings. In any event, a mere commercial interest in the outcome would probably not be enough—he must have rights or liabilities in respect of the performance of a specific act, which will be directly affected by the declaration of the court.

Offences

Any person who falsely represents that anything disposed of by him for value is a patented product or process commits an offence. It is also an offence for any person to represent in respect of any article disposed of for value by him that a patent has been applied for if no such application has been made or any such application made has been refused or withdrawn. For each offence, the penalty is a fine not exceeding RM15,000 or imprisonment for a term not exceeding two years, or both. It is a defence for either offence described above to prove that due diligence has been used to prevent the commission of the offence.

Any person who makes or causes to be made a false entry in the Register, or a writing falsely purporting to be a copy or reproduction of any such entry in the Register, or tenders or causes to be produced in evidence any such false writing commits an offence. Penalty for this offence is similarly a fine not exceeding RM15,000 or imprisonment for a term not exceeding two years, or both.

Patent agents

All new applicants for patents, who are neither resident nor domiciled in Malaysia, must appoint patent agents to act on their behalf in all proceedings before the Patent Office. Every patent agent must be registered under the 1983 Act. Any person who carries on business, practises, acts, describes himself, holds himself out or permits

CHAPTER 10

SECURITIES LAW AND THE
REGULATION OF FINANCIAL MARKETS*
by Low Chee Keong

INTRODUCTION

The central policy objectives of Vision 2020 are the building up of a progressive, prosperous and united Malaysia, with the country attaining the status of an industrialised developed country by the year 2020. The development of efficient, vibrant and innovative financial markets is central to the attainment of these objectives, as significant capital investments are required to achieve national growth targets. Approximately RM170 billion and RM380 billion will be required to fund the various undertakings by the public and private sectors respectively in the five-year period between 1996 and 2000. Should current financing patterns continue, the latter sector is expected to raise at least 40% of its requirements through financial markets. To ensure that this demand is satisfied, a sound domestic investor base must be established in tandem with the implementation of policies to attract and retain foreign funds.

Securities, unlike goods, are created rather than produced. They have no intrinsic value and are merely choses in action, namely, legally enforceable rights or interests in something else. A security conveys to its holder an interest either as an owner or a creditor of the issuer. Accordingly, the valuation of a security represents the claim which the investor has on the issuer. The financial position and the ability of the promisor to meet its obligations determine the value of a bond or a note, while shares are valued by the market perception of their worth, as reflected by the profitability and future prospects of the issuer, and the willingness of these parties to pay for them.

The regulation of the marketing and sale of securities differs from that of transactions in other goods. As most goods are produced, distributed and consumed, the central thrust of regulation focuses on ensuring that the ultimate consumer is protected against dangerous articles and unscrupulous producers who may practise false advertising or non-competitive pricing. Unlike goods, securities are

---

* The information in this chapter was correct at 31 March 1997.

unique in that they may be created and issued in unlimited amounts at virtually no cost. Financial markets provide a forum through which securities may be traded. The liquidity of such markets allows investors to make, and realise, their investments, and also provides the issuer with cheaper sources of generating funds to facilitate the implementation of its business plans. If the market is operating efficiently, the price of the securities will reflect the profitability of the issuer and its ability to meet its financial obligations.

The decision to buy or to sell securities at a given price and time is dependent upon pertinent information with respect to the issuer, and it is on this premise that securities regulation is based. The regulation of securities markets is seen as necessary because, by their nature, securities often do not have a readily ascertainable value, as is the case with tangible property. Because the value of securities depends on the financial position and the future prospects of the corporation which has issued them, or more particularly, on the market's assessment of their value, the legislation requires a certain degree of public disclosure of relevant information and the maintenance of proper markets in securities. The common law provides the basis of the law dealing with securities, as is the case with company law in general. In particular, the law of contract is relevant and, because purchasers of securities usually deal through agents or brokers, the law of agency is also applicable.

The legal landscape of securities regulation in Malaysia has been significantly transformed since the establishment of the Securities Commission in 1993, and is governed by a number of pieces of legislation, namely:

- Securities Industry Act 1983
- Securities Commission Act 1993
- Securities Industry (Central Depository) Act 1991
- Futures Industry Act 1993
- Companies Act 1965

The interrelationship between the foregoing may be illustrated by the diagram below.

The principal features and application of each of the five statutes are discussed in the ensuing paragraphs.

SECURITIES INDUSTRY ACT 1983

The trading of securities is regulated by the Securities Industry Act 1983 (SIA), which has as its preamble:

OVERVIEW OF SECURITIES AND FUTURES REGULATION IN MALAYSIA

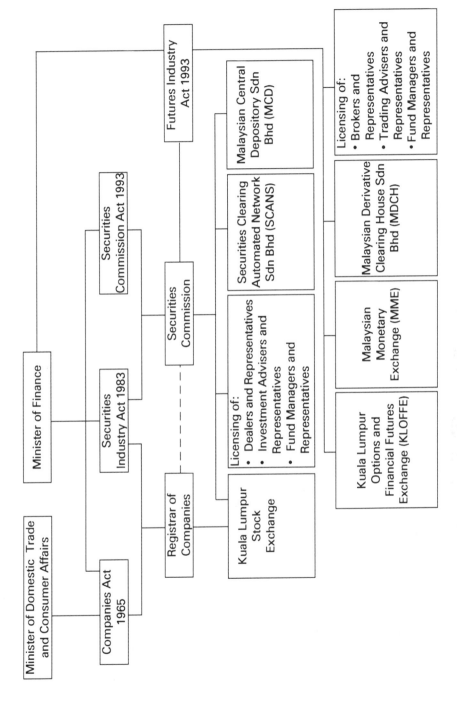

An Act to make provisions with respect to stock exchanges, stock brokers and other persons dealing in securities, and for certain offences relating to trading in securities, and for other purposes connected therewith.

The term 'securities' is extensively defined in s 2(1) of the SIA to mean 'debentures, stocks and shares in a public company or corporation, or bonds of any government or of any body, corporate or unincorporate, and includes any right or option thereof and any interest in unit trust schemes'. The SIA replaced its less effective predecessor, the Securities Industry Act 1973, and in 1997 comprises the Principal Act of 1983, the amending legislation of 1987, 1991, 1993 and 1996, together with the combined effects of the enactment of the Securities Commission Act 1993 and its amendment in 1995. The ambit of the SIA extends to four principal areas:

(1) The formation and conduct of stock exchanges and clearing houses.

(2) The relations between stock exchanges and the issuers of securities.

(3) The licensing and conduct of persons involved in the securities industry.

(4) Improper market practices.

Regulation of Exchanges and Clearing Houses

A stock exchange is a market place for the securities of corporations and governments, providing the means by which shares, debentures, options and bonds may be bought and sold. This market comprises two interrelated parts: the primary market where new issues of securities are sold, and the secondary market in which outstanding issues of these securities are traded. One of the most important characteristics of a listed security is that it enables its holder to sell it quite easily at the prevailing price. The fluidity brought about by the markets makes such securities more attractive to investors, which in turn facilitates further raising of capital by the company. In a broad sense, a stock exchange provides a mechanism whereby available funds may be channelled into productive uses.

Stock exchanges across the region, including Malaysia, have historically been privately run and were, until the 1970s, relatively unregulated by legislation. Each stock exchange promoted the philosophy of self-regulation and reserved for itself the mandate to make its own rules to regulate its members and the companies whose securities were listed on the exchange. Its members were the stockbrokers through whom trading in securities is carried out. The first formal organisations for stockbrokers in Malaysia can be traced to June 1930 with the establishment of the Singapore Stockbrokers' Association, which was subsequently renamed as the Malayan Stockbrokers' Association. However, public trading of shares only commenced in 1960 with the establishment of the Malayan Stock Exchange. The inclusion of Singapore as a State of Malaysia in 1963 necessitated another change of name to the Stock Exchange of Malaysia and Singapore so as better to reflect the markets served by the organisation. The subsequent political changes of the mid-1960s and the splitting of the Stock Exchange of Malaysia and Singapore made it necessary to re-establish a Malaysian stock exchange, culminating in the formation of a new public company known as the Kuala Lumpur Stock Exchange (KLSE) in 1976 under the provisions of the Companies Act 1965.

The KLSE aspires to be a world class stock exchange. Its principal objectives include:

(1) The provision, regulation, and maintenance of such facilities as may be required for conducting the business of a stock exchange by the creation of a fair, orderly and efficient securities market.

(2) The setting of rules to regulate member companies.

(3) The operation of a clearing house and a central depository system for the stock exchange, functions which in 1997 are carried out by two separate subsidiaries, namely, Securities Clearing Automated Network Services Sdn Bhd (SCANS) and Malaysian Central Depository Sdn Bhd (MCD) respectively.

(4) The establishment of just and equitable principles in business transacted on the stock exchange.

(5) Acting as the arbitrator in the settlement of disputes arising in the course of business between its members, and between its members and non-members.

(6) The promotion and protection of the interests of its members and of the investing public having dealings on the stock exchange.

Section 7 of the SIA provides that only current existing stock exchanges may establish, operate or maintain a stock market. A new stock market may only be established with the consent of the Minister of Finance if an application is made in the prescribed form and manner with consideration to the factors set out in s 8(2). The KLSE is a public company limited by guarantee with its own Memorandum and Articles of Association empowering it to make rules and regulations which cover two broad aspects: regulations governing the members, and rules to be complied with by listed companies. The rules of the KLSE regarding membership include rules for determining how someone becomes a member, how someone ceases to be a member and disciplinary powers over members. It also sets out the rules to govern the trading activities of its members, including clearing and settlement, brokerage and the proper administration for trading on margin accounts.

Members of the KLSE may be individuals or corporations with a shareholding in a stockbroking company. This differs from other jurisdictions because eligibility for membership is determined by ownership in a stockbroking company, that is, one which carries on the business of dealing in securities. The Articles of Association of the KLSE limit its membership to 250, comprising a maximum of 200 natural persons and 50 corporations. Foreign nationals may only be admitted to membership with the approval of the Minister of Finance. There is no equivalent restriction for corporate members as they need only have shareholders' funds of at least RM100 million and hold at least 51% of the equity of the stockbroking company. The Articles also provide for the exercise of some degree of discretion by the Minister of Finance with respect to eligibility for admission as corporate members.

Although the KLSE may exercise the rights under its Articles to make such amendments to its rules as may be necessary to facilitate its smooth functioning as a self-regulatory organisation, s 9(3) of the SIA requires it to obtain the written approval of the Securities Commission (SC) before any such amendment becomes effective. In addition, the SC is empowered to amend such rules by written notice to the KLSE pursuant to s 9(4).

The KLSE operates through a number of departments and its organisational structure reflects its front line self-regulating role which may be illustrated by the diagram below.

In 1997 the KLSE Committee consists of nine people, five of whom are elected to represent the members of the KLSE, while the other four, including the Executive Chairman, are appointed by the Minister of Finance under s 8(3) and (4).

The KLSE has, since 1995, undertaken some significant liberalisation measures to consolidate its position as the first among ASEAN countries, third in the Asia-Pacific region, and regularly within the top 15 globally in terms of market capitalisation. These measures include the introduction of graduated commissions, the lowering of contract stamp duty and further reduction in costs for trades coming in from foreign broking firms. Eligible broking houses are now

STRUCTURE OF KUALA LUMPUR STOCK EXCHANGE

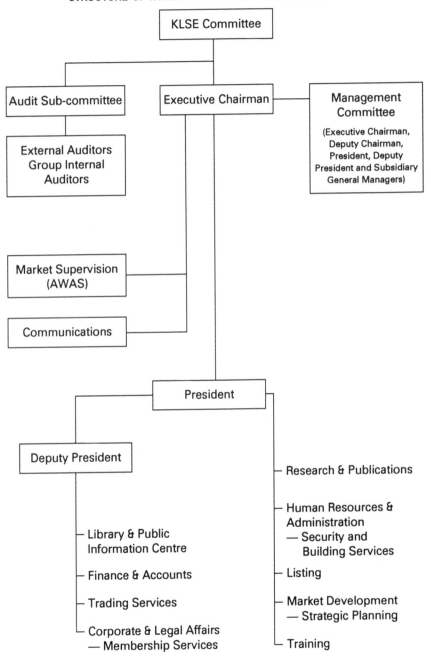

permitted to operate unit trust schemes, and the ceiling on the listing of broking houses has also been lifted. The KLSE will also consider applications for the listing of infrastructure project companies and closed-end funds provided these meet with the requirements of the SC's Guidelines for Public Offerings of Securities of Infrastructure Project Companies and the Guidelines for Public Offerings of Securities of Closed-end Funds respectively. The listing of foreign companies will also be progressively allowed, commencing with those which are Malaysian-owned or controlled. In addition, the establishment of two independent rating agencies, Rating Agency Malaysia Berhad in May 1991 and Malaysian Rating Corporation Berhad in September 1996, should provide the necessary impetus for the development of the corporate debt market and should further enhance the status of the KLSE as a leading regional exchange.

The KLSE has maintained a fully automated trading system since 1987 with share price information disseminated on a real-time basis through MASA, the acronym for 'Maklumat Saham' which is the national language for share information. The system is continually enhanced, culminating in the introduction in 1994 of WinStock, an integrated information system which shows the three best bid and offer prices for each stock together with the quantity at each price. Two types of orders may be entered: market orders for execution at the current best price, and limit orders which allow the investor to set a limit on the acceptable execution price. Matching is then done by the System on Computerised Order Routing and Execution (SCORE), which does so initially by price and then by time. Market orders are accorded priority over limit orders. SCORE will then send out confirmation detailing the names of the broker and counterparty broker together with the trading room slip number (TRS), which is used for settlement purposes. Enhanced risk management and increased efficiency in operations were brought about by the introduction of the WinScore (Broker Front-End) system in early 1996. This system enables stockbrokers to monitor their exposure on a real-time, on-line basis and subjects each order to limit checking before being allowed into the system, thereby preventing overtrading by dealers and their clients.

Securities Clearing Automated Network Services Sdn Bhd, a wholly-owned subsidiary of the KLSE, acts as the central clearing house for contracts between stockbroking firms. Central depository services are provided by Malaysian Central Depository Sdn Bhd, a 55% owned subsidiary of the KLSE. The full implementation of the Central Depository System (CDS), which was launched in November

1992 to increase the efficiency of the settlement and clearing systems, should alleviate the problems associated with theft, forgery and loss of share scrips. The operation of the CDS is governed by the Securities Industry (Central Depository) Act 1991, pertinent features of which are discussed below.

Relationship Between the KLSE and Issuers of Securities

The KLSE administers and reviews the Listing Requirements of the Stock Exchange which are both additional and complementary to the common law and statutory obligations of publicly-listed companies. These rules perform two principal functions. First, they set out the initial listing requirements which must be complied with by companies seeking a listing of their securities on either the Main Board or the Second Board of the KLSE. The object of the latter is to enable companies which are not large enough to satisfy main board listing requirements to have access to an equity capital market. The establishment of second board markets therefore enables a wider range of companies to raise share capital from the public while increasing the range of investment opportunities for investors. All second board companies are required to comply with financial reporting requirements, including a half-yearly report, a final report for each year and an annual report. This is designed to offer to investors similar protection as occurs in the case of companies listed on the main board.

Secondly, the rules impose on companies strict continuing obligations which supplement the disclosure requirements of the Companies Act and, if not complied with, may render them liable to removal from the official list. These rules are set out in Parts 2 and 3 of the Main Board and Second Board Listing Requirements respectively. The KLSE maintains and enforces a corporate disclosure policy, designed to ensure the perpetuation of a fair and orderly market, which requires all listed companies to:

- make immediate public disclosure of all material information concerning their affairs;
- ensure the timely release of such information to the public in a manner designed to maximise public dissemination;
- promptly and publicly clarify any rumour or report which may have an effect on the trading of their securities;

229

- make inquiries into any unusual market activity in their securities and to thereafter make such appropriate announcements as may be necessary in the circumstances; and
- refrain from unwarranted and unnecessary promotional disclosure.

In addition, the policy on insider trading requires company insiders to refrain from trading their securities on the basis of non-public material information and for such further periods as may be necessary for the investing public to evaluate the information after its public dissemination.

The KLSE Listing Requirements are reinforced by the Policies and Guidelines on Issue/Offer of Securities issued by the SC, the latter of which set out the following quantitative requirements for initial public offerings with effect from 1 April 1997:

	Main Board		*Second Board*
Issued and paid up capital Ordinary shares of RM1	Not less than RM50 million		Between RM10 million and RM50 million
Profit track record	*Either*		
Minimum number of years	3	5	3
Minimum average per year	N/A	N/A	RM2 million
Minimum achieved per year	RM4 million	RM2 million	RM1 million
Aggregate over said period	RM25 million	RM25 million	N/A
Basis of calculation	After tax	After tax	After tax
Profit forecast Minimum to be achieved	RM6 million		RM2.5 million
Basis of calculation	After tax		After tax
Business operation Minimum number of years in operation	5		5

The Listing Requirements are the strongest elements in the regulation of listed companies in Malaysia and have received judicial and legislative recognition. Section 100 of the SIA enables an application to be made by the SC, the Registrar of Companies or the

KLSE to the court for an order that the rules of the stock exchange be complied with.

Licensing and Conduct of Persons Engaged in the Securities Industry

One of the major ways in which the SIA regulates the securities industry is by requiring persons engaged in the industry to be licensed, which enables supervision of such persons and their activities. Section 12 prohibits people from carrying on a business of dealing in securities unless they hold a dealer's licence. Similar restrictions are imposed under ss 14 and 15A to ensure that people do not act or hold themselves out as investment advisers or fund managers unless they hold an investment adviser's or fund manager's licence respectively. Representatives of such dealers or investment advisers or fund managers, such as their employees or agents, are also required to be licensed under ss 13, 15 and 15B respectively. Contravention of any of these prohibitions will attract a maximum penalty of RM1 million and/or 10 years' imprisonment.

An 'investment adviser' is defined in s 2(1) to include a person who carries on a business of advising others concerning securities; or a person who, in the course of a business, issues or publishes analyses or reports concerning securities.

The foregoing definition specifically excludes:

- banks as defined under the Banking Act 1973 or the Islamic Banking Act 1983;
- authorised public trustee companies;
- registered life insurance companies;
- lawyers or accountants in public practice where investment advising is solely incidental to the practice of their professions;
- dealers or exempt dealers whose carrying on of that business is solely incidental to the conduct of their business of dealing in securities;
- proprietors or publishers of newspapers and periodicals not principally concerned with giving advice on securities; and
- licensed fund managers, whether exempt or not, whose carrying on of that business is solely incidental to the conduct of their business of managing a portfolio of securities for other persons.

The SC assumed the functions of licensing and supervising licensed persons, as well as for the promotion and maintenance of integrity of such persons, in the securities industry through a series of legislative reforms in 1995. The recently released Guidelines for Application of Licence Under the Futures Industry Act 1993 set out the criteria for futures traders, and similar guidelines are being negotiated with the KLSE for the securities industry. The SC has also proposed the creation of dual licences which would allow stock-brokers to trade in futures and derivatives. This would enable stockbrokers to persuade their cash market clients to trade futures, thereby providing an impetus to improve liquidity on both the Kuala Lumpur Options and Financial Futures Exchange (KLOFFE) and the Malaysian Monetary Exchange (MME), which are discussed under the heading of Futures Industry Act 1993 below.

Section 17(1)(d) provides the SC with some degree of discretion in deciding not to grant and/or renew licences as specified under ss 12–15B where it is of the opinion that the applicant has failed to satisfy the minimum criteria set out in the Schedule to the SIA. The elements revolve around the need to ensure as far as possible that such persons are fit and proper to hold the offices for which they have applied, taking into account the character of the individual and the interests of the public. Such licences are generally not granted in cases where the applicant has committed an offence involving fraud or dishonesty or violence, or is not suitably compe-tent; or where the SC has reason to doubt his or her soundness of judgment, or to believe that the applicant will not perform his or her duties efficiently, honestly and fairly. The SC is also allowed to take into consideration any business practices of the applicant to determine if these are deceitful, oppressive or otherwise improper, regardless of the fact that they may be lawful. Section 17(2) specifies that such a refusal to grant or to renew the licence may not be effected without adhering to the rules of natural justice.

Section 18 empowers the SC to impose certain conditions and restrictions upon the granting or renewal of such licences. Such condi-tions and restrictions may include conditions relating to the limitation of liability that may be incurred, the lodgement of additional security and the maintenance of a minimum level of assets. Licences are granted on a renewable basis for periods of one year unless they are surrendered in writing pursuant to s 28A, or revoked or suspended under s 27 at any time prior to their expiration, suspension being subject to the rules of natural justice. Revocation or suspension of a licence may be effected by the SC should its holder breach any of the provisions under s 27(1) and (2), which include death, insolvency, contravention of securities laws, the failure to adhere to any condition which may have been imposed upon the licence, and causing the SC to be of the opinion that he or she is no longer a 'fit and proper' person to hold such a licence. The consent of the Minister of Finance is required if the sanctions imposed under ss 18 and 27 involve a licensed dealer. All appeals with respect to licences are heard by the Minister of Finance, whose decision is final under s 28.

The holders of a dealer's licence must comply with the requirements regarding accounts and audit as set out in Div 1 of Pt VII of the SIA. Dealers must keep proper accounting records containing such information as is necessary to allow for a determination of their financial position and to facilitate the preparation of true and fair profit and loss accounts and balance sheets. They must also keep a trust account with a bank, into which they pay all money held in trust for clients. Money is deemed to be held in trust for a client if it has been received from a client, but does not include brokerage or payment of previously delivered securities, and may only be withdrawn for the purposes of payment to the client, defraying brokerage or other proper charges, or for other authorised payment. Section 46 specifically prohibits the use of such funds in trust accounts for the purposes of payments of the debts of a dealer. The committee of the KLSE is empowered under s 59 to impose any further requirement to the above as it thinks fit. Similar requirements, which are subject to control by the SC, are imposed upon fund managers under Div 2 of Pt VII.

All dealers, fund managers, the KLSE and recognised clearing houses (collectively the 'relevant person') must appoint an auditor who is independent of them. These parties are required to lodge their auditor's report in manner prescribed by Forms 20, 21, 22 and 23 of the Second Schedule to the Securities Industry Regulations 1987 with the SC and the Registrar of Companies (ROC) within three months of the end of their respective financial years. The auditor is under a duty to determine whether the relevant person has breached any securities laws, undertaken irregular transactions which may jeopardise the interests of his or her clients, failed to meet the minimum financial requirements, or is potentially insolvent. The auditor is under a statutory duty to lodge a written report with the KLSE, SC and ROC after becoming aware of such matters relating to dealers, and to the SC and ROC in all other cases. The SC may appoint an independent auditor to examine the affairs of the relevant person and thereafter to submit his or her report to the SC, the costs being borne by the relevant person. Such an appointment may be effected where the relevant person fails to submit the auditor's report within the time stipulated, or upon the receipt of a written application of a client of the former. Obstruction of the auditor in the performance of his or her duty is an offence which attracts a maximum penalty of RM1 million and/or a term of imprisonment of 10 years.

Section 39 requires all licence holders to state their interest in any securities they recommend by written circular, contravention of which is an offence, with the sanctions being a fine not exceeding RM1 million and/or a term of imprisonment not exceeding 10 years. Section 40A provides for civil liabilities to arise from such breaches, or where it is proved that the licence holder has no reasonable basis for making such a recommendation. The objective standard of proof is applied by s 40A, which appears to supplement any legal action under other non-statutory avenues including misrepresentation and breach of duty.

Section 61 requires the KLSE to establish and maintain a compensation fund consisting primarily of contributions by each member firm and income from investments. The operation of the fund is governed by Pt VIII of the SIA and is administered as a separate bank account by the committee of the KLSE. The purpose of this fund is to compensate persons who suffered pecuniary loss as a result of defalcation or fraudulent misuse of moneys in the course of business by a broker or the insolvency of a member company as set out in s 72. This provision effectively overturns the decision in *Daly v Sydney Stock Exchange Ltd* (1986) 4 ACLC 283. In that case, an investor had placed money on deposit with a stockbroker after receiving advice to do so from an employee of the stockbroker. The broker was in financial difficulties at the time, subsequently becoming insolvent and unable to repay the deposit. A claim for compensation from the fidelity fund failed on the ground that there had been no defalcation by the broker. A failure to repay a debt is not a defalcation where the relationship is that of debtor and creditor.

Prohibited Market Practices

The SIA creates a fair, effective and efficient market place by attempting to prevent its abuse through improper market practices and the establishment of false markets for securities. These provisions may be grouped under three broad categories: short-selling, market manipulation and false information, and insider trading. Breach of any of these provisions attracts a maximum penalty of RM1 million and/or imprisonment of up to 10 years.

Short-selling in the context of the securities market is the practice of selling securities when they are not owned by the seller at the time of the sale. Section 41 renders it an offence for any person, whether as agent or principal, to sell securities when he or she does not have a presently exercisable and unconditional right to vest the securities in the purchaser. The foregoing is, however, subject to some exceptions, namely, where the seller:

- has reasonable grounds to believe that he or she has such a right;
- is a broker who specialises in dealing in odd lots for the particular security;
- has entered into a contract to buy the securities but has yet to complete the transaction; or
- undertakes such transactions in the form and manner prescribed by the KLSE, on the proviso that the seller is not an associate of the body corporate that issued or made available the securities in relation to the sale. This allows short selling to be conducted in a regulated manner which has the dual advantage of enhancing market liquidity as well as providing for the protection of investors. Investors should also take cognisance of the Guidelines on Securities Borrowing and Lending in Malaysia issued by the SC and the KLSE Rules on Regulated Short Selling, the latter being implemented in September 1996 with an initial group of 50 approved stocks.

The other main prohibitions, broadly categorised as market manipulation and insider trading, are set out in Pt IX of the SIA which is headed 'Trading in Securities'. Sections 84 and 85 prohibit market manipulation, that is, the creation of a false or misleading appearance with respect to the price or activity of any securities on the KLSE. This may arise where transactions are entered into for the purposes of raising, lowering or stabilising the price of securities with the intent of inducing another person to enter into the market, or through fictitious transactions which do not involve any change of ownership. Section 86 extends the prohibition to the making of false and misleading statements which are likely to induce persons to enter the market or to affect the price of the securities. Similar prohibitions against inducing a person to deal in securities are set out in s 87, while s 87A makes it unlawful to use deceptive devices whether directly or indirectly in connection with the sale or purchase of any securities. However, although heavy sanctions are imposed to deter such practices, there are no corresponding provisions for the imposition of civil liability.

The prohibition against insider trading is contained in ss 89 and 90 which are titled 'Dealings by Officers in Securities' and 'Prohibition on Abuse of Information Obtained in Official Capacity' respectively. Although not extensively defined, the prohibition has a potentially wide application as it refers to the securities of any body corporate, which would not only include companies, but would extend to issues by unincorporated bodies and the government. Furthermore, it applies equally to dealings in securities other than on the KLSE. Persons are deemed to be connected with a body corporate if they are its officers, agents or employees. Officers include any director, secretary, privately appointed receiver and manager, or liquidator in a voluntary winding up of the company, including those who occupied that position within the past 12 months. The definition of an agent includes persons with whom the company has had a professional or business relationship over the past six months, such as its auditors, bankers, lawyers and stockbrokers. Such persons are prohibited from securities dealing based on non-public information acquired in connection with their positions, which information, if disseminated, would materially affect the price of the securities. This prohibition extends to causing or procuring others to deal in those securities, thereby preventing the insider from either benefiting indirectly, or enabling others to so benefit. If convicted, such persons will also be subject to civil liability under s 89(1), the quantum of damages payable being the approximate difference in the price of the securities had the information been made publicly available.

SECURITIES COMMISSION ACT 1993

The SC was first proposed by the Minister of Finance in 1988 in response to the need to revitalise capital markets in Malaysia following the global sharemarket crash of October 1987. One of the principal objectives in setting up the SC was the desire to create a central 'one stop' authority for the regulation and development of capital markets. A task force comprising representatives of the relevant regulatory authorities, including the Central Bank, the ROC, the Foreign Investment Committee, the Capital Issues Committee and the Attorney-General's chambers, was set up in 1991 to examine the issues pertaining to the structure of the SC, its objectives, powers and functions.

The structure subsequently adopted for the SC is based largely on the Australian Securities Commission and the Securities and Futures Commission of Hong Kong, both of which regulate the securities as well as futures markets. In late 1992 the Federal Parliament passed the Securities Commission Bill, the Futures

Industry Bill and the Securities Industry (Amendment) Bill thereby establishing the SC on 1 March 1993. Both the Capital Issues Committee and the Panel on Take-overs and Mergers were dissolved on that day to give the SC the role of central market regulator. Its mission statement compels the SC 'to promote and maintain fair, efficient, secure and transparent securities and futures markets and to facilitate the orderly development of an innovative and competitive capital market'.

The SC is a body corporate, with its nine members appointed by the Minister of Finance. The nine comprise an Executive Chairman, who is responsible for the day-to-day administration of the SC, four members to represent the government, and four other persons who must not hold full-time office in any publicly-listed company. Members are appointed for an initial period not exceeding three years but may be reappointed at the end of their term of office unless they resign, are removed from or vacate the office during their tenure. The SC is empowered to meet as often as is required by circumstances for the performance of its functions, with five members forming the requisite quorum. It has wide discretion with respect to the delegation of its powers and the establishment of committees to facilitate the performance of its functions. In the exercise of its power to delegate the SC had, as at the end of 1996, constituted four divisions, the Issues & Investment Division, the Market Supervision Division, the Research & Development Division, and the Finance, Human Resources & Administration Division, all of which report directly to the Executive Chairman. In addition, three units were established within the Office of the Chairman, the Corporate Affairs Unit, the New Building Project Unit and the Internal Audit Unit, the last of which also reports directly to the SC (see diagram below).

The SC has extensive powers, set out in ss 15(3) and 16 of the Securities Commission Act 1993 (SCA), to include 'powers conferred upon it by or under the securities laws' and 'all such powers as may be necessary for or in connection with, or reasonably incidental to, the performance of its functions under the securities laws'. The functions of the SC were significantly extended with the enactment of the securities and futures reform package of 1995 comprising the Securities Industry (Amendment) Act 1995, the Futures Industry (Amendment) Act 1995 and the Securities Commission (Amendment) Act 1995. These include responsibility for the maintenance of market integrity, enforcement of the relevant Acts, Codes and market place regulations, the protection of investors and the enhancement of the

237

ORGANISATION CHART OF SECURITIES COMMISSION

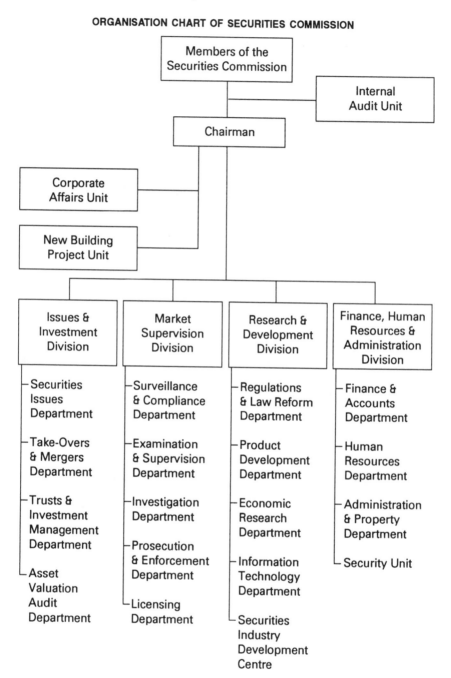

reputation of Malaysian markets through sound, considered and innovative development, for both the securities and futures markets. The SC is also entrusted with the responsibility for licensing, and supervising, intermediaries in the securities industry and with the maintenance of the integrity of such licensed persons.

The enactment of the Future Industry (Amendment & Consolidation) Act 1996 has further enhanced the powers of the SC to incorporate supervision over the commodity futures industry. As such, control of futures trading, whether financial or commodity-based, now comes within the ambit of the SC under the substantially expanded Futures Industry Act 1993.

To provide for a more effective regulatory environment, the SC is empowered to appoint investigating officers to ascertain whether an offence has been committed in breach of securities laws. The investigating officer has extensive powers, including the right to enter a place or building, to search, seize or take possession of articles and documents, as well as to call for the production of books and documents. He or she may orally examine any person connected with the matter being investigated and such persons being examined may not refuse to respond on the grounds of self-incrimination. The record of examination is admissible as evidence in court proceedings which may only be initiated with the written consent of the Public Prosecutor.

An illustration of the effectiveness of these provisions is the investigation conducted by the SC in September 1995 on the operations room of the Malaysian Issuing House (MIH) on allegations of irregularities in the balloting for the Great Wall Plastic Berhad initial public offer. The investigation revealed that some 40% of the applications were not included in the first ballot, thereby necessitating the subsequent conduct of a 'proper' second ballot, which led ultimately to the imposition of a RM1 million fine on MIH for making a statement which was false or misleading under s 87A(c) of the SIA.

In line with the globalisation of securities markets, the SC is allowed to render such assistance as it deems fit to any foreign supervisory authority exercising similar functions. This is achieved through the signing of a bilateral Memorandum of Understanding with its counterparts, including the Australian Securities Commission and the Securities and Futures Commission of Hong Kong.

An important role undertaken by the SC is the vetting, and approval, of all corporate proposals made by public companies. The Policies and Guidelines on Issue/Offer of Securities which took effect from 1 January 1996 mandate issuers to obtain the approval of the SC before undertaking any of the following proposals:

(1) Public offerings of securities whether or not with listing and quotation on a stock exchange.

(2) Issues of securities arising from corporate restructuring, mergers and acquisitions, schemes of arrangement or compromise, employee share option schemes, private placements, and bonus, rights and special issues.

(3) Issues of debt securities.

(4) Issues of warrants, convertibles and call warrants.

Debt securities dominated the fund-raising scene in 1994 and 1995 with a total of 94 issues attracting RM36,624.6 million from investors representing approximately 56.3% of all funds raised, or to be raised, in the Malaysian capital market for the two years combined. The SC was also active in considering proposals for initial public offerings during this period, approving 77 and 62 out of 109 and 112 applications in 1994 and 1995 respectively.

In seeking to promote a strong and healthy securities market, the Policies and Guidelines place great importance on the due diligence and professional responsibility of those involved with the issue, including the professional advisers, the promoters and the directors of the company. This requires the maintenance of high standards of disclosure and accounting. The formulation of the guidelines allows the SC to ensure a fair and consistent application of policies, with the resulting transparency serving the interests of investors.

SECURITIES INDUSTRY (CENTRAL DEPOSITORIES) ACT 1991

As trading volume on the KLSE increased, it became evident that the Fixed Delivery and Settlement System, which called for the physical delivery of scrips, was becoming progressively inadequate. Its manual delivery and clearing procedures had numerous disadvantages—principally risks associated with human error, forgery, theft and loss of scrip. Another weakness with the system was that the selling broker could only be paid when the scrips were delivered to SCANS, the central clearer for the KLSE, a process which could take up to five market days following the date of the contract.

The Securities Industry (Central Depositories) Act (CDA), which comprises the Principal Act of 1991 and the amending legislation of 1996, was enacted in response to this deficiency. It established and implemented a more efficient clearing and settlement system, the

CDS, a scripless share trading system based on a computerised book entry system which is operated by MCD, a 55% owned subsidiary of the KLSE. The CDS immobilised all physical scrips of companies listed on the KLSE in a vault under the control of the MCD. These are stored in the form of jumbo certificates in the name of MCD Nominees Sdn Bhd. The MCD is deemed to be a bare trustee in relation to the deposited securities, with the investor retaining all shareholder rights as beneficial owner of the same. As such, one certificate represents the holdings of all the shareholders rather than the latter holding the same in board lots.

Trading practices remain essentially the same, with investors instructing their brokers to buy or sell, the principal difference being the procedural requirement for investors to provide their CDS account numbers. Transfer of ownership of scrip is effected by means of a book entry, while settlement for these transactions is effected by transfers of cash through the banking system.

The central feature of the CDS is the requirement that investors open CDS accounts, into which they must deposit their shares, to enable them to trade in the listed securities. The implementation of the CDS does not prevent investors from holding scrips outside of the system. It simply prevents them from trading in the same, since transfers of ownership in securities may only be effected through the CDS. The physical delivery and receipt of scrips is dispensed with under the CDS as the seller's account is debited and the buyer's account correspondingly credited for each transaction. The CDS automatically recognises the investor with a credit balance of shares in his or her CDS account as the beneficial owner of those shares, thus eliminating the requirement for registration. A further advantage of the CDS is that it provides for the automatic crediting of entitlements in the form of shares into the investor's account while facilitating the remittance of dividend cheques directly to the investor by the share registrar.

CDS accounts may be opened through an authorised depository agent (ADA), as defined in s 13, which includes the KLSE, SCANS, stockbroking companies, commercial or merchant banks, and finance houses. Individual investors are only permitted to open one CDS account with any given ADA, although they may do so with as many ADAs as they wish, while corporate investors are allowed to maintain multiple accounts with the same ADA. The CDS maintains a central record of investors' beneficial interests. Acting as, or holding oneself out as, an ADA without the authorisation of the central depository is an offence under s 13(4) punishable by a fine of up to

RM10 million and/or a term of imprisonment not exceeding two years.

The MCD maintains the account balances of investors within the CDS. Advices of account transactions such as transfers or withdrawals are sent directly by the MCD to the investor. Statements of accounts, setting out the details of all transactions within the CDS account, are issued on a monthly basis to the investor unless the account is inactive for that particular month. In addition, half-yearly statements in June and December are sent to the investor regardless of whether there has been any activity during the period. Investors may also obtain a printed ad hoc statement detailing all transactions with their ADA for a nominal fee. However, only details of transactions conducted through the particular ADA will be available, as the system does not allow access to investors' CDS accounts maintained with other ADAs.

The CDS accounts show only the quantities of shares held, not their values. Investors must ensure that they have sufficient shares in their CDS accounts by 12.30 pm on the fifth market day after the transaction or contract date, that is, T+5, otherwise a buy-in will be initiated against the investors by the MCD. Purchases of shares under the CDS are credited to the accounts of investors on T+5 but may not be utilised until they have been paid for.

CDS account holders may also pledge their shares as collateral for loans by transferring these shares into their bank's CDS accounts. This dispenses with the need to withdraw physical scrip, thereby saving costs and minimising risks. In addition, the CDS account may be used for applications for public issue of shares. The MCD will credit the account of successful applicants prior to the actual listing of the shares to ensure that the investor is able to trade on the first day of listing.

Part IV of the CDA sets out the secrecy provisions which compel the MCD and the ADAs to take all reasonable security measures to ensure that the CDS accounts are not accessed, altered, disclosed or disseminated without proper authorisation. As the duty to maintain secrecy and restrict disclosure of information is vital to the success of the CDS, heavy sanctions are imposed under s 43(3). These include a fine not exceeding RM3 million and/or a term of imprisonment of up to five years. As a further security measure, access to the computer system is regulated by s 46 and the CDS does not provide for the linking of accounts where the investor maintains more than one. A breach of s 46 is an offence punishable with a fine not exceeding RM10 million and/or a term of imprisonment of not more than 10 years.

Disclosure of information is only permitted under the circumstances prescribed in s 45 which include:

- written permission by the investor;
- the application of insolvency laws;
- facilitating duly authorised investigations of offences;
- assisting the Minister of Finance in the exercise of his power;
- enabling the Central Bank and the Securities Commission to discharge their functions;
- enabling the stock exchange and auditors of the CDS to discharge their functions;
- allowing for the collation of information in a manner which does not reveal the identity of the investor; and
- where it is required in the interests of the investor or in the public interest.

As a further safeguard, the MCD maintains a compensation fund to reimburse investors for losses brought about by any wrongdoing due to professional negligence, fraud by a staff member or a computer-related crime.

THE FUTURES INDUSTRY ACT 1993

The success of the Kuala Lumpur Commodities Exchange (KLCE) in setting the global reference benchmark for palm oil pricing in the cash market through its highly liquid trades in crude palm oil futures provided the necessary impetus for the authorities to initiate a feasibility study into establishing a financial futures market in Malaysia. This eventually led to the enactment of the Futures Industry Act 1993 (FIA), as amended by the Futures Industry (Amendment) Act 1995, which established two separate exchanges, the KLOFFE and the MME, to provide for the regulation of the trading of financial futures and options. The KLCE became the third exchange within the ambit of the FIA in 1997 with the passing of the Futures Industry (Amendment & Consolidation) Bill 1996. The ensuing paragraphs provide an overview of the organisational structure and operational framework of the KLCE, KLOFFE and the MME.

The Kuala Lumpur Commodities Exchange

The KLCE was established in 1980 to provide commodity traders with effective risk management facilities coupled with a pricing mechanism. Futures contracts traded on the KLCE include crude palm oil, tin, cocoa and rubber, resources for which Malaysia is renowned, the most active being crude palm oil futures. The rules of the KLCE are modelled on those of larger and more established futures exchanges and are not altogether different from those practised by the KLSE taking into account the different markets serviced by the two organisations. As with the KLSE, self-regulation is promoted within the KLCE, and to this end the latter has set up the Business Conduct Committee to discipline any of its members found to have violated the rules of the Exchange.

All trades are conducted and executed through the floor of the KLCE on an Open Outcry competitive trading system and must be registered and cleared by the Malaysian Futures Clearing Corporation (MFCC), a clearing house which is jointly owned by the KLCE, its clearing members and a consortium of local banks. This requirement allows the MFCC to guarantee the financial performance of all futures contracts traded on the KLCE, a factor which has led to increased investor confidence in trading through the KLCE, given the financial security provided. The MFCC is able to extend such assurances as all its members are compelled to provide adequate collateral to cover their potential liabilities, a system which is effected through the collection of deposits and margins on a daily basis.

The operations used to be governed by the Commodities Trading Act 1985 which provided for the statutory establishment of a commodity exchange under Pt V and the control of matters pertaining and connected to the trading in commodity futures contracts. The establishment of the Commodities Trading Commission pursuant to Pt II and the office of the Commissioner of Commodities Trading under Pt III provided the regulatory framework entrusted with the responsibility for the supervision of the KLCE and the commodity futures industry.

These functions have since been assumed by the SC following the enactment of the Futures Industry (Amendment & Consolidation) Act 1996 which repealed the Commodities Trading Act 1985 and brought the control of commodities futures within the purview of the SC.

The Kuala Lumpur Options and Financial Futures Exchange

The establishment of KLOFFE in December 1995 responded to the growing sophistication of investors by opening up new opportunities for more effective portfolio management. KLOFFE is a self-regulating organisation with the mandate to provide a market place for trading in futures and options, commencing with stock index futures based on the KLSE Composite Index. Trading on KLOFFE is conducted through KLOFFE Automated Trading System (KATS), a fully integrated computer system which provides both trading and clearing functions. KATS minimises both the costs and the risks associated with manual systems, and provides for increased transparency in the market as all traders have access to the same information at the same time.

The management of KLOFFE is vested in its board of directors comprising nine members as set out in s 5 of the FIA. Two are elected by the futures brokers, four are elected to represent the shareholders of KLOFFE and another three are appointed by the Minister of Finance. The term of office of the government nominees is determined by the Minister, who also retains the discretion under s 5(2A) to vary the composition and numbers of the board, while the other directors have their tenure determined by the constitution of the company. The Minister appoints the Executive Chairman from the members of the board, and approves of his or her salary and remuneration which is paid by KLOFFE.

The principal regulators of KLOFFE are the Ministry of Finance and the SC. The latter is entrusted with responsibility for regulating and monitoring the industry as well as for the licensing of its participants. Persons who must be licensed by the SC include:

(1) Futures brokers, which must be companies incorporated under the Companies Act 1965, and their representatives.

(2) Futures trading advisers, who may be companies or individuals, and their representatives.

(3) Futures fund managers, who may be companies or individuals, and their representatives.

Applicants for the various licences must meet the Guidelines for Application of Licence under the Futures Industry Act 1993 issued by the SC, pertinent details of which are highlighted below.

- Futures brokers must:
  (a)   maintain a minimum Bumiputra equity of 30%;

(b) encourage an employee composition which is at least 30% Bumiputra;

(c) meet the financial requirements of the exchange and as specified under the Futures Industry Regulations 1995 which set a minimum paid-up capital of RM4 million;

(d) obtain approval in principle for admission from the exchange;

(e) obtain a certification on its risk management system and financial credibility, management appraisal and capital adequacy from the exchange; and

(f) appoint an applicant for the futures broker's representative licence.

- Futures trading adviser (Corporation) must:
    (a) maintain a minimum Bumiputra equity of 30%;
    (b) encourage an employee composition which is at least 30% Bumiputra;
    (c) maintain a minimum paid-up capital of RM500,000; and
    (d) appoint an applicant for the futures trading adviser's representative licence.

- Futures trading adviser (Individual), futures broker's or futures trading adviser's representatives, and local members must:
    (a) either possess suitable academic qualifications or have exceptional experience to compensate for the lack of the former;
    (b) be above 21 years of age without a criminal record and not have been adjudicated a bankrupt;
    (c) have sound financial standing and have passed the Malaysian Options and Futures Registered Representative (MFORR) exams; and
    (d) possess knowledge in the futures industry.

Contravention of the licensing requirements is an offence which attracts a fine not exceeding RM1 million and/or a term of imprisonment of not more than 10 years.

Futures brokers are direct members of KLOFFE, the practical significance of which is that they can carry out trades on the exchange whether on behalf of another person or on their own account. They also ensure that the trades are cleared through the Malaysian Derivative Clearing House (MDCH), which serves as the clearing house for both KLOFFE and the MME. The management of the MDCH is vested in its board of directors comprising nine members as set out in reg 9 of the Futures Industry Regulations 1995. Two members are elected by each of KLOFFE and the MME, two each from the corporations which are the affiliates of KLOFFE and the MME, and the final person is appointed by the Minister of Finance.

Clearing of trades is facilitated in one of two ways: by the broker being a member of MDCH, or by the broker maintaining a clearing agreement with such a member. The trading practices expected of a futures broker are set out in Pt V, being ss 49–56, and include the provision of timely information to clients and prospective clients, the requirement that the broker segregate the money and property of its client from its own, and the sequence in which orders are to be sent and carried out. Section 55 allows the SC, or KLOFFE with the approval of the SC, to fix or limit the volume of transactions which may be conducted by a broker.

A futures trading adviser may not conduct business as a broker, serving principally as an adviser to investors desirous of participating in the futures and options markets. The advisory role includes the business of advising other persons about trading in futures contracts or engaging in the publication of futures reports. All recommendations made by advisers in relation to trading in futures contracts must be reasonably based having regard to the needs and financial situation of the investor, and to the subject matter of the recommendation. Section 52B(3) allows the investor to claim damages from the adviser where it can be established, on the balance of probability, that the loss was occasioned by the adviser making the recommendation without a reasonable basis.

A futures fund manager engages in the business of offering to any person for subscription, or inviting any person to subscribe for, participatory interests as defined in Div 5 of Pt IV of the Companies Act 1965. This defines a person to be a futures fund manager where he or she raises money from investors so as to apply it, whether in part or in its entirety, in the trading of futures contracts. Employees of a futures fund manager are referred to as futures fund manager representatives.

As with the futures broker, advisers and fund managers in the futures industry and their representatives must comply with the relevant trading practices as set out in Pt V. Failure to comply renders the person guilty of a breach which is punishable with a fine of up to RM1 million and/or a term of imprisonment not exceeding 10 years.

Investors and speculators need not conduct their trades through brokers as the current framework provides for two types of membership of KLOFFE: trading members and local members. Trading membership is attained by subscribing to a RM1 'A' preference share and must have, as the purpose of membership, the conduct of the business of a licensed futures broker. Local members may only trade on their own behalf and have no access to the clearing facilities, which must be effected through an MDCH member. As local membership is not governed by the FIA, such members need not be licensed.

Section 58 of the Act requires KLOFFE to establish and maintain a fidelity fund consisting of, inter alia, contributions from its members, income from investments and contributions made by KLOFFE. The operation of the fund is governed by Pt VI of the FIA with the purpose being to compensate persons who have suffered monetary loss in the circumstances outlined under s 66A(1) including defalcation and fraudulent misuse of money or property entrusted to a broker. As the nature of the remedy is compensatory, the quantum paid cannot be greater than the applicable amount as ascertained under the business rules of KLOFFE.

Malaysian Monetary Exchange

MME is a wholly-owned subsidiary of KLCE which provides trading facilities in interest rate and currency futures and operates under the jurisdiction of the SC. It is governed by the FIA in the same manner as KLOFFE and has three categories of membership, namely, broker, non-broker and individual. Their relationship is highlighted by the chart below.

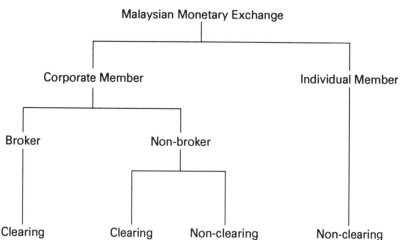

The MME commenced operations in May 1996, and persons involved in the MME are subject to the same licensing requirements as those in KLOFFE as both are governed by the FIA.

Clearing facilities are provided by MDCH, which is jointly owned by the MME and KLOFFE. Clearing members are authorised to register trades on their own account, for their clients or for other non-clearing members, and are required to lodge a minimum security deposit of RM1 million with MDCH. In addition, the MDCH establishes minimum initial margin levels which, together with the security deposit, serve as a performance bond to cover for its potential exposure to price fluctuations. Non-clearing members may trade either on their own account or for the account of their clients but their trades must be cleared through a clearing member. Individual members or 'locals' must also clear their trades through a clearing member but may only trade on their own account.

Trades in financial futures, which will initially be centred on the three month Kuala Lumpur Inter-Bank Offered Rate (KLIBOR), are conducted in the trading pit of the MME on an Open Outcry system with simultaneous display on the trading screen. KLIBOR futures were chosen to enable the MME to be the only exchange to offer a hedging instrument on ringgit interest rates. It is modelled on the successful Eurodollar contract traded on the Singapore Monetary Exchange (SIMEX), and is anticipated to serve as a prelude to the introduction of more complex derivative products such as interest rate swaps and forward rate agreements.

The MME is managed in the same manner as KLOFFE, by a board of nine as prescribed under s 5 of the FIA. Transparency is attained through the MME's Trade Allocation and Confirmation System (MTACS), which displays details of trade and allows members to confirm, designate, allocate or reject daily trades to which they are recorded as a trading party. To protect the integrity of the market place the MME has implemented a series of safeguards including:

(1) Adoption of a single slip system which bears the details of the trade initialled by both buyer and seller.

(2) Administration of collection of margins from member firms and settlement between clearing members on a daily basis by the MDCH.

(3) Financial surveillance which requires broker members to submit certified financial statements annually and interim financial statements and reports as directed by the MME and MDCH.

(4) The conduct of routine and random inspections.

(5) Intra-day monitoring of price movements.

(6) Allowing the Audit and Compliance Division to have daily access to specific account position information through the requirement that members report their own position and that of their customers once a predetermined level is reached.

These safeguards allow the MME to impose a limit on the positions which a person or persons may hold or control in any one contract, or for all contracts combined, by preventing a concentration of positions. Such measures are necessary to ensure a level playing field for all investors through the reduction of risk of manipulation and cornering of the market place.

THE COMPANIES ACT 1965

To some extent it is artificial to regard the regulation of companies and the regulation of the securities industry as separate areas of law. The two areas can be seen as being complementary, as the Companies Act provides for disclosure and regulates various aspects of securities including:

(1) The regulating of fund-raising activities through the prospectus provisions, ss 37–47.

(2) Restrictions on the allotment of shares pursuant to ss 48–50.

(3) Provisions regulating 'participatory interests' as defined under Div 5 of Pt IV of the Act (ss 84–97), which allow the holder the right of participation in the returns from the investment.

(4) Part VI of the Act with respect to accounts and audit.

(5) Part X which deals with the power of investigation into the affairs of companies.

The Act is administered by the ROC, who is in turn assisted by the Regional, Deputy and Assistant Registrars, all of whom are appointed by the Minister of Domestic Trade and Consumer Affairs. The principal function of the ROC is to ensure that corporations and their officers comply with the provisions of the Act. The ROC has been accorded extensive powers of enforcement under ss 7B, 7C and 7D, which allow him or her to enter into premises, to seize documents which may be used against the corporation or its officers, and to compel the oral testimony of any witness without providing protection against self-incrimination. The withholding of cooperation with, or obstruction of performance by, the ROC in the discharge of his or her duties is an offence under the Act.

There is some overlap between the functions of the ROC and those of the SC. The ROC comes principally within the purview of the

Minister of Domestic Trade and Consumer Affairs, and is responsible for all companies incorporated in Malaysia. The ROC also regulates the affairs of foreign companies having a place of business in Malaysia under the provisions of Div 1 of Pt XI of the Act (ss 329–343). The SC is entrusted with the administration of the principal securities and futures legislation in Malaysia, namely, the Securities Industry Act 1983 and the Futures Industry Act 1993, and comes under the control of the Minister of Finance.

Although it appears that the ROC has a wider jurisdiction, given his or her control over all companies, it should be noted that the ability of private companies to issue securities is restricted by s 15 which prohibits both invitations or offers to the public to subscribe for shares in, or debentures of, the company and for the deposit of money with the company. As such, the ROC may be viewed as complementing the SC, particularly in the area of compliance which includes the registration of prospectuses and the requirement for annual statutory audits of companies.

CONCLUSION

The legislative reform package of 1995 has enhanced the regulation of financial markets in Malaysia and brought the SC closer to being the central securities regulator. It is particularly significant that the SC now performs an integral aspect of market regulation, namely, the licensing and supervision of intermediaries in both the securities and futures markets. The move towards a disclosure-based system of regulation, the expansion of the scope of market proposals which require the approval of the SC and the transformation of the Malaysian Code on Takeovers and Mergers into subsidiary legislation backed by criminal sanctions for breach of its provisions are further evidence of the determination of the Malaysian Government to consolidate the position of the SC.

None the less, the system may be further streamlined by reducing the overlap between the SC and the ROC. The former should assume all functions with respect to securities, which would include the registration of prospectuses. This would have the dual advantage of avoiding any ambiguity with respect to their respective jurisdictions and of further enhancing the role of the SC as the central 'one stop' authority in the regulation and development of capital markets.

The internationalisation of securities markets will provide the Malaysian equity, futures and debt markets with a variety of key opportunities for expansion. For example, due consideration may be given to the proposal by the Philippines Stock Exchange for the creation of a regional stock exchange since the Minister of Finance approved the listing of Malaysian-controlled foreign companies on the KLSE. The linking of the markets will provide the opportunity for new products to be traded on different exchanges and in different time zones. As a step towards this end, cross-listing of shares could be considered, with settlement effected in the currency of choice.

KLOFFE and the MME stand to benefit immensely from the series of policy announcements in 1996 aimed at increasing the liquidity of the futures markets. These include the eventual introduction of a dual licensing scheme which will allow remisiers to offer futures contracts to their clients, and the increase in the number of market makers. In addition, plans are afoot for the launch of index options by KLOFFE in 1997. None the less, there is a need for the introduction of new and flexible products to stimulate market activity, as only the KLSE Composite Index and the three month KLIBOR are, as at 30 April 1997, traded on KLOFFE and the MME respectively. Examples of such products include a number which were introduced by the Chicago Board Options Exchange (CBOE) in 1993: equity options with customised strike prices, time to expiry, exercise style and/or method of expiry value determination, longer dated equity options, tailor-made currency options and flexible arrangements for interest rate futures. The launch of the Hang Seng Asia Index, in which the KLSE Composite Index is a constituent, presents a further opportunity from which derivative products could be traded.

The establishment of two independent rating agencies for corporate debt securities will allow Malaysia to capitalise on the growing regional need for long-term funding within the private debt markets. The increasing importance of asset securitisation provides yet another avenue for growth, and the myriad types of assets which may be securitised should be a boon for the market which has thus far been dominated by the mortgage-related activities of Cagamas Berhad.

Another significant development in 1997 is the proposal to establish the second stock exchange to be called the Malaysian Exchange of Securities Dealing and Automated Quotation, or 'MESDAQ', under s 8(2) of the SIA. Contrary to a common misconception, MESDAQ will not be an over-the-counter market, although it was originally conceived as such. Its structure will be that of a recognised stock exchange with rules to provide for, and to enforce, the principle of fair play. It will be owned by its members who will pay a fee, in the form of seat money, to MESDAQ for the right to trade in the quoted shares. These members will be in the same position as stockbrokers who are members of the KLSE.

The primary intention for the establishment of MESDAQ is to provide a quotation for high technology based companies and other high growth small enterprises which have strong potential for growth but lack the necessary track record to seek a listing on the KLSE. However, to ensure growth of the economy and investments in the country, at least 70% of the funds raised through a quotation on MESDAQ must be invested in Malaysia. In doing so, MESDAQ will provide a strong impetus and strategic capital market support for the development of the Multimedia Super Corridor (MSC), the most innovative project to be undertaken within the region. The successful implementation of this proposal will contribute significantly towards the promotion of technology-intensive industries and lay the foundation for a strong base of indigenous research and development efforts in line with the requirements of Vision 2020. In the longer term, MESDAQ will be the platform to provide a Nasdaq-like market function for similar companies from within the Asian region.

However, whatever the developments, the markets will only be as sophisticated as their investors. Therefore, an integral requirement is that the proposed changes are implemented in tandem with enhancement of education programs. Increased knowledge of the regulatory environment and of the products offered leads to an increased confidence in the same. The establishment of the Securities Industry Development Centre (SIDC), and the Research Institute of Investment Analysts Malaysia (RIIAM), by the SC and KLSE respectively are but two concrete examples of the importance which the principal market regulators place upon investor education. The dual objectives of the SIDC are to create awareness of the role and functions of the SC, and to educate the public on the developmental changes in the capital market. The significant impact of the SIDC is evident in its corroboration with KLOFFE and the MME to structure the Malaysian Futures and Options Registered Representative examination syllabus, which examination all applicants for licences under the FIA must pass. RIIAM, an affiliate of the KLSE, pursues enhanced investment research standards and has contributed positively to the increasing level of knowledge of the investing public through its numerous courses, seminars and workshops. It has also cooperated with the Royal Melbourne Institute of Technology to pioneer the Diploma in Investment Analysis program, which in 1997 remains the only course of its kind in Malaysia. The importance of education cannot be overstated and the authorities should ensure that education is readily and easily available to everyone, as increased transparency is a condition precedent for increased liquidity of the market place, thereby further consolidating the status of Malaysia as a premier regional financial centre.

CHAPTER 11

DISPUTE RESOLUTION
by Vinayak Pradhan

Malaysia's commercial legal system, which is rooted in the common law, allows commercial disputes to be resolved either privately or publicly. Public resolution remains the favoured process, although there is a growing shift to private resolution, particularly of disputes which have an international flavour whether because of the parties involved or because of other factors.

THE COURTS

The source of judicial power in Malaysia is the Federal Constitution, Part IX of which deals with the Judiciary. Article 121 provides for the creation of the High Courts of Malaya and of Sabah and Sarawak, as well as such inferior courts as may be provided by federal law. The courts are now restricted to such jurisdiction and powers as may be conferred by or under federal law, so that when questions relating to jurisdiction arise, these have to be identified by reference to particular legislation. Prior to 10 October 1989, the Constitution generally provided for the judicial power of the Federation to be vested in the two High Courts.

The two main statutes relating to the courts are the Courts of Judicature Act 1964 and the Subordinate Courts Act 1948. The former regulates, inter alia, the powers and jurisdiction of the High Courts, the civil jurisdiction being conferred by ss 23 and 24. Section 23 in essence confers jurisdiction to deal with matters arising under, or related to, the territorial sovereignty of that area of Malaysia of which each High Court is part, or where any one of several defendants resides or has its place of business. Section 24 deals with specific areas such as divorce and matrimonial cases, bankruptcy, companies, guardianship of infants and of other incapable persons, and probate and administration. Significantly, it also confers like jurisdiction in matters of admiralty as is had by the High Court of Justice in England under the United Kingdom Supreme Court Act 1981. Of importance also are ss 23(2) and 25(1) which preserve the jurisdiction of the High Court existing prior to Malaysia Day (16 September 1963). This included the jurisdiction and powers conferred by the Courts Ordinance of the Federation of Malaya 1948, the first section of the Second Schedule of which conferred jurisdiction and authority identical to that exercised by the Chancery and King's Bench Divisions of the High Court of Justice in England, which would necessitate reference, inter alia, to the United Kingdom Law of Property Act 1925. The High Court additionally has the powers stated in the Second Schedule to the Courts of Judicature Act 1964, the matters enumerated including those relating to prerogative writs, distress, partition and sale of land, interpleaders, injunctions, interest, enforcement of judgments, transfer of proceedings and vexatious litigants.

The High Court has jurisdiction to deal with monetary claims for an unlimited amount and is empowered to award judgment for any sum it chooses. However, if a claim is for a monetary sum which is within the jurisdiction of the Subordinate Courts and does not contain any prayer for relief which only the High Court can give, eg an injunction or a declaration, the filing in the High Court of proceedings which are within the jurisdiction of the Subordinate Courts will result in the High Court staying these proceedings and transferring them to the Subordinate Court.

One must then turn to the Subordinate Courts Act 1948. This legislation creates and defines the jurisdiction of the different levels of courts which, in order of descending power are the Sessions Court, the Magistrates' Court and, in West Malaysia only, the Penghulu's (Village Headmen's) Courts. In addition it creates the office of Justices of the Peace (except for Sarawak), who have, in West Malaysia, such powers not exceeding the powers of a Second Class Magistrate, as may be conferred by any written law, and, in Sabah, powers and duties conferred upon them by any written law.

The quantum of the claim is the major, though not the sole, jurisdictional dividing line between the High Court and the Subordinate Courts, and between the various Subordinate Courts inter se. Thus the Penghulu's Court has jurisdiction to hear claims in relation to a debt or liquidated demand not exceeding RM50 provided that all parties to the proceedings are persons of an Asian race speaking and understanding the Malay language. A First Class Magistrate's jurisdiction now extends to claims of up to RM25,000, in addition to jurisdiction to hear civil appeals from the Penghulu's Courts within the same territorial jurisdictional area. A Second Class Magistrate has the power to deal with debts or liquidated demands not exceeding RM3000. The monetary limit of the Sessions Court's jurisdiction is RM250,000 generally, with unlimited jurisdiction in respect of motor vehicle accidents, landlord and tenant distress, and the recovery of immovable property unless there is a bona fide question of title involved, in which case the consent of the parties is required.

The non-monetary limitations on the jurisdiction of the Subordinate Courts is set out in s 69 of the Act. This provides that the Sessions Court shall have no jurisdiction in relation to immovable property (except as stated in the preceding paragraph), the specific performance or rescission of contracts, injunctions, the cancellation or rectification of instruments, the enforcement of trusts, for accounts, for declaratory decrees except in interpleader proceedings, for probate and administration of deceased estates, when any question of the legitimacy of a person is in question, guardianship and custody of infants, unless specifically conferred by any written law and where the validity and dissolution of a marriage is in question unless specifically provided in any written law.

The additional powers of the Sessions Courts and Magistrates' Courts are conferred in the Third Schedule to the Act. These include powers to stay or dismiss proceedings because of a multiplicity of proceedings or where the matter is res judicata, to stay proceedings where there is in effect no connection with the local jurisdiction of the court, to transfer proceedings to a court of coordinate jurisdiction, to allow service of process extra-territorially in Singapore or Brunei or, with the leave of the High Court, elsewhere, in relation to service, set-offs, discovery and interrogatories, subpoenas and warrants for arrest, committal for contempt, attachments before judgment, poor litigants, costs, enforcement of orders, discharge, variation and suspension of orders and the execution of orders of a Muslim Religious Court.

Rules of Court have been promulgated pursuant to both the Courts of Judicature Act 1964 and the Subordinate Courts Act 1948 to regulate the procedure of these courts. These are the Rules of the High Court 1980 and the Subordinate Court Rules 1980. They are similar in philosophy but not identical in content or form. The Rules are based on English rules of practice and procedure. The Rules of the High Court were initially brought into force in 1957 in substitution for a then-existing Civil Procedure Code which had its origins in the Civil Procedure Code of India. The procedural system reflects the inherited common law adversarial process.

ARBITRATION

Special Factors

Court delays have often been advocated as a principal reason for opting for arbitration. There has, however, been an improvement in court processes, the result primarily of the appointment of an increased number of High Court Judges and of Judicial Commissioners who have all the jurisdiction and powers of a High Court Judge and who would usually expect confirmation as a High Court Judge within two years of appointment as a Judicial Commissioner. In at least one court in Kuala Lumpur full trials are being scheduled within less than a year of the filing of court proceedings. None the less, it still generally holds true that, on the assumption that both parties are seriously intending a quick resolution of their dispute, arbitration is the speedier process. Some disputes, notably those relating to the construction industry, because of the vast amount of technical detail and controversy usually involved, are more efficiently handled in an arbitration. The flexibility of the arbitral process, the particular expertise of the arbitrator, and the privacy and confidentiality are well-known factors favouring arbitration.

In Malaysia there are four other considerations which have been raised as reasons for opting for arbitration. The first of these is of particular relevance to the foreign investor and relates to the language of the courts. Until March 1990, s 8 of the National Language Act 1963–67 allowed for the use of either Bahasa Malaysia, which is the national language of Malaysia, or of the English language or both in any court proceeding, with a proviso that the court could, either on its own notice or on application of a party to the proceedings 'after considering the interests of justice', order the proceedings to be conducted either wholly in the national language or wholly in the English language.

The March 1990 amendment provided for all proceedings to be in the national language with the court, however, having the power to order, either on its own motion or on application and 'after considering the interests of justice', that the proceedings be conducted partly in the national language and partly in the English language.

The amendment thus requires proceedings to be in the national language with the court's discretion to allow proceedings to be partly in English depending on the judge's appreciation of what the 'interests of justice' are. Most judges are judicious enough to recognise that the linguistic competence of counsel, the original documents being principally in English, and any existing foreign element are 'interests of justice' factors which persuade them to have the proceedings conducted primarily in English. There are a few judges, however, whose inflexibility on the matter is a cause for concern, particularly to foreign litigants who would like to have lawyers of their choice and be able to follow the proceedings.

Thus, a party entering a contract who would like a dispute to be resolved using a language of its choice is better off opting for arbitration and ensuring the provision in the arbitration agreement of a clause stipulating the language of its choice.

The second factor in relation to the flexibility of the arbitration process is the statutory exclusion of the Evidence Act 1950 from arbitration. The Evidence Act defines and regulates the reception of evidence in judicial proceedings. Section 2 of the Act excludes the Act's application from proceedings before an arbitrator and s 3 clarifies that arbitrators are excluded from the operation of the Act even though they are legally authorised to take evidence. Arbitrators are thus not bound by the technical rules of evidence and may, for instance, allow some amount of hearsay.

The third factor in this regard is the freedom of a party not to have a Malaysian lawyer representing it in the arbitration and to have a foreign lawyer or even a non-lawyer acting as a lay advocate. The issue arose in *Zublin Muhibbah Joint Venture v Government of Malaysia*[1] where an American attorney intended to participate in the cross-examination of the government's witness in the arbitration, to which the government took objection. The High Court granted a declaration effectively allowing the American attorney the right of participation. Interestingly, the Bar Council did not oppose the application. Judgment was delivered by the present Chief Justice of Malaysia, Eusoff Chin J, then sitting as a puisne judge. He said, inter alia:

> An arbitral forum is not a court of justice in Malaysia as envisaged by the Legal Profession Act 1976. It is a private tribunal. Subject to s 12 of the Arbitration Act 1952, the arbitrator is appointed by the parties to an arbitration agreement to adjudicate on certain specific facts before him, and ultimately to settle the dispute between the contracting parties arising out of their contract. The parties who may appear before the arbitrator are those provided for by the arbitration agreement, or if the agreement does not so provide, then the provisions of s 13 of the Arbitration Act 1952 shall apply.

The fourth factor is that parties may opt for a system which allows the arbitral process to continue completely free of any intervention from the court. This is dealt with under the next heading.

The Kuala Lumpur Regional Centre for Arbitration

Independence for the countries colonised by Britain did not see a natural end to colonial domination. In relation to the administration of justice, the view was predominantly Anglophile with a deep-seated notion that English judges and English lawyers do 'better justice' than locals. Most colonies have, however, now done away with appeals to the Judicial Committee of the Privy Council. So far as the private resolution of commercial disputes was concerned, arbitration was London-centric. This was one of the reasons, if not the principal reason, why a United Nations body, the Asian-African Legal Consultative Committee (AALCC),[2] decided to set up, in 1978, three regional centres for arbitration, at Kuala Lumpur, Cairo and Lagos.

These centres were a major step in the institutionalisation of arbitration processes. Support from Malaysia came from the-then Deputy Prime Minister of Malaysia (since 1981, the Prime Minister), Dato Seri Dr Mahathir Mohamed, who, in his address at the First Conference on International Commercial Arbitration for the Asia and Pacific Region at Kuala Lumpur in July 1979, said:

> On behalf of the Government of Malaysia I wish to reiterate our full support to ensure the success of this centre. I also wish to give the assurance here that the government will respect the independent functioning of the centre as an international arbitral institution.

This promise of independence has been given statutory effect in s 34 of the Arbitration Act 1952 which was added to the Act by a 1985 amendment. Section 34 reads as follows:

> (1) Notwithstanding anything to the contrary in this Act or any other written law but subject to sub-section (2) in so far as it relates to the enforcement of an award, the provisions of this Act or other written law shall not apply to any arbitration held under the Convention on the Settlement of Investment Disputes Between states and Nationals of Other states 1965 or under the United Nations Commission on International Trade Law Arbitration Rules 1976 and the Rules of the Regional Centre for Arbitration at Kuala Lumpur.

(2) Where an award made in an arbitration held in conformity with the Convention or the Rules specified in sub-section (1) is sought to be enforced in Malaysia, the enforcement proceedings in respect thereof shall be taken in accordance with the provisions of the Convention specified in sub-section (1) or the Convention on the Recognition and enforcement of Foreign Arbitral Awards 1958, as may be appropriate.

(3) The competent court for the purpose of such enforcement shall be the High Court.

The effect of this amendment is to exclude the supervisory jurisdiction of the High Court over arbitrators and arbitrations from the two kinds of institutionalised arbitrations referred to therein which may conveniently be called ICSID arbitrations and KLRCA arbitrations respectively. The court's jurisdiction is not excluded from the enforcement of awards which must be undertaken in accordance with the New York Convention Act 1958 so far as KLRCA arbitrations are concerned. The Washington Convention Act provides for enforcement of ICSID awards.

This statutory exclusion of the court's jurisdiction from arbitration is unique. In other jurisdictions where there is a possible exclusion of the ordinary right of recourse to courts, the relevant statutory provision is an enabling one which allows the parties to contractually specifically exclude the court's jurisdiction. A distinction is made in some other jurisdictions between domestic arbitration and international arbitration, with exclusive agreements in relation to the former valid at the time of the commencement of the arbitration and in the latter at the time of the creation of the contract. The Malaysian provision creates the bar to the court's doors as an incident arising out of the choice of the rules of the arbitration and does not require the parties to specifically agree on the exclusion.

Two cases have decided that the statute means what it says: *Klockner Industries-Anlagen Gmbh v Kien Tat Sdn Bhd & Anor*[3] and *Soilchem Sdn Bhd v Standard Elektrik Lorenz AG.*[4] In *Klockner* the claimants in the arbitration, Kien Tat Sdn Bhd, went into liquidation while the reference to arbitration was in progress. The respondents, Klockner, then applied to the High Court for an injunction to restrain the arbitration from proceeding because of Kien Tat's liquidation. The learned judge declined to go into the merits of the application which raised the issue whether Kien Tat had the capacity to continue with the action because of the provisions of the Companies Act. The learned judge, Dr Zakaria Yatim J[5] (as he then was) had no doubt that s 34 of the Arbitration Act excluded the court's jurisdiction to deal with the question. He said, at 185:

> In my opinion the crucial words in s 34 are '. . . the provisions of this Act and other written law shall not apply to any arbitration held under . . . the Rules of the Regional Centre for Arbitration at Kuala Lumpur'. It is clear that under the section, the court cannot exercise its supervisory function as provided in the Arbitration Act 1952, in respect of such arbitration. Neither can the court exercise its supervisory function over such arbitration under any other written law. The words 'written law' have been defined in s 3 of the Interpretation Act 1967, to mean the Federal Constitution and State Constitutions, Acts of Parliament and subsidiary legislation made thereunder; ordinances and enactments and subsidiary legislation made thereunder, and any other legislative enactments or legislative instruments. 'Written law', therefore, includes the Companies Act 1965.
>
> Therefore, the question of capacity or locus standi of a party to the arbitration, the question of security for costs, or the issue of pleadings before the arbitral tribunal, cannot be determined by the court by virtue of s 34. These are issues which the arbitral tribunal has to decide and the court cannot and will not interfere with the proceedings of the tribunal. The function of the court is confined only to the enforcement of the arbitral award if the award is sought to be enforced in Malaysia.

In reaching his decision, the learned judge did take into account the presumption that the court's jurisdiction should not be excluded except by clear words. He said, at 185:

> It has been said that the jurisdiction of the courts must not be taken to be excluded unless there is quite clear language in the Act to have that effect. See dictum of Evershed MR in *Goldsack v Shore* at 712. In the present case, I agree with Datuk Dominic Puthucheary that the words in s 34 are 'plain', clear and precise. Reading the clear language of the section I am of the view that the section excludes the court from exercising its supervisory function under the Arbitration Act 1952 or under any other written law, including the Companies Act 1965, in respect of arbitrations held under the Rules of the Arbitration Centre.

Soilchem Sdn Bhd v Standard Elektrik Lorenz AG came before the courts after Soilchem's claim in the arbitration was dismissed by the arbitrator. The Arbitration Act provides for the remedy of setting aside the award on grounds including those of errors on the face of the award and of the arbitrator's misconduct of himself or the proceedings, misconduct being a technical word understood in a non-pejorative sense. Section 34 of the Act, however, excluded the Act from the arbitration, thus taking away the statutory remedy. Soilchem thus framed its application to the court to set aside the award by invoking the inherent jurisdiction of the court which, it claimed, entitled the court to set aside the award on the grounds of error and misconduct. Soilchem sought certiorari relief and obtained, on the usual ex parte application, leave for the motion for certiorari to issue. Lorenz then moved to strike out the application on the grounds that the provisions of s 34 had totally excluded the court's jurisdiction.

Soilchem maintained that the arbitrator had misconducted himself and the proceedings, that the award delivered by the arbitrator was wholly erroneous in law and in fact, that it was irrational and unreasonable and was one which no reasonable arbitrator would have arrived at.

Soilchem further argued that *Klockner* was wrongly decided. While Zakaria J's reasoning was not directly faulted, it was contended that Zakaria J, who had been involved in the setting up of the centre when he was with the Attorney-General's Chambers, and who had referred, in his judgment in *Klockner*, to two of his published articles in the centre, had prejudged the issue.

Soilchem's further submissions were that the court's jurisdiction could not be excluded except by clear words and, as s 34 did not expressly exclude the remedy of certiorari, it was available.

The response of the learned judge, Abu Mansor J, to this was brief. He said:

> After considering the submissions of both counsel, I am clear that the policy of the Arbitration Act 1952 was obviously to exclude cases that are before the Regional Centre for Arbitration at Kuala Lumpur. I have no doubt as to the purport and meaning of s 34 of the Act. It was meant to exclude the jurisdiction of this court in such cases. I am clear on this and I apply the judgment of Zakaria Yatim J in *Klockner Industries*.

Given the clear words of s 34 and these judicial pronouncements, what protection exists when an arbitrator misconducts himself or commits errors in his award? A limited remedy is provided by the UNCITRAL Rules which allow a party to challenge an arbitrator if it has justifiable doubts about the arbitrator's independence. The challenge must, however, be made within 15 days of knowledge of the fact which gives the grounds for the challenge. If the arbitrator declines to step down, the appointing authority, which will generally be the Director of the Regional Centre, will decide the matter. This does not appear to be satisfactory. For a matter as serious as the disqualification of an arbitrator because of lack of independence, prudence would ordinarily dictate the creation of a respectable panel to decide on the issue rather than a single individual, however eminent that individual may be.

Apart from the question of independence, no other challenge is possible, and even obviously erroneous awards will stand. Awards may, however, be challenged at the enforcement stage on the same grounds as that which apply to New York Convention awards.

LAW AND PROCEDURE

The law relating to arbitration in Malaysia is the Arbitration Act 1952 which is similar to the United Kingdom 1950 Act.

This Act recognises the authority of an arbitrator appointed pursuant to written agreements to refer present or future disputes to arbitration whether or not the arbitrator is named therein, with the authority of the arbitrator generally being irrevocable except with the leave of the High Court. When three arbitrators are appointed, the third is the umpire who only enters into the adjudication arena if the other two cannot agree on their decision. Where the contractual machinery for appointing an arbitrator or a replacement arbitrator breaks down, the High Court has jurisdiction to appoint an arbitrator or replacement arbitrator. Sections 9, 10, 12, 25 and 26 empower the High Court, in certain circumstances, to appoint or set aside the appointment of the arbitrator, umpire or third arbitrator or to order an umpire only to enter into the reference as if he were the sole arbitrator.

Most litigation in relation to arbitration will revolve around s 6 of the Arbitration Act. Ultimately, an arbitration agreement does not exclude the jurisdiction of the court to determine the dispute between the parties. Thus an aggrieved contracting party can make its claims in court. It is then open to the other party, the defendant in the court proceedings, to invoke the arbitration clause and ask for a stay of the court proceedings pursuant to s 6 of the Act. The main reason for doing so would be the prospect of getting summary judgment in court, which means judgment being given on affidavit evidence without a trial. This is available only in clear cases where there is no question of fact to be tried and where the legal issues are clear cut and can be addressed without difficulty.

A much-litigated position is thus the situation where a plaintiff seeking a quick judgment in court is met with the defendant's application to stay the court proceedings and have them referred to arbitration. Three cases from the highest court in the country have now established clear principles in relation to the granting of a stay:

Perbadanan Kemajuan Negeri Perak v Asean Security Paper Mills Sdn Bhd,[6] *Seloga Jaya Sdn Bhd v Pembinaan Keng Ting (Sabah) Sdn Bhd*[7] and *Tan Kok Cheng & Sons Realty v Lim Ah Pat.*[8]

These cases provide that a party seeking a stay must show to the court on affidavit evidence that, from the time the proceedings were commenced up to the time when the exercise of the court's discretion was sought for the grant of a stay, the defendant has been ready and willing to do all things necessary to have the matter arbitrated. To do this the defendant must show there is a dispute, even if not full-blown, which is covered by the arbitration clause. The court will not look into the bona fides of the defendant. Early in the proceedings there is little that a defendant needs to do except to swear or affirm a formal affidavit reciting his readiness and willingness to have the dispute arbitrated. Once this is done, the onus shifts to the plaintiff to satisfy the court that he should be allowed to continue with the action. Although the final decision on whether or not to grant a stay of proceedings is a matter of discretion, the court will normally hold the parties to their bargain and allow the stay of the court proceedings.

Arbitration clauses come in extremely varied forms. At one end of the spectrum is the provision for a single arbitrator with no provision for how his appointment is to be effected and with no mention of any procedural rules. At the other end are clauses spelling out the manner of appointment of each arbitrator and specifying the procedural rules for the arbitration. The rules most commonly used in Malaysia are the UNCITRAL Rules and Institute of Engineers (IEM) Rules of Arbitration. Most arbitration is undertaken without any applicable procedural rules, with the parties allowing the arbitrator full freedom on procedural matters.

Except where the applicable rules specifically provide, pre-hearing procedures are at the discretion of the arbitrator. The usual practice is for the arbitrator to convene a preliminary meeting at which he satisfies himself as to his jurisdiction by seeing that the referred dispute falls within the provisions of the arbitration clause. Directions are then given for the arbitration. These include the delivery of pleadings, which are the Points of Claim, the Defence and Counter-claim, the Reply and Defence to the Counter-claim and the Reply to the Defence to the Counter-claim. Discovery and inspection of documents are part of the arbitrator's normal directions. All documents, including internal confidential memoranda, are expected to be disclosed, with privileged documents being confined to solicitor-client communications and documents created, upon the dispute between the parties arising, for the purpose of the arbitration.

Unless specified in rules applicable to the arbitration, eg UNCITRAL or IEM, the procedure for the hearing is determined at the first or any subsequent preliminary meeting. Unless the arbitration can be disposed of by documentary evidence, there is a tendency to follow common law adversarial procedure with the claimant first presenting its case and the defendant then responding with its case after the conclusion of the claimant's case.

Witnesses are generally examined, cross-examined and re-examined orally, although there is a growing tendency to obtain advance written depositions to replace or reduce the length of an examination-in-chief. The Arbitration Act provides the arbitrator with the power to administer oaths and the High Court with the jurisdiction to issue subpoenas. Fees of witnesses are part of allowable costs which, pursuant to the Act, are at the arbitrator's discretion. A reasonable fee is normally awarded. As stated earlier, the formal rules of evidence are not applicable to arbitration by virtue of the provisions of the Evidence Act 1956 and arbitrators are left with the flexibility to deal with evidence in a practical, and not overly legalistic, manner.

The right to counsel exists independently of the provisions of the Act, but this may be waived. As mentioned earlier, the right of representation is not confined to local counsel, and foreign lawyers or non-legally qualified persons may represent parties to an arbitration.

The Arbitration Act 1952 provides that awards are deemed to be final and binding unless a contrary intention is expressed in the arbitration agreement. The Act confers the arbitrator with jurisdiction to make interim awards which also have a final and binding effect. The 'final and binding' character of the award does not preclude judicial review, and awards may be set aside or remitted for consideration on various grounds, including the misconduct of the arbitrator or errors of law appearing in the award. The Act also provides for the award to be enforced in the same manner as a judgment or order of the High Court.

As the provisions of the Act do not apply to ICSID and KLRCA arbitrations, judicial review of these is excluded. Enforcement of awards of these arbitrations is undertaken pursuant to the provisions of the Washington Convention or the New York Convention.

'Misconduct' is a technical word which does not per se carry any moral stigma so far as arbitrators are concerned. Applications to set aside an award or to remove an arbitrator for misconduct will succeed when the arbitrator conducts himself or the proceedings in such a way that raises a reasonable apprehension that the arbitrator is not independent, or where the rules of natural justice have been breached. In so far as the arbitrator's independence is concerned, the test is one of perception and it is not necessary to show that the arbitrator is actually biased in order to set aside an award or to remove him.

So far as errors of law are concerned, the error must appear on the face of the award or on a document clearly incorporated into the award. The mere reference to a document in the award does not necessarily incorporate the document, as it may have been referred to only for convenience. If documents are incorporated and if the award clearly contains errors of law, the award may be set aside and may additionally be remitted for the arbitrator's reconsideration. The term 'error of law' does not only encompass the application of a wrong principle of law; errors in the interpretation of a contract are treated as errors of law.

The Act also provides for the opinion of the High Court to be given on questions of law arising in the course of the arbitration, such opinion being binding on the arbitrator. This could be done either on the application of the parties or on the arbitrator's own motion, and takes the form of the arbitrator stating a case for the court's consideration. If a party requests the arbitrator to state a case, the arbitrator need not accede to the request, but he must give the party an opportunity to go to the High Court to see if that court will direct the arbitrator to state a case. Failure to do so would be misconduct.

The Limitation Act 1953 applies to arbitration as it does to actions. The Act prescribes periods of limitation from the date of accrual of the cause of action. Arbitration is commenced essentially when notice requiring the appointment of an arbitrator is given. A limitation period of six years is prescribed for the enforcement of an award.

The 1980 United Kingdom Act, which has been the model for similar legislation in Singapore and in Hong Kong, has not been followed in Malaysia and neither is there any report of a move on the part of the government to consider reviewing the position relating to arbitration and to comprehensively amend the Act or to re-enact the law.

ALTERNATIVE DISPUTE RESOLUTION (ADR)

The rising cost and length of arbitration, particularly in complex construction disputes, and at times a tendency to follow court procedures in arbitration, have resulted in attempts at alternative methods of resolving disputes. This could take various forms. For instance, it could be made a condition precedent to any court or arbitration proceedings for the parties to sit together and negotiate a settlement of their dispute either by themselves or in the presence of an adviser; to appoint a person or persons who would attempt to speak to both parties either at the same time or on different occasions, without the parties getting together, to try and narrow the areas of dispute between the parties and to have them settled. Even if these provisions are not in the contract, if the parties are sensible and have a genuine desire to resolve their dispute, an agreement for mediation or conciliation can be arrived at after the dispute arises.

The terms 'mediation' and 'conciliation' are more often than not used inter-changeably and it will be convenient to refer to them collectively as mediation. There seems to be a need for mediation to be extended in Malaysia, although it is perhaps too early for the other ADR device—the mini trial. As there is no legislation in relation to ADR, its use is a matter of contract.

Parties seeking ADR processes must ensure that their agreements to do so are carefully drafted. These agreements should provide for the specified type of ADR as a condition precedent to either arbitration or litigation. Ideally they would provide for a set of rules to regulate the ADR process, to define its parameters and to provide for the preservation of confidentiality of information obtained, as well as the immunity of the mediator for any action. In this connection the UNCITRAL Conciliation Rules and the American Arbitration Association Mediation Rules are useful guides.

There are no formal mediation and conciliation procedures in Malaysia, apart from a reference to conciliation in the Convention on the Settlement of Investment Disputes Act 1966, which only governs disputes between a Contracting State (to the Convention relating to the Act) and a national of another Contracting State.

---

1 [1990] 3 *MLJ* 125.
2 The AALCC is an inter-governmental organisation with 41 members from Asia and Africa and two permanent observers (Australia and New Zealand).
3 [1990] 3 *MLJ* 183.
4 [1993] 3 *MLJ* 68.
5 Dr Zakaria Yatim was partly responsible for setting up the centre. At the commencement of the case he offered to decline to hear the case, but neither counsel accepted the offer and both requested him to hear the matter.
6 [1991] 3 *MLJ* 309.
7 [1994] 2 *MLJ* 97.
8 [1995] 3 *MLJ* 273.

INDEX